BREAKING
WITH
TRADITION

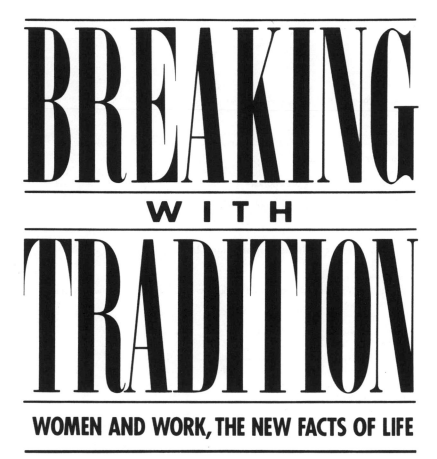

BREAKING

W I T H

TRADITION

WOMEN AND WORK, THE NEW FACTS OF LIFE

FELICE N. SCHWARTZ

with Jean Zimmerman

WARNER BOOKS

A Time Warner Company

Warner Books, Inc., 1271 Avenue of the Americas, New York, NY 10020
W A Time Warner Company

Printed in the United States of America
First printing: March 1992
10 9 8 7 6 5 4 3 2 1

Library of Congress Cataloging-in-Publication Data

Schwartz, Felice N.
    Breaking with tradition: women and work, the new facts of life Felice N. Schwartz with
Jean Zimmerman
        p.   cm.
    Includes bibliographical references.
    ISBN 0-446-51600-7
    1. Sexual division of labor—United States.   2. Dual-career
families—United States.   3. Working mothers—United States.
I. Zimmerman, Jean.   II. Title.
HD6060.65.U5S39   1992
306.3′615′0973—dc20   91-50418
                                                                                                              CIP

Book design by Giorgetta Bell McRee

For Bus,
   With gratitude for half a century of love, support and pride.

ACKNOWLEDGMENTS

I am grateful to so many people—more than I can name here—for offering the support, information and perspective that contributed to the making of this book.

First, in the world of Catalyst, I'd like to thank Gloria Markfield for her firm hand on the Catalyst tiller, and for her vigilance in protecting the serenity of my "book days."

I couldn't have done it without the solid research generated over the years by Catalyst's staff, whose high standards insured an infrastructure for my ideas—and especially, Wendy Hirschberg and her staff in the Information Center, for invaluable assistance in tracking down data and confirming facts.

Erika Pretell and Carla Geiersbach deserve special mention for the concern they brought to organizing my life.

I want to express my gratitude to Catalyst's Board of Directors for their support of this endeavor and the Board of Advisors for discussing with me many of the issues that are at the heart of this book.

Thanks, also, to Dick Lewis, Cam Starrett, Hank Lebed, Fran Bonsigneur and Deborah Pines for their careful reading and critique of the manuscript—and to Tony and Jim who reviewed portions of the book, not only as my sons but as the fine writers they are.

My own three families gave me the opportunity to look to the future by observing their lives in the present.

Warm thanks to Diane Crispell, who talked through complicated demographic trends until I understood them.

Thanks also to the faculty and students of Wharton, Kellogg and Tuck. Their candor stimulated my search for answers.

My appreciation to Jamie Raab for her belief in this book and her perceptive editorial hand. And to Joy Harris for her encouragement and skillful advocacy.

Gratitude beyond measure to the working women and men who speak with me wherever I go. I hope this effort is worthy of all theirs.

Most of all, to Jean Zimmerman, my profound appreciation for her fine intelligence, sensitivity and judgment, skill, hard work, and friendship.

CONTENTS

FIGURES

BREAKING
WITH
TRADITION

INTRODUCTION

*T*hree years ago I published an article about women and business in the *Harvard Business Review* and had a wild roller-coaster ride as the media and then the public took off with it. For thirty years, as founder and president of a national not-for-profit organization called Catalyst that works with business to effect change for women, I had acted behind the scenes. Now, suddenly, I found myself in the middle of a very public controversy that coalesced around a pejorative catch-phrase I didn't invent: the mommy track.

During the months-long debate stimulated by my article, I found myself repeatedly challenged on points I had never made and with which I did not agree. I couldn't dismiss these challenges easily. They forced me to examine my own beliefs. I had to face squarely the reality I saw in my daily work and, further, to look back over my three decades of experience in order to understand the origins of that reality.

This book grew out of that experience. In it I've tried to answer three questions: What's really going on now for women and men at home and on the job? What's wrong? How can we make it work? Most important, this is a book about solutions that will work for women, their employers, and their families—and *why* these solutions work.

I am convinced that we stand on the brink of making as much progress during the coming decade as we have over the thirty years since large numbers of women began to enter business and the profes-

1

sions. The feminist movement that was ignited in the early 1960s legitimized the anger of women. It enhanced awareness of women's potential beyond full-time homemaking, and it motivated women to want to do something different with their lives. But it didn't give any direction to individual women eager to enter the workplace. Nor did it look at what had to happen in society in order to facilitate the change that needed to take place.

We now need a revolution of the same magnitude as the upheaval that freed women from the confines of the home. This one has to start not with women, but with employers. Policymakers have to begin thinking in a profoundly different way about the people they hire, develop, and retain.

Women, too, must take another difficult step. They must recognize that through their decisions and their actions they can take much more control over the developments in their careers and in their family life.

I believe we must forge a radical new partnership between women and employers. Throughout my career I've often wished that the people who run companies and the people who work in them could have more opportunities to eavesdrop, if you will, on the conversations of "the other side." It would help them understand that their interests are shared. And it would help them talk to one another in a way that would be heard and understood.

I had that in mind in approaching this material. Unlike some books, this one is targeted not for one specific audience, but for a variety of people who generally think of themselves as being in different camps. In fact, I wrote with four specific types of readers in mind. First is the top executive of an organization, whether that means the corporate chief executive officer, the managing partner at a professional firm, the president of a university, the head of a government agency, or someone who runs his own small business. Since the reality today is that these are primarily men, I use the masculine pronoun throughout. Second is the human resources officer, who is responsible for initiating those company policies that concern people. Third is the manager, whether male or female, who puts these policies into practice. The fourth audience is comprised of women and men at work and at home.

The book is divided into parts, and some of the parts seem to address one type of reader more explicitly than another. However, I hope that readers from the different groups will take the opportunity to "read over the shoulder" of the others. In my experience the prerequisite to change is an understanding of the needs of others and of the attitudes that derive from these needs. It is necessary to put oneself into the mind of the other, so to speak, in order to recognize what will cause him or her to change.

In the first part my objective is to expose the pattern of silence that conceals the experience of women in business and the professions and the way in which women are perceived by men in leadership and management positions. The disparity is enormous, but it is not discussed. This conspiracy of silence prevents us from identifying the problems that exist and, therefore, from analyzing and addressing them. I then trace the progress women have made over the period spanning my mother's and my granddaughter's generations. My purpose is to show that although women have been greatly empowered by such factors as greater education and smaller families, they continue to experience the private pain of "intruders" in the world of work created by men for men. The first part of the book concludes with a discussion of the controversy that erupted over my *Harvard Business Review* article, because I think that experience illuminates the nature and genesis of the explosive emotions surrounding the changing role of women.

The second part of the book consists of only one chapter, which describes the trends—the forces of change—that I believe will sweep women into the mainstream of business and the professions.

Throughout part 3, I am talking with the man at the top, in order to convey the degree to which the talent of women in business is wasted. From my experience in talking with corporate leaders, I go on to discuss many of the questions executives often have about women in the workplace so that I can answer them within earshot of women and in a manner that I think will help to move things forward for everyone concerned. Then I discuss what I believe must change if companies are to capitalize on the most talented individuals at every level.

Part 4 speaks to women and men in an effort to clarify their roles in effecting change—the distance they must travel to meet their employers and partners halfway. And it is designed as well to define for employers what they can reasonably expect from their employees.

I've often been accused of being too optimistic about issues related to women and the work force. The implication, it seems, is that I take the reality, which is pretty dismal, and dress it up with a cheerful attitude. But for me optimism can be a form of realism. It means looking squarely not only at the here and now, but also at what is possible. What is possible nearly always differs significantly from what is happening in the present. But it can nonetheless be practical, not pie in the sky.

In 1945, when I was twenty years old and just graduated from college, my belief that what appears to be intractable can often be changed led me to start an organization that helped open higher education to black students. Two years later, the National Scholarship Service and Fund for Negro Students placed 750 black students in colleges and universities that had not yet begun to move towards integration.

I founded Catalyst in 1962. My goal was to expand the options of women and to facilitate their entry into the work force. The need for this effort became apparent when I was pregnant with the second of my three children. My husband and I moved to a suburban community. There, the wasted talent of the women I grew to know had a powerful impact on me. My sense of their frustration was made more acute by virtue of an unusual opportunity I had enjoyed in my late twenties—I helped get a family manufacturing business back on its feet. Unencumbered by too much knowledge, I was able to go from one area to another within this metal etching and embossing company: from purchasing, to production control, to cost accounting, to negotiating a labor contract with seventeen male shop stewards. It was the equivalent of a graduate degree in manufacturing, and it was a solid base for my work with the business community over the following three decades.

In starting Catalyst, that experience served me well in another way: I knew that women could do more than raise their children and support their husband's careers—because I had done it. I was convinced that many other women could, too.

From the beginning, the experience I have had in running Catalyst has taught me something about what motivates people to change. In the best of all worlds, a change in a person's values and attitudes precipitates a change in behavior. More often, in my experience, a person's behavior changes because his or her self-interest is served. I welcome change that opens options for women regardless of the motivation that sets it in motion.

In the early days at Catalyst, I couldn't tell employers that women were essential to their business. It simply wasn't true. Until recently women's ability to pursue careers was more important to their need to support themselves and their families and to their own fulfillment than to the needs of business. Catalyst's first, carefully worded statement of purpose was "To bring to our country's needs the unused capacities of educated women who want to combine family and work." We had to put Catalyst's definition in terms that were acceptable and nonthreatening for that specific era and in a context that would move corporations to respond. In those days that meant introducing the idea that through combining family and work, women could better serve society—not that they would be forging full-time, lifelong careers in business, which could be construed as abandoning their families.

Today Catalyst identifies emerging issues affecting women, conducts both quantitative and qualitative research, and publishes reports that are broadly disseminated throughout the corporate and professional communities to suggest the options companies have in addressing those issues. Additionally, the organization serves in an advisory capacity to many major companies and firms.

Only in the last five years has it begun to be possible to focus explicitly on why it is in corporations' interest to respond to women. Today what works for women also works for business. Women and their employers need not see themselves as adversaries. Their interests are mutual.

My experience in working to effect change for women has been in the corporate sector. That was a deliberate choice. I have never been intrinsically interested in large corporations or in women at the managerial level, but rather in opening options for all women. To that end I have long felt that change in the corporate arena would prove the best fulcrum for change for all women. Progress at the upper levels of business, where women are more visible, will translate to progress throughout the workplace.

I therefore hope that the ideas in this book will have relevance for those who do not aspire to the executive suite, for smaller companies, for women in the public sector, in academia, the professions, and the not-for-profit world, and for those who haven't yet embarked on their careers. And although this book focuses mainly on women, I believe it also speaks to men in their work and in their family roles. We have all been affected by the tremendous changes of the last half a century in both these areas. I hope that this book will help to open career and family options for women and men everywhere.

I believe that equality can be achieved for women in the American workplace. We can't estimate whether we will eventually see equal numbers of women and men in all the top jobs or, for that matter, at all hierarchical levels, from top to bottom. That literal, "utopian" form of equality may never come to pass, if only because men and women—on the basis of socialization or biology or other reasons—reject it.

The goal we must strive for is equality of opportunity, so that women and men can pursue the career and family options they choose, unrestrained by the strictures of gender. Whether or not half the CEOs in the corporate community are ultimately female, any young woman who wants to compete at that level should be entitled to a fair shot. Only then will business reap the talent of women and the competitive advantage it can provide.

June 1991

PART I

Breaking the Silence

CHAPTER ONE

The Riddle of the Rings

*I*n the spring of 1990 I had the opportunity to spend some time at the Wharton School of Business. A campus group called Women at Wharton had invited me to address the student body, and this occasion allowed me to schedule additional meetings with small groups of women and men enrolled in the business school, with the dean, and with some of the faculty.

My purpose was fairly broad. I wanted to explore the plans, perceptions, and expectations of America's next generation of managers and future leaders. I wanted to know how they hoped to make their lives work, how they dreamed of combining the professional and the personal. Their vision of the status quo is, after all, a reflection of the degree to which women have been successfully integrated into the mainstream of business.

I followed the Wharton visit with two others, to the Amos Tuck School of Business Administration at Dartmouth and to the Kellogg Graduate School of Management at Northwestern University. Thus, within the space of a few months I visited three of what are generally regarded as the top ten MBA programs in the country.

For this immersion in the culture of business students I was well rewarded. Hearing these young people talk, it seemed to me we were naturally evolving toward a world in which women and men will be

9

able to choose freely what they want to do with their lives. I came away with a clear sense that the young women I spoke with, every bit as much as the young men, were intent on making a real contribution to American business and did not see that goal as incompatible with spending real time with family. The young men seemed determined to have closer relationships with their children than many of their fathers, perhaps, had had with them. They didn't expect to be house husbands, they weren't saying that they intended to be the primary nurturers of their children, but they wanted to play a vital part.

My sense, in short, was that both men and women wanted careers and they wanted family. True, they weren't thinking terribly practically about how they might balance the two—in fact, they seemed to me overly confident that business would allow them to put this new way of life into practice. Still, at least they were dreaming of a new way of combining roles, and that's the first step toward making it happen.

I noted another change as well. The young men, who were no doubt fairly traditional in terms of work ethic, values, and political views, seemed genuinely to accept the idea of women as equals. They looked forward to working side by side with women as professional colleagues and spoke earnestly of finding a marital partner with whom they could found an egalitarian relationship.

If these shifts in aspiration and attitude had been all I observed at Wharton, I probably would have gone away feeling fairly sanguine about the pace of change that's taking place. Unfortunately I would soon learn that steady, ineluctable progress, as attractive as that analysis might be, was not the whole story.

I had another experience while I was at Wharton, one that struck me first as anachronistic, then as profoundly disturbing. It happened when I was talking with a group of Wharton women. Suddenly one blurted out that it was common practice for married women in the MBA program to remove their wedding bands before going to job interviews.

To this day that image haunts me: a young woman about to leave her apartment to face that formidable rite of spring common to all top-flight business schools, the corporate recruiting interview. The woman I visualize is a natural. Extraordinarily talented, top-tenth percentile in her class, a comer. The best and the brightest may be a cliché, but it is a cliché that could have been coined to describe her.

She picks up her portfolio and her suit jacket, checks her look in the mirror, turns to kiss her husband good-bye. At the door she hesitates a moment. Thoughtfully she looks down at her wedding band. Then she slips it off and shuts it away in a dresser drawer.

The image struck me as nothing short of a violation of all the "progress" that had so impressed me throughout the day.

Why? I thought. Why does the woman who removes her ring feel compelled to make such a gross compromise of her self? What does her action say about how young professional women today are approaching the workplace? What does it say about the corporate workplace itself, that it could command a compromise so vast?

To try to understand the implications of that image, I spent the better part of several months bringing up the subject with every thoughtful person I could think of, including professional women, corporate leaders, students, and academicians. It was a journey that led me in the direction of any number of "correct" answers—and yet, ultimately, no answer. Still, as I shared the riddle of the rings with people whose judgment I respect, I found a way of thinking about the issues that helped to shape the concerns of this book.

AN IMPERFECT STRATEGY

My initial reaction, as I've suggested, was dismay. I may be old-fashioned, but it seemed to me that to hide your wedding ring is to disavow a central part of your identity. As a person who has been married for forty-odd years, I know that I feel naked without my wedding ring. Nothing, I felt, should require that degree of self-abnegation.

My feelings must have showed, because the women who told me about the rings started interrupting each other to give their rationale. "You don't want to jeopardize your getting the job, so you're not going to wear it," was the dry explanation of a student in her late twenties.[1] Why would being married endanger your hiring prospects? It was patently obvious to these women: recruiters will not offer the plum jobs to those women they believe will have commitments to their families. Understandably enough, these women didn't want discrimination to play a part in their evaluation.

There was another element in their behavior that became clearer as we spoke. It seemed that the response of these young women was based in large part on expedience, on trying to avoid discomfort in the interview situation itself. In other words, they anticipated bias on the basis of maternity. They knew how incensed they would be to confront that bias. They didn't want to have to expend energy on that reaction in the course of the interview. If they could avoid it by hiding a wedding ring, fine.

It seemed the prospect of experiencing an intense, and endemic, level of bias was so much a given, so much a fact of life, that all they could imagine doing in response was to roll with the punches. It was more an aggravating inconvenience than a cause for alarm or offense. The students I spoke with were impatient, perhaps, or anxious—but the rings scenario didn't make them angry. I think they were more disturbed at me for suggesting there might be an alternative course of action.

A wave of discouragement hit me. These Wharton students, after all, are truly the elite. They have gone through a succession of fine screens to prove their caliber: first excelling in college, then proving on-the-job ability in an interim professional position, then getting into this highly selective MBA program, and, finally, surviving the rigors of the business curriculum itself. The interview is a challenge, sure, but a challenge these women have proven themselves eminently qualified to meet.

To me, the real tragedy lay not in their response—after all, they'd always find some excellent opportunity—but in its implications for the countless young women across the country who are not among the elite. If the woman who is potentially so successful feels she must deny so profound a part of herself—if she's thinking, How can I hedge this? How can I protect myself from this kind of preconception?— what about all the other equally able young women who aspire to business careers but have not had every advantage? What about the woman who attended the business program not at Wharton or Kellogg or Tuck, but at some less prestigious school? What about the woman who wasn't able to afford a graduate degree but pursued her business education at a small college? What about the woman who had to go to work right out of high school but had the moxie to try to further her career options by attending night courses in business at the local community college? Any of these women might well be brilliant. All are in a significantly weaker competitive position in the recruitment marketplace.

I saw a flaw in the students' reasoning. It seemed to me that one mistake they made was believing that through their action they could break the link in their recruiter's mind between them and questions of maternity, child care, relocation—the whole panoply of "women's issues" that might be triggered by the sight of a wedding band. I asked the women at Wharton if they imagined that interviewers registered only the information that potential recruits deliberately gave them. Did they think that unless they announced explicitly that they might at some point get married or start families, interviewers wouldn't draw that connection?

Said one unmarried student:

> They probably do think that. But if they know you're married [already] and they know you're a certain age, they think it's going to happen sooner rather than later. If Leigh walked in and said, "I'm married, I'm thirty-two," they'll say, "Okay, she's going in three years." If I walk in and say I'm twenty-five and unmarried, they'll say, "Okay, we might get six or seven out of her."[2]

In other words, the recruiter's degree of suspicion would be calibrated roughly to the relative likelihood and chronology of each candidate's having a child and subsequently leaving the company.

That seems unrealistic, I told the students. The recruiter is not secretly factoring the odds that one or another woman will leave and assigning jobs on that basis. For most executives, even those at companies we think of as better than average, the woman who removes her ring is already suspect, by virtue of her gender alone. No matter whether he sees a ring or not, he is more likely than not thinking some variation on the old formula: "Woman = Baby = No commitment."

There is a way to get around the formula, I told the students. Why don't you go in and find an opportunity to address the issue of how you plan to have both career and family? That is the way to bring out your commitment. That is the way to replace the preconception of the interviewer with a recognition of your value. Then you will be in just as good a competitive position as the woman without a ring or the one with a ring who makes no reference to it.

About six months prior to the Wharton visit, I had participated in a panel discussion with a number of professionals who had given thought to issues of women in the corporation. The moderator, television journalist Fred Friendly, engaged the panel participants in a mock interview, assigning himself the role of editor at a great newspaper. Each of us in turn would play the part of a young woman recently graduated from the Columbia School of Journalism and eager for a job on his paper.

Friendly began the interview with a panelist who happened to be a well-known ardent feminist writer and advocate. He asked almost immediately whether she planned to have a child. "What kind of question is that to ask?" she demanded. "It's not relevant to my qualifications for this job."

Then Friendly pushed farther. "I really need to know," he said. "What are your plans?" She refused to answer, pointing out that his question was a violation of Title 7 of the Civil Rights Act of 1964 and that she could take legal action against him. The discussion ended abruptly.

Eventually it was my turn to be interviewed. My prospective employer started to ask me the same question, but I jumped in feet first and announced that I did plan to have children, but I was twenty-two and on fire with journalism, ready to give my all and establish myself at his company. "Will you leave the paper when you have a child?" he said. I told him that I was sure I would want to be very much involved in the life of my child, but that my career was critically important to me. I might want to return to work very quickly or take some time off. If I had the opportunity to work part-time I would very likely do so for a finite period, after which I could return to my former fast pace. In any case it would be obvious to him when I did, because I planned to communicate with him openly throughout the process. By responding in the way I did, I believe I moved the exchange from confrontation to facilitation.

When I finished telling the Wharton students this story, it scarcely prompted a great ovation, but it did seem to penetrate their consciousness. Indeed, four or five women came up to talk about it with me after our group discussion ended. They thought my suggestion made some sense—then asked what I would think if they didn't bring up the subject of their work and family plans in the first interview but did so after they were offered the job. They wanted to take some kind of action but couldn't see risking as much as I was suggesting.

I could understand their caution. Given the heightened awareness of sex discrimination that has resulted from a generation of consciousness raising, most students are aware that discussion of personal issues during an interview can easily segue from the realm of the vaguely uncomfortable, to the socially impermissible, to what is genuinely illegal. Thus many of the women with whom I spoke advanced another argument, following "We have to!" with "It's ideologically correct." Why should recruiters be allowed an iota of visual ammunition—a wedding band—which might lead to discriminatory hiring decisions?

I knew that there was more than a shred of realism in this approach. Neither the climate of the average job interview nor the present hardnosed corporate environment is exactly conducive to dialogue about individuals' family needs. Midlevel managers who conduct interviews for companies are generally no more sensitized than their colleagues to dealing appropriately with the entry of women into the workplace.

The discomfort of these recruiters—or worse, their sexist assumptions—can lead to grotesque incidents. One true story recently circulated on campuses involved an interviewer from a prominent financial services company, who asked women in interviews if they would get an abortion if they got pregnant.

With these experiences in mind, career counselors at business schools encourage recruitment candidates to steer interview conversation away from "personal" questions. One Wharton student said the guidance office had coaxed her to destigmatize her credentials: "I was told that if my résumé went out with what was obviously a married name, I would never get a single letter from the résumé book."[3] It turns out, not surprisingly, that these same counselors had been influential in advising married women to remove their rings.

Although I sympathized with the students' predicament, I could see the recruiter's vantage point as well. Consider, for example, the recruiter who genuinely wants to hire women. No doubt he wants to see them shine in their performance once they are on board, as it reflects well on him when the people he brings in excel. These days the recruiter might also be female and have some personal motivation as well to further the status of women in the work force. Nonetheless, no matter how "correct" are many recruiters' intentions, the way that the corporations that most of them represent are now structured—with little flexibility offered to working parents—employees with home responsibilities are more likely to fail.

The recruiter is getting a strong message from his employer that the environment for women isn't likely to change any time soon. He wants to sort out the candidates that he can hypothetically retain somewhat longer. The standard against which he's going to measure recruits is whether they can make it in the climate of his company, now, today, inflexible as it might be. He's just doing his job.

One paradox contained in the riddle of the rings concerns the typical job tenure of professional employees today. The expectation of life-long loyalty has all but vanished from the employer/employee relationship and isn't generally a primary concern in the campus recruiting interview. According to the law of averages, it's fairly unlikely that any recruitment candidate out of graduate school will be around long enough to have the opportunity to leave the company she's interviewing with on the basis of maternity. But the message to women nonetheless goes out: Prove that nothing will stand in the way of your single-minded, unending commitment to our company. It is as if the expectation of lifelong commitment has been artificially resuscitated to apply only to women.

My first reaction to the behavior of the students had included a measure of disapproval. After thinking about their concerns and those of the recruiter, I couldn't judge the students so harshly. Theirs still didn't seem the best approach, but obviously they were dealing with a complex, difficult double bind in the only way they knew how.

There was something strange in this. Earlier in our discussions, the young women had projected a confidence in their future employers' receptivity to their needs as mothers and professionals that had struck me as unrealistic. Here, it seemed, was a deeper truth. It might be on an unconscious level, but they had been totally imbued with a message that achieving as professionals and having families were two incompatible goals—so incompatible, in fact, that it was necessary to conceal any hint of desire for the two. In safe quarters, in a controlled, private setting such as the discussion groups with me, or among themselves, they could divulge the terrible secret of their dreams. In an interview, however, the disclosure would constitute an irremediable transgression.

Keep in mind that although most of these students have held short-term jobs in companies, they remain relatively inexperienced. Few of them, we have to assume, have seen firsthand any examples of discrimination on the basis of sex. They don't need to have had endless job experience to sense the reality of the corporate response to women, because it is absolutely pervasive. Beneath all the rhetoric about "utilizing the talent that women bring to the mix" is an intransigence when it comes to leveling the playing field for women. And business students are getting a clarion call to dissemble.

At about the same time as the Wharton visit, I had a meeting with the head of human resources of a medium-size company. Because we had worked together for some time, he trusted me enough to confide opinions he would probably never divulge publicly. Women, he said, weren't committed to their careers and couldn't be depended on. He said he would never rely on women as a central resource: "As long as I can get a satisfactory man who will work full-time for life (and I assume as much for all men), I'll take him every day of the week over a much better woman." The Wharton students would never hear a policymaker say as much, but they were acting as though they'd overheard that executive.

Deception, for young female recruits who get that message, has become a strategic necessity. Its basic principle: Delay dealing with the issues of career and family until you absolutely must. Students are too smart to imagine this is a perfect strategy, but it's the best they have on hand.

It shouldn't be imagined that male business students employ the same strategy as their female colleagues. A young man knows that his single status won't increase his reliability in the eyes of a prospective employer. Quite the opposite: it's thought that the need to support a family will enhance his commitment to the company. I even heard that some men borrow wedding rings to wear to their recruiting interviews.

Why, when I spoke with them earlier, had the students not told me, "It's impossible—I can't even think of combining family and career"? I think it's because they're getting that message only on a subliminal level. They're responding to the prohibitions of business—which go unstated but are nonetheless very evident—without having absorbed the fact that they exist, and that if the way business is structured continues, they are not going to attain their dreams.

The grad students are willing to buy the party line that business is moving ahead. It gives them hope, and they are at the loins-girding stage of their careers, when they are making every effort to be hopeful. Still, they can't help but respond to the real message unconsciously—and their response is cynical. They're saying privately, "I am determined to lead the life I want, which will include a successful career and a fulfilling life as a wife and mother." They're saying through their actions, "I don't believe that my desire to combine the two roles will ever be tolerated."

The irony is that they're playing into the intolerance through their actions. In the best of worlds the interview is a two-way process, one in which the candidate is also evaluating his or her prospective employer. If a student doesn't feel able to bring up the subject of the company's response to its employees who want to combine career and family, or its interest in advancing women, she misses an opportunity to learn something essential about her future employer.

Isn't it terribly important, I asked the Wharton students, to find out the number of women at senior levels? To investigate the programs and policies the company has in place to unclog the channels for women's advancement? Even to ask about the climate in general for women? Do you really want to work for a company that doesn't believe working women should have children or, at least, wants to keep the number of mothers in their company to a minimum—whether or not you yourself are planning a family?

It was discomfiting to hear the most promising members of the new generation reduced to taking crumbs from the corporate table.

> I think the thing that I'm counting on is just that I'm working at a company next year that doesn't have a whole lot of women at the senior level, but I think it's the kind of place where they just treat people nicely, you can just tell. I feel like it's the kind of place where I can make change in terms of flexible arrangements five, ten years down the road. I think at this point, that's all I can hope for. I don't feel like I can do a lot about it before I'm in there. I have to sort of make myself valuable before I can do anything.[4]

By now it had grown clear to me that because of the overwhelming risk of bias, women simply could not be expected to raise these questions as individuals. So at the end of a day of mulling it over, when I got up to speak to the student body and faculty in the Wharton auditorium, I made another proposal. What if the whole graduating class were to get together and formulate one or two questions that they would *all* ask their recruiters? "What are your work and family policies?" perhaps. And "Tell me about the number of women you have at the senior levels." Surely no company could afford to discount an entire class of Wharton graduates.

Then the students all got up and applauded, because they could feel the security they'd get from approaching the issue en masse.

And that's what a social movement is. It's dictated by the impact of numbers.

This was an attempt at a solution, at least. But as I thought about it, I realized that it could only be a partial answer.

If all the students at Wharton were to bring up the same two questions, it would solve one problem, that of getting information about the company that they might go on to work for. It could help them avoid some mismatches and disappointment later on. But even if all the students felt strong enough to ask any two or three or fifteen questions, it would leave other, deeper, more difficult issues unaddressed. It wouldn't resolve any individual student's relationship with her employer or the question of what constituted each one's responsibilities toward the other. We're living in a time when there are no absolutes in terms of expectation on either side, because individuals have tremendously varied goals. We have to figure out a way of understanding one another, first, and then of meeting each other halfway regarding commitment.

CAREER SUICIDE

I took the riddle of the rings to a group of young associates at Catalyst. These women are all feminists; several were educated in women's colleges. As members of Catalyst staff, they are steeped in issues of women and work. Their job is to be out in the field all the time, conducting research in companies, probing these issues. I wasn't sure what their reaction to the rings scenario would be—though part of me thought they would take "my" side in finding the idea of removing one's wedding band dismaying.

Instead, to my surprise, I found a firm consensus: given what we know about the conditions for women in the overwhelming majority of companies today, it makes sense for a woman to remove her ring. True, the associates were uneasy about denying one's marriage. But conditions are harsh, they told me, and women can't sacrifice their paychecks to fight the system. They repeated the graduate students' thinking that it's better from a strategic standpoint to integrate yourself into the corporate culture, earn respect, then effect change from within.

Within days after my visit to Wharton, *The Wall Street Journal* ran a "Labor Letter" item about some of these questions. The article said that I was urging women to confront these issues at interviews and asked various people to comment on my approach. Among those who disagreed was Madelyn Jennings, a senior vice-president of personnel I respect. She said, "Employers might as well start asking men if they have a family history of heart attacks."[5]

Her comment reinforced my sense that there is a deeper issue here we're not addressing. After all, babies are not heart attacks. Why would she equate the negative impact of a predictable, onetime physical crisis, which affects only a small percentage of men, with the sequence of welcome events in the lives of nearly all women that includes marriage, children, building a family?

The *Journal* item prompted a call from a long-standing Catalyst board member, Christine Beshar. The first woman to become a partner at the law firm Cravath, Swaine & Moore, Beshar had a traditional European upbringing and never actually attended law school but instead read for the law. An independent, strong-minded person, she has three grown daughters, all of whom are also professionals.

She told me that two of her daughters, lawyers both, had come over for dinner the night before, and this question had dominated the conversation. Frankly, she said, both of them think you've got to be out of your mind to bring up the subject of family plans in an interview. The expression Beshar used was "career suicide." A job candidate foolhardy enough to say she was planning to have children, either verbally or through the signal of her wedding ring, would lose out to the one who didn't wear a ring or who refused to discuss children. She would certainly lose out to any male candidate.

Beshar is well aware that women are being shut out of management because they can't survive with the current attitudes, policies, and practices of the male-dominated corporate climate. She agreed that the turnover of women when they have children is a tremendous problem. Yet she was sure that the stakes are too high to force the issue in a job interview.

I began to see a catch-22 take shape. Women in corporations experience problems that need addressing. The problems cause them to perform less reliably and effectively than their male peers. Recruiters know this but cannot raise issues of commitment in interviews for fear of litigation. Women MBAs can't reveal anything about themselves that might suggest their needs as women, for fear of being penalized. So the questions don't get raised, and they are never addressed.

I still had no answer to the riddle of the rings. It was beginning to seem, however, that everyone but me felt that taking off your ring for an interview was an unpleasant but unavoidable requirement.

JUST DO IT

So I took the rings scenario to other thoughtful people, and suddenly the reactions swung in a new direction. For example, I broached the subject at a committee meeting with five well-known professional women, among them two presidents of women's colleges. All professed themselves shocked at the "dishonesty" inherent in the situation.

Bryn Mawr president Pat McPherson observed, "When I spoke at Wharton, the students asked such naive questions—questions that Bryn Mawr sophomores might ask, but certainly not graduates—questions about how we managed to have babies and careers." What I think she was saying: Women's college graduates don't even understand anxiety about combining family and work. They are properly self-confident.

I found that response troubling. McPherson's "just do it" mentality assumes that women can triumph over the status quo through the sheer force of their competence and will. Her view has been borne out by studies that track the achievements of women's college graduates. Of the 31 women members of Congress, for example, 13 attended women's colleges, as did one third of women on the boards of Fortune 1,000 companies and 36 percent of the highest paid female officers and directors at Fortune 1,000 companies.[6]

Young women are ill served if we extrapolate the experience of single-sex college graduates to the situation of all women—for two reasons. First, the women's college population is minuscule in comparison with the total number of women leaving school and entering the corporate world. The vast majority of young women don't have that confidence bred into them by their college experience, though many have equivalent competence. Second, although any young woman, no matter where she was educated, may enter the job interview with a great deal of confidence intact, no amount of confidence alone can topple the barriers for women that are endemic in the corporate environment as it exists currently. Thus, assuming that women can "just do it" perpetuates the idea that women should adapt themselves to an unchanged status quo.

In the reactions of these accomplished women, I sensed a strange disassociation occurring. There was an almost disingenuous quality in the extent to which some of these sophisticated commentators were "surprised" by what they were hearing.

"I didn't even register 'babies' when you talked about the rings. That only occurred to me a few minutes later," said Ellen Futter, president of Barnard College.

Shock was also the predominant reaction among a group of high-level professional women at a Capitol Forum meeting. I asked them to write down their response to the rings scenario, along with a brief explanation of their reaction.

The comment of Candice Shy Hooper, an attorney at Davis Polk & Wardwell, was fairly typical: "It's stupid; it can't be based on an understanding of their own real interests in life. Appalling." Why? "I am surprised—shocked—that kids with that kind of education are thinking in such convoluted terms about their futures and themselves. I can't believe the lack of confidence it shows."[7]

All in all, the reactions of these thoughtful, distinguished individuals brought to mind a sense that they believed themselves to be beyond the issues, that the business students in question were displaying a sort of immature bad judgment, a mistake made in the heat of their business adolescence. It was troubling mainly because it wasn't necessary: "It's silly. Grow up. Join the real world."

Their attitude intrigued me. I myself had disapproved of the act of removing one's ring. But the motivation behind that act seemed more honest than that of those individuals who advocated wearing one's ring as if there were no risk involved.

I visited the Smith Management Group, a program that is a sort of mini-MBA for women with around fifteen years of corporate experience. Participants are chosen to attend because they are among the highest-achieving women in their companies. Here, I thought, was an opportunity to get another corner on this question.

I asked the group to indicate how many would definitely wear their wedding rings into the interview, and it seemed every hand shot up.

In the words of one, "If the company can't take you for what you are, you don't want to work for them anyway."

As refreshing as I found their attitude, I had to interpret their confidence with a twinge of skepticism. I had a suspicion that they could be so definitive in part because they were at a stage of their careers when they had already established their credentials. They had lost the urgency and sense of danger that the young women felt.

Then, after a number of women commented, one woman stood up and made a speech that bears repeating.

> As you get older, you know things that you will or you won't do. But when you're really young, and you're trying for a position, we might all sit here and say, "No, no, no, I'm not going to do it." But realities are another thing. You're out there trying to compete, and you *want* that position. You're not going to get it if you wear the ring. That might sound terrible. But that's a fact of life. It happens, and it happens a lot.[8]

There was something marvelous about her honesty. Here she was, standing up before a room filled with seventy-three of her peers, articulating something that was in total disagreement with everything that had already been said. You could not hear her talk without knowing that here was a woman of high principles, courage, and integrity. Yet she was saying, "I'd take my ring off."

PLAYING TRICKS WITH REALITY

Plato has a ring parable, too, a famous one. What would you do if someone gave you a ring that rendered the wearer invisible? Within this seemingly simple query is a fundamental ethical question: How would you act if the strictures of society were removed—in other words, if no one could see you? Would you steal and cheat and run wild?

The riddle of the rings is simple in a way but conceals more than one difficult moral question. To what extent should companies that have ostensibly objective hiring procedures bring to bear another set of criteria—criteria that remain unverbalized but are pervasive? How much should women be forced to comply with these criteria? How much willed blindness, willed silence, is acceptable in order to achieve your own ends, whether those ends include getting the plum job, for women, or finding women who can match the male model and so survive a corrosive climate, for recruiters? Most important, where can this deception on both sides possibly lead?

Companies compromise their integrity by allowing recruiters to screen candidates on the basis of their future family commitments. This strikes me as especially true in the better-than-average companies, where initiatives are being taken to remove the barriers to women's advancement. There are questions of ethical double-dealing on the side of the students as well. Business students of the kinder, gentler 1990s are extremely aware of the fate of the Ivan Boeskys of the world. These days ethics are an integral part of the business curriculum. Unethical behavior is considered to be bad form as well as bad business. So why do so many find it morally acceptable to render invisible their identity as women and mothers-to-be by removing their wedding bands?

I met with some of the faculty at Tuck to explore the ethical facet of the rings question. "The first ethical decision you make is the choice you make of your employer." So said Ronald Green, Adjunct Professor of Business Ethics. If you're unmarried one day and married the next, what does that do to undermine the relationship? "It involves you in the kind of compromise and self-deception that is a terribly poor way to start a professional relationship."[9]

When the job candidate removes her ring, her act lets her employer off the hook as much as it lets her off the hook. It allows the issue to continue to be a nonissue—which is basically wrong, because the degree to which the workplace will change to accommodate family is critical.

Practicality, righteousness, moral indignation. These were some of the reactions I heard. What struck me as equally telling was a response of astonishment coupled with mild dismay.

"That is wild," was the spontaneous reaction of Dean Colin Blaydon at Tuck.[10] He could see students' logic, he said, but thought that the behavior was an overreaction. He conceded that a degree of judging whether a woman is committed or uncommitted goes on in any interview. But it's "playing tricks with reality" to remove one's ring, and the deception could recoil harmfully. A simple "Why do they have to do it?" was the response of Dean Donald Jacobs at Kellogg.[11]

Why indeed? The plaintive question brought me back to my own original feeling of dismay, which had sparked this quest. I'd come full circle—a vicious circle, one where the only answer is "Because that is the way it is."

IN A BOX

Of all the comments I heard, one rang most true.

I happened to be meeting with the partners at a high-powered law firm. Our discussion focused on the killing pace of the firm, and our stated objective was to explore how women with family commitments could be enabled to stay longer, given that pace. The head of litigation explained why women, in his view, were less than ideal as a talent resource: "When a woman works for us, she's got to be absolutely driven. She's got to be ready to pick up and go anywhere, at any time, for a case." One of his young associates, who hadn't yet made partner, disagreed. "Wait a minute," he said, "not all our litigation cases take five months out of town. Also, if you talk with the individual up front and say, 'Litigation takes this kind of commitment,' then if she wants to be in litigation, she will work her family around that commitment. But let *her* make that choice."

That prompted the partner in charge of recruiting on campuses to say: "That would be a good idea—but we can't talk about it. We're in a box."

We're in a box. That comment, it seems to me, captures the essence of the situation. We're trapped by a phenomenon I came to think of as a conspiracy of silence about issues related to women and the corporate workplace.

I undertook this quest hoping that if I spoke with enough smart, concerned people, I might find an answer to the riddle of the rings. But I didn't. I couldn't. There is no answer within the current framework of women and business. Everybody has a point, yet it's all a waste and a fraud.

Nearly everyone I spoke with was, however inadvertently, invested in preserving the silence. That included those students who took off their rings, of course. It included recruiters themselves. It extended to the people who professed not to see the problem or who minimized its importance.

I found another truth in all my discussions with people. Whatever approach we've taken up until now is not going to free us from the box we're in. To get out of the box, to break the conspiracy of silence, we have to do something entirely different.

And it's not just students and recruiters who are trapped. Through all my conversations, I came to feel that if I could distill the problems of women and business in general to just one salient image, it might be that promising young woman—she who is truly the elite, who has had every good fortune—marching off to her job interview with nothing but empty space around her ring finger. To me, the image has come to invoke a chain reaction of conflicts and uneasy compromises that still make women's role in the paid workplace so volatile.

It begins with an environment that refuses to bend to accommodate the presence of women. This results in the absence of any kind of message from employers that women are valued. That leads to a lack of trust, where women view any potential employer as an adversary. Soon we are deep into a mechanism of denial, a pattern of omissions, outright lies, and casual deceits. If I just pretend I am not married, not a potential mother, *not a woman*, maybe the problems will go away.

But they won't.

CHAPTER TWO

The Conspiracy of Silence

A revolution has transformed the workplace and the home. The massive entry of women into the paid work force has created a way of life that in our society's famous split-second memory has already been taken for granted. Until the last few decades it would have appeared so radical as to be unthinkable.

At some level we all know that the revolution has taken place. After all, we've witnessed the tremendous changes between our own lives and those of our parents and our grandparents. But at the most immediate, everyday level, we fail to comprehend.

This is the ideal picture we've drawn of ourselves. Side by side, women and men create goods and provide services. Side by side, they run our government. Side by side, they care for children, and side by side, they do the essential chores of the home. Partners, not each doing their separate half, but doing it all together.

To at least some extent, the ideal is based on the real. Never in the history of the United States have the roles of women and men been so far from polarization, so close to being shared. Never before have the choices of what to do with one's life been so unbound by that most invidious of traditional straitjackets, the stricture of gender.

Yet something is grievously wrong.

27

Women still find themselves blocked in their career advancement and stymied in their efforts to combine work and family. Men are unable to satisfy a new yearning for more connection with their children. Companies recruit and train talented employees, only to see them fail because they are thwarted by lack of opportunity and corporate inflexibility.

We've put this revolution, this fantastic machine, in motion, but we haven't provided the fuel it needs to run.

Clearly, radical change is in order. This will require nothing less than transforming the way we envision the workplace. Employers will have to articulate the human requirements of jobs in a way that's never before been attempted. Individuals will have to go beyond rethinking the old roles at home to the harder work of actually adopting new patterns of behavior. We'll begin to make difficult choices about how we want to lead our lives as self-determinate individuals.

Incredibly, though we've just started, we're midway to a time when women and men will have equal opportunity to do what they want with their lives. Women, after all, have gradually gained a solid foothold in the business arena over the past thirty years. Business leaders have an expanded awareness of women's abilities and of their own need for precious human talent. If you count hopes and dreams and expectations as progress, we might even be farther than halfway there. But what we really need now is a huge push, nothing less than a second revolution, in order to facilitate the change that has begun.

The issues we must now address are mind-boggling in their scope and complexity. We can't go on the way we have been—living new lives in the old patterns. Yet somehow women and men and their employers have all swallowed the idea that women's complete assimilation into the workplace will somehow just evolve.

In order to complete the revolution that's already under way, we have to examine the problems so that we can address them. Certainly a number of issues *are* being discussed now. The problem is that they are always raised in private, among women or among men, but not together. We have the situation of many people talking and not much being communicated.

A TALE FROM THE FRONT

The business students I spoke with at Wharton hoped that once they demonstrated their talent on the job, they would find a more opportune time to place their stamp as women on the corporate environment. In order to suggest the limitations of that approach, I want to zero in on the experience of one professional woman about ten years after receiving her MBA at Harvard.

Corporate leaders should not dismiss the story I'm about to tell as something that happens in some other terrible company. I have talked with many of the CEOs at companies where serious initiatives are being undertaken to address some of the issues created by women's entry into the workplace. Even at these companies, even when the chief executive feels that he is really moving the status quo for women ahead, the self-fulfilling prophecy of failure regarding women is still taking place.

Let's call our heroine "K.," with a nod toward Kafka, since her story borders on the surreal. At first K. thought her nightmare maternity leave experience was simply personal, a quirk in the system, something that happened because she had a small-minded boss. "Weird," as she described him. She came to believe the things that happened to her during her maternity were systemic—they were due to the misguided policies of her company. I also believe they were systemic, but I would widen the circle of culpability to business as a whole.

Actually K. had two maternity leave experiences at the same company, both bad. It was not until her second baby that she concluded her treatment couldn't be a coincidence. K. thought she knew why things went wrong the first time around. She was the victim of unfair comparisons. Her boss had had a child the same year, in July, while she had her baby in April. First child, first onslaught of Pampers, first night feedings. The curious mixture of exhaustion and euphoria that is parenthood could have given manager and subordinate something in common. But there was one crucial difference. Her manager's wife was a full-time homemaker.

It made all the difference in the world, at least in the boss's perception of her. After K. returned from maternity leave, he stopped assigning her meaty projects. She confronted him, and he was baldly unapologetic.

"He said, 'Well, I really think you should be home with your baby, and you really aren't going to get any good projects. I don't want to burden you, I don't want to pressure you.' "[1] He had observed his wife engaged in the heroics of raising an infant and couldn't imagine how K. was managing to do that job at the same time as her job at the bank. He figured he was doing K. a "favor" by cutting back her work. Killing her with kindness.

End of discussion, and the end of what had been a better-than-average working relationship. K. had no problem getting a transfer to a different department—her credentials were that good. She took the quickest way out of a certain career dead end.

By the time the second baby was on its way, two years later, K. felt confident her first experience had been an aberration. She had proved her value to the firm. Why, the company was even installing a $30,000 computer system in her house, tied in to the mainframe, for the duration of her maternity leave. Then something began to go awry.

"Two days before I was due to have my baby," she recalled, "they said, 'We'd like you to take a new job.' And they explained the new position to me. And I said, 'Well, that's very nice, but I'm not interested, thanks anyway. It just doesn't appeal to me.' "

K. was being politic. Underneath she felt that the proposal was a way of pulling the rug out from under her. Her current job was central to the life of the department. The position she was being urged to take was "a very risky one in that if you were going to downsize, it would be a job you could get rid of real quickly."

The saga continued. "They came back to me the day my daughter was due and said, 'You're going to take this job.' " Management's explanation: " 'We don't think you're being well utilized in your current job, and this'll provide you with a lot more opportunity.' " Seeing no other option, she accepted the new position.

The baby came. The executive went home. What happened next? "They never called, never did anything. I heard absolutely nothing."

No communication. No work assignments. The expensive computer system never got booted up.

Two or three days before K. was due back on the job, still without a word from her boss, she began to get nervous. She called and got her boss on the phone. " 'So what am I going to be doing when I get back?' And he said, 'Oh, you're coming back?' "

Up until the last weekend of K.'s maternity leave, she still had no idea what she might be doing when she returned to the office. All her boss would tell her was, " 'Well, come in on Monday. We'll find something for you to do.' "

"Essentially, they took my job and gave me a very small piece of it and gave a subordinate the rest of my job." She adds, "But it isn't keeping me occupied, and it certainly isn't going to represent a career advancement."

It's called "constructive discharge." The firm makes your life so miserable that you leave.

K. explains her theory.

> They just make the decision that they know what's best for you, and they know what's best for your children. I think they're trying to make it okay if you decide to quit. Part of it's to cover themselves, probably, and part of it is because they sincerely believe, given it is their wives' situation not to work, and they know how hard it is to take care of kids, that you're not going to be dependable, you're not going to be able to meet the demands of your job.

On the surface, this appears a clear-cut, us-against-them story. But I see more than a hint of collusion on K.'s part. She set up unreasonable expectations by volunteering to work during her disability leave—the reason for the expensive computer hookup. She probably would have followed through if the company had called her during this time. But they didn't. Because she was frustrated and angry at them for cutting her out of the loop, she didn't call them, either. The whole situation reinforced her boss's prejudices about working mothers.

> I sincerely believe that the senior management at the bank should be made aware of the discriminatory practices that are going on there, but then I sit back and I look at it and I say, a) "What good does that do me on a personal level? I could get fired," and b) "I'm not coming to them with a solution, other than saying, 'Do you realize there's a problem here?' " And if one of my employees came to me with a business-related problem, I'd probably say to them, "Think up a good solution and we'll see what we can do about it." But I don't know what I'd tell senior management about it, other than "Stop what you're doing."

More hints of collusion. I will not confront the company about its policies because it may expose me to an unacceptable level of career risk.

Yet when I spoke with K., she told me that what she really wanted to find at this point in her career was a part-time option. That, of course, she was not in a good negotiating position with her company at this point. And she couldn't go to another company and expect to find a part-time position with the same degree of challenge and responsibility that she had at the company where she had proved herself.

In short, K. was in a box, along with her employer, and there was no way out.

A TWO-SIDED COIN

Here is another story that suggests the uneasiness, the indirectness, even the self-censorship, with which employers feel they must approach issues they don't know how to deal with.

Recently the head of human resources at a Fortune 500 financial services company recounted an experience he had had now that some of his top people are women. He told me that three of his most valued professionals—great deal makers, each of them—had returned from maternity leave with a resolution to reduce their workdays from sixteen to nine hours in order to devote more time to their families. He said that of course the time limitation would preclude deal making, but that all three were excellent administrators.

"What adjustment," I asked, "did you make in their compensation?"

He looked surprised. "None," he replied. He hadn't felt comfortable bringing up the subject, because it could expose him to the possibility of litigation.

Some time afterward, at a business function, I found myself in conversation with a high-ranking woman whom I discovered had worked at the same firm. She told me that she had recently had a baby and had reduced her hours—and it became apparent that this must be one of the same women the human resources executive had described. It turned out that she had subsequently left the company.

When I asked why, she replied that she had felt she was no longer pulling her weight and it was only a matter of time before it would be found out that she was not performing to the level of salary she was bringing home. Unwilling to suffer the blow to her professional reputation that would result from dismissal, she had chosen to resign.

This tale has a happy ending. The executive managed to rearrange her status at the company and was now acting and being compensated as a consultant. Both she and the company had taken a hard look at what she could deliver and what it was worth in dollars. An arrangement—possibly a temporary arrangement—was made to the benefit of both, allowing the company to retain and capitalize on her talents and commitment while responding to her family needs.

Situations like this one pose difficult questions for women and their employers. Yet it is perhaps too easy to assume, as many do, that the difficulty of the interaction means we are doomed to failure.

To get out of the box, it might help to understand how we got into it in the first place.

ORIGINS OF THE SILENCE

It started with the conditions under which the huge wave of women entered business twenty-five years ago. At that time there were two parallel worlds occupied by men and women. There was men's world, the paid workplace, and women's world, dominated by home and family. Women entered the work force in an era when they weren't perceived to be needed, when they weren't thought of as able to function effectively in business, and when men and many women thought they should be home tending the hearth and raising the children.

Despite the negative reception they received, women persisted, driven by their frustration with the purely domestic function they were told was rightly theirs. When they pounded on the door of business, made legislative gains, and were propelled into the workplace by the force of economic necessity, men had to respond. But they did so reluctantly.

Few members of the corporate community viewed women's presence in their world as anything but an intrusion. Men saw no benefit in women joining them as equals in the workplace. They really had no bottom-line need for women to staff their companies—the baby boom had yielded up a surfeit of male talent. On a more profound level, men resisted women's incursion because it changed a status quo they'd always known and been comfortable with. In that status quo, women were romantic partners or secretaries or, most important, wives, providing an essential support system in the home.

Only grudgingly did the men who ran companies make a place for women in the ranks of business. They would let them in, but they would do only the minimum required to facilitate their employment. Because men had no thought of the value women might bring, and no apparent need for them to enter their world, they lacked an incentive for dismantling the barriers obstructing women's advancement or easing women's difficulty in adding a second job to their prior full-time responsibility of maintaining the home. And women got a clear message. Those who wanted to succeed in the men's world had better be prepared to do so on men's terms.

Few women at that time were in a position to object. The qualifications for success in business had been established by men. If women couldn't play by their rules, they wouldn't be permitted to play at all.

There was another reason women obeyed this dictum. When the wave of women entered the work force in the 1960s, it was with the conviction that the world of home and family was less rewarding, less glamorous, less prestigious, than the world of work. There was the pervasive idea that men led a better life—they had mental stimulation, challenging relationships with their colleagues, a sense of measurable accomplishment, autonomy, growth, power, money. They were truly enviable. Equality with men came to mean sameness with men.

This emphasis on sameness was a new theme in the old struggle for sexual equality. At other times in history—the fight for female suffrage in the 1920s, for example—women based their appeal for equal treatment on the reasoning that they brought different, even superior, traits to the public arena. Perhaps this was because until the advent of contemporary feminism, women's world had been fairly isolated from that of men. For the most part they had no firsthand knowledge of men's world and therefore little desire to join it on any terms. They didn't want to enter the male world, so they didn't have to conform to the male model.

Now, however, beginning in the mid-1960s, the women who entered the business mainstream were better educated and more autonomous than their feminist precursors. Their expectations had been forged in their exposure to the world of ideas during college and by the work experience many had during World War II. They hungered to take part in the world beyond their own sphere. When they were told that they had to make it on men's terms or not at all, that didn't sound like an unreasonable condition.

For the most part, therefore, those who entered the world of work were willing to recast themselves in the male mode. They felt victorious to be admitted into men's world at all and hardly thought to insist that companies implement changes to help them succeed. They wanted to prove that they could do it exactly as men had always done it, and it was a source of pride for those who could.

At the same time, corporate men held on to their traditional views about women's proper place and role. Privately, at a deep level, men still clung to their belief that what was right for men differed from what was right for women. They continued to think of the roles and behaviors of individuals as inherently male or female. Though they accepted the reality of women in the halls of business, they still experienced a dissonance.

"There is no spectacle on earth more appealing than that of a woman cooking dinner for someone she loves," wrote Thomas Wolfe a half century ago. To this day men continue to believe that women are uniquely equipped to stay at home and care for their children. No one, they feel, can love a child as much as its mother. Few men in the country would get up at the podium and say, "I really think women should be home while their children are young." But many men really feel in their hearts that women should stay home.

I remember my father used to tell me I'd make a great mother—an athletic tomboy, I looked neither mature nor maternal. Throughout my adolescence I swam and rode competitively to my father's applause. Yet in that period he just knew I was going to be a wonderful mother. It never occurred to him that there could be a contradiction in this. Motherhood was so central to his idea of a woman, and I was so central to his idea of perfection, that it would happen.

In business, men's beliefs about women do not end with their nurturing qualities. Today they can't help but know that women are as able intellectually as men. Still, their gut reaction is to doubt that a woman can direct an enterprise as effectively, analyze a problem as incisively, or negotiate a settlement as definitively as a man.

Though corporate leaders do not articulate these underlying beliefs, they act on them every day. And the convergence of their traditional thinking, the ground rules they refuse to change, and the inevitable differences that women bring have led to a self-fulfilling prophecy of failure for women and for business—which is perpetuated and worsened by the fact that none of these things can be talked about.

Just beneath the conscious level simmers policymakers' lingering belief that women are a higher risk to employ than men. Because of this perception of added risk, the people who run companies are not yet ready to look seriously at the changes that are needed in the corporate culture to enable parents, especially mothers, to function as freely, to be as productive, and to have the same opportunities for growth as those employees without parenting responsibilities. They don't think it's relevant to them, or they're not sure how to deal with it, so they deal with it as little as they can. The risk could be removed or at least minimized if the problems women faced were analyzed and addressed, but no one is talking about them, so we stand at an impasse.

Women know from their first entrance into the gleaming headquarters of the Company that although male senior managers pay public tribute to the need for women in the work force, their underlying feelings are more ambivalent. Many women take umbrage at the negativity they sense in corporate leaders' attitudes. They grow alienated, resentful. Nonetheless, because women want so much to pursue careers and because they don't want to or cannot forgo the income their work provides, they quickly get with the program.

A brutal logic transforms the approach of all but the unusually brave or fortunate into one common strategy: Deny any hint of gender-related difference. It's the same strategy employed by business students when they put away their rings before interviews. And, like the students, women within companies do not relish the approach of denial. They buy in when this appears the only tenable course of action.

The results of this conspiracy of silence, placid on the outside and adversarial underneath, are all around us. A woman's detour to start a family can, in the minds of male top executives, lead altogether logically to total derailment of her career objectives. At the same time these policy planners are resistant to making any change in policy that would give women the flexibility they need to balance family and a career. Then, because women are socialized to rear children, since they want to be active players in their children's lives, and their desire to do so is condoned by their employers, their leaving is legitimized. Hence we see a senior manager's frustration, but not surprise, when a female highflier announces she wants to cut back or quit in order to spend more time with her kids.

To top this, many men think that the problems of children today are primarily a function of women's absence from the home. Believing this makes them more inclined to accept what they consider to be the reality of women's need to cut back at work to spend time with their families—they think society benefits from it. The net result of all this: Employers do not address the need for policies and practices that will enable women, or men, both to work and be responsible parents.

The self-fulfilling prophecies go on and on.

- Corporate leaders' preconception that women don't take risks and are not cut out for technical jobs leads them to shunt talented women away from line positions that are essential to running a business.
- Male managers overlook women for transfer opportunities because they believe the women won't want to relocate so women don't gain the lateral experience they need to make policy as a senior executive.
- Men who supervise women often are not comfortable giving them the candid performance evaluations, with constructive suggestions for growth they need, if they are to move up as rapidly and as far as their male colleagues.
- Male managers see the insensitive behaviors to which women are subjected by colleagues, clients, and customers, then are surprised and disappointed when it hinders their ability to deal with these same colleagues, clients, and customers.

In each case women feel they can't call attention to themselves by asserting their needs. In each case, when women don't advance as far as they might have, don't fulfill their initial promise, men tell themselves it was never meant to be.

Women have moved into the world of work, and they will never again go home on a full-time basis. What that means is that the workplace now contains the family—whatever responsibilities women had in the home are now the concerns of business. If we talk about the factors that are negatively affecting women, we can either accept them as natural and inevitable, or fix them, or some combination thereof.

Once again, though, when we don't acknowledge the issues, we can't analyze them. When we don't analyze them, we can't address them. The conspiracy of silence allows a perpetuation of the self-fulfilling prophecy of failure.

In the meantime, employers don't yet view women as a leadership resource, so they undermine their productivity and block their advancement. Women in turn see employers as adversaries. The entire scenario is a lose-lose proposition for women and for employers. There is a lack of trust, of openness. Deceit prevails. Everybody suffers, but all we can do is despair. There is no place for solutions, because it is a closed system of failure.

There is only one thing we can know for sure. Our current approaches are getting us nowhere. And it won't work for anybody until we find some common ground. The critical first step, though, might be the most difficult—to admit that we've got a problem.

CHAPTER THREE

What Aren't We Talking About?

*I*n today's corporate world, we find ourselves surrounded by Voltaire's optimists, beset by "the mania of maintaining that everything is well when we are wretched." We spend the bulk of our energy denying rather than dealing with the problems that impede working women.

This was brought home to me recently when I watched a television news segment that featured two women and a man, all senior-level executives, in a discussion about women's status in business today. I'd looked forward to the program because I knew one of the guests, a CEO who has a reputation for moving things forward.

One after the next, the guests maintained that the barriers women faced were either nonexistent or insignificant. One of the women, for example, was asked. "How about the old-boy network?"

"I really don't think that's been a problem," she replied.

"The old-boy network is really more of a shared business network," volunteered my friend, the CEO. I am sure that he thought he was doing the right thing by denying the specter of an exclusionary all-male network. In his eyes the problems for women are not great. Anyway, it would be somehow "not nice," demeaning of women, to suggest that anything was holding them back.

"Nothing's simple," said the second female guest, a vice-president at Boeing, when pressed to say whether women faced any obstacles at all. "It's a challenge." Then she qualified her statement: "But it's a challenge for *everybody*."[1]

Now, her industry, the aerospace industry, would be close to the bottom of any list of where companies stand regarding women's career advancement. If anyone has had a chance to experience massive barriers to women's upward mobility, it's someone like this woman, who has reached a senior level in such a traditionally male-dominated company. Yet neither she nor the other female guest on the panel, an officer of a prestigious old-line banking firm, were willing to publicly air problems women face.

And I thought to myself: If we deny the problems, how in the world can we open up the old-boy network to let women in? How can we make sure that women have just the same career opportunities as men, if we pretend we've already resolved these issues?

The reticence of these executives about the old-boy network isn't just an isolated event. A wider pattern of silence about issues surrounding women and the workplace permeates our culture. The playing field in corporate America is by no means even for both sexes. *But no one wants to talk about it.*

Again and again we deny the issues and problems and, quite simply, the realities that we must address if we want to move ahead. Women and men think that talking about these things will lead to bad outcomes, when in fact it is only by talking about them that we can find solutions.

So let us look without flinching at the things we usually deny.

WOMEN HAVE BABIES

Sometime last year I brought a team of Catalyst specialists to meet with a skeptical chief executive of a large manufacturing concern to discuss how we might be able to help his company. We talked about the importance of women's leadership development, about the usefulness of concrete data about his work force, about the barriers faced by women. As we talked I felt that although the CEO might be somewhat interested, in an abstract sense, in the issues of women and business, nothing in our discussion had fully engaged him. Finally he interrupted the presentation and asked a simple question: What's really the issue here?

My response was visceral: Babies, babies, and babies. And suddenly his interest soared.

I think we can safely attribute his renewed interest to my having broken with the party line about maternity. It was a relief that someone could admit the fact that women have babies. But why did I focus on this one issue when corporate women face so many difficult barriers? Why did I start by talking about babies?

First of all, because women have babies and men don't. It's the one immutable difference that women bring with them wherever they go.

Second, because women are in the workplace to stay. It follows that employers cannot effectively advance women until they accept maternity as the predictable, manageable event it can be. Until they do, business will suffer.

Third, because until we stop asking women themselves to deny this central facet of their lives, women will suffer most of all. Now that working women have proven their smarts, their career commitment, and their indispensability to business, why are we asking them to sell their souls to stay in the game? Surely now women can ask that employers go halfway—that companies do whatever it takes to allow maternity and business to coexist productively.

Because until babies, babies, babies have a place on the business agenda, we will all continue to fail.

It sounds so simple, but it's not happening now.

We have, in our time, chosen not to discuss—or even, legally, to permit discussion of—this most basic difference between men and women. It's not that no one thinks about it. In many employers' minds, women are natural mothers who don't belong in business at all, or they are managers who have no maternal identity. There is little room for overlap. This paradox puts pressure on those women— and it is a majority, as 85 percent of women have babies—who are mothers.

Employers, again, rarely make their views explicit. They don't need to. The message women get is clear and simple. "What bothers me is that most people out there really don't want mothers to be working," said one money manager I spoke with, who "put herself on the slow track" for five years to raise her daughter.[2]

Women join their employers in denying the impact of maternity, knowing it would be career suicide to do otherwise. They struggle to conform to the baby-free image that is required for career success, whether it means forgoing motherhood altogether, choosing their maternity dresses with great care, or truncating their parental leave allotments so as to make a rapid-fire return to the office. In private they struggle to achieve the toughest balancing act of our age, but publicly they feel compelled to say the role of superwoman suits them fine. "When you first come back to work," said Denise McLaughlin, a first vice-president at J. Henry Schroder Bank & Trust Co. in New York, "people will ask, 'And how's the baby?' You better be prepared with a very short answer: 'Everything is perfect.' "[3]

We compel working women to pretend that maternity is not a big issue, whereas it is central to life.

The fact that women have babies doesn't alter the quality of their work. It has absolutely no corollary in terms of women's level of commitment to their careers or their ability to perform their jobs. Except—and this is a big exception—if maternity goes unacknowledged, unplanned for, unmanaged.

When you look more closely at the reality of maternity in the workplace, you see it is a continuum made up of four interrelated stages: pregnancy, childbirth, parental leave, and child care. The degree to which each new mother is affected by the four depends on various factors that no one can control, such as her health in pregnancy, the nature of the delivery, the health of the child, and the availability of good child care that she can afford. All four stages are multifaceted and merit a great deal of discussion and planning. As it is now, all four are obscured by the conspiracy of silence.

Pregnancy

The conspiracy of silence about pregnancy begins even before a woman starts to "show."

"I'm waiting as long as I can to change into maternity clothes," one member of a working mothers group announced at a meeting in New York City last June. The executive reasoned that a long-awaited transfer opportunity would be decided any day. She worried, she confessed to the crowded room, about the deceit involved in not telling her boss about her pregnancy. To a woman, the group shouted in chorus: "Don't give ground until you have to!"[4]

Women regularly delay announcing their pregnancies, especially if they are awaiting a job offer, promotion, transfer, or some other career advancement that they fear might hinge on their demonstrating that they are just like their (male) competitors.

> When I learned that I was pregnant, I had a senior position in my company. I was going through a salary negotiation at the time, and I purposely did not let it be known that I was pregnant, because I knew that if my boss knew, he would factor that into his mind-set about me. He would say, "Well, she will be in a debilitated state, she won't be able to look for another job, she's going to need the time off, so her leverage is less." Women know that the reality is that when they are pregnant, and when they first have their children, they are perceived to be in a weakened position. Which in some senses, they are. So they don't want to draw attention to it.[5]

When the time comes that they must discuss their physical condition with their supervisors, many women feel apprehensive, embarrassed, even apologetic about what is for many the most joyous event of their lives.

Eventually, of course, every pregnant woman reaches a point when she can no longer outfit herself in "civilian" clothes. Then she must really do the impossible: conceal a physical reality that grows daily.

Pregnancy doesn't necessarily incapacitate. But it makes a difference in how one feels. Some women are energized; for most it is a happy period. But if you have to pretend that this enormous adventure is not happening, it can be a terrible burden.

The maternity clothes of choice in professional circles, for example, are those that best conceal the pregnant form—they are not chosen for the degree of comfort they provide. Women who carry their pregnancies to term in corporate offices must deny the fatigue that comes simply from carrying the extra weight, as well as the discomfort that accompanies the final prepartum trimester. For example, the logical approach to edema, elevating your feet or, when sitting through a long meeting, standing up and walking around, is rarely viewed as acceptable for women in a business setting.

Also inadmissible are the emotional counterparts to these physical sensations, whether anxiety about the delivery, worry about handling the new responsibility of mothering, or joy about becoming a parent.

Childbirth

The corporate community, faced with the physical reality of childbirth, has managed to acknowledge it by putting it into a neat little prefab category: postpartum disability. Maternity's importance has been reduced to that of a broken ankle.

Not that all working mothers receive even this finite time allotment to recover from childbirth. Only those companies with a state mandate to offer disability coverage for any medical condition are required to include postpartum disability in their provisions.

Never mind that childbirth is an exhausting experience—emotionally as well as physically; that at the end of six weeks, the average baby—and, hence, its mother—still wakes three or four times during the night. Never mind the difficulties of finding qualified, affordable child care that would allow the new mother to return to work with the confidence that her child is being appropriately cared for in her absence. According to a 1990 study by Hewitt Associates, unpaid parental leave beyond the disability period is offered by just 44 percent of employers.[6]

We don't talk about these things because it's so clear how monumentally difficult the experience is for nearly all working mothers. The reality is that almost any new mother needs a significant amount of time to make the adjustment to parenthood and then, to make the transition back to her job, combined with parenting responsibilities. Employers don't want to admit the reality because they don't know how to respond to it. Women don't want to assert any demand for time beyond the six weeks that is minimally responsive to their physical needs, out of fear it might undermine their career advancement.

Women know that companies will not tolerate uncertainty about their female employees' career plans after having babies. The clear signal of this intolerance is that most of the companies that do provide disability to reimburse employees for their maternity expenses do so only if the employee is unquestionably planning to return to work. The result is further mutual duplicity.

The vast majority of women who take leaves of absence to have their babies assume they will return to their jobs. They are invested in having a career and, further, are driven to keep their jobs by economic necessity. But even if a woman has doubts about whether she wants to return to her job, she will probably assure her employer that she plans to. She well knows that unless she pledges to return from leave within a predetermined time period, she will not receive coverage, and she will not be able to afford medical care. Even the individual who is ambivalent about whether she will return feels compelled to promise that she will indeed be back.

Then, also, she knows that expressing any ambivalence about her intention to return could dismantle the all-too-fragile image of single-minded career commitment. It doesn't take much to confirm her employer's suspicion that she hasn't got what it takes to go the distance. One slip, one acknowledgment that she has a primary commitment in addition to her career—to her family—and her hard-won reputation could be smashed.

The truth is that no matter how conscientious, no matter how career committed, a woman is, she can never know for certain what she'll do until she has given birth and experiences her desire to be with the baby. Given the dearth of part-time opportunities, many mothers decide to stay home with the child, even if it involves great financial sacrifice. They make the decision only after they have given birth, long after they have begun their leave.

For this reason there is inevitable uncertainty in the situation. But because we can't prepare for it, the outcome is often stressful for women. It can be devastating for employers. Consider the predicament of the employer. The woman is constrained from expressing her ambivalence about whether, and when, she will return from her leave. Her colleagues cannot plan effectively for coverage of her work. If she doesn't return, it leaves the office short-staffed, scrambling to find a replacement. It's not her fault—she was forced to squelch her true feelings. What could have been a manageable event becomes a crisis.

Because employers insist that women state unequivocally their post-maternity plans, and because many of them can't, it ultimately undermines the long-term relationship between a company and the women it employs. The comment of a thirty-two-year-old manager of market planning and development suggests the shadow it cast in her company.

> Once you start to show, people start to look at you differently. "Are you okay—are you feeling okay?" They almost start to expect that you're going to call up the next day and say you can't show up because of one reason or another. Which I did none of. But you know, it's kind of an interesting thing that so many women throughout their pregnancy

do so many things like that, whether they're valid or not valid, so it gives the ones who don't sort of a stereotype. They say they're going to come back. And then they milk every cent out of the company that they possibly can, and then nobody can rehire anybody until they know that they are coming back or not coming back and so that's what people expect virtually all women who go out on maternity leave to do.[7]

When a woman fails to return, it's not only a surprise and a disappointment for her boss. She feels guilty. The employer feels he's been burned again. But has he been betrayed, or has he forced the woman to betray him?

Parental Leave

Employers don't want to talk about providing even unpaid leaves beyond whatever length of disability is required by law. Women are also afraid to bring up the idea. I often hear corporate leaders and women boast about how soon some stellar woman came back to work after she had her baby. But useful as this speedy return may be in the short term, the long-term outcome can be destructive.

Knowing that to preserve their career momentum they must disassociate themselves from maternity as swiftly as they can, women often go back to their jobs before they are ready physically, mentally, or emotionally. The outcome can be traumatic for the mother. She has little opportunity for bonding with her child and returns to work feeling resentful, guilty, sad, and frustrated about leaving the baby so soon. Think about the issue of breast-feeding. The woman who returns to work so quickly must abandon this most natural of mothering functions.

The too swift return to work can also be unproductive for the employer. "I returned while still fuzzy-headed," said one high-level woman from a major corporation at a Catalyst focus group discussion. "I don't know how much I cost the company." She had returned to her job two weeks after the birth of her child.

Given a work environment where both employee and employer are unwilling to discuss longer parental leaves, the postleave experience is likely to be a lose-lose situation for both.

Child Care

Let's think for a moment about a typical new mother.

She welcomes the stimulation of her job after six weeks of being at home with her baby. Still, like most new parents, she craves time with the infant who has stolen her heart. Her career has always been central to her dreams and expectations, to her identity—so, too, she now realizes, is her child. At the same time, her upbringing has conditioned her to welcome the role of nurturer of her child. In most cases she, not her husband, must research, choose, and monitor a safe, affordable child care arrangement and to communicate with the child care provider. It also becomes her job to pick up the child at a center every day if that is the form of care the couple has selected. If not, if she can afford at-home care, she has more open-ended coverage, but caring for the child after hours is still likely to be her responsibility primarily. She returns to her job, but these dual responsibilities exhaust her.

She quietly begins to put in fewer hours at the office. Superficially all is fine. But look more closely and you will see that she arrives at the office later and leaves earlier. Without special arrangements she is unavailable for early or after five meetings. The change is not huge: instead of eight A.M. to six or six-thirty P.M., she now arrives at nine or nine-thirty and must leave shortly after five to pick up the baby. She knows this reduction in hours won't last forever, that before long she'll be back gung ho. In the meantime she makes up for some lost time by working smart and by bringing her briefcase home on weekends.

She worries that her boss is aware of the change. But she never mentions it. She comes to work hoping that if her boss hasn't said anything, he may not be noticing and everything may be fine.

Of course, it's not fine. Her boss can't help but notice that his ace performer is no longer available for last-minute, pre-or postwork meetings and emergencies. But he doesn't know what to make of it.

He doesn't know that this period of distraction will be finite because neither he nor she has broached the subject. Gradually, though, over the course of this first crucial year of parenthood, his traditional views lead him to imagine that her commitment flicked off, like a light switch, when she had her baby. Rather than talking with her about her performance or her needs, he begins to assign the important projects to others. Silently he crosses her off his list of those with unlimited potential.

She resents it when she's passed over for the good projects, the promotions, the raises. She becomes embittered and loses interest in the job. Her commitment to the department dims. She begins to think about leaving the company. Her manager will be sad to see her go, but he'll be relieved as well—until he recognizes that in all probability, given the demographic realities, he will replace her with another woman who will also have a baby.

These are components of maternity that corporate women face singly and treat silently, crossing their fingers that no higher-up will mistake their parental obligations for lack of commitment to their jobs.

Denying that women have babies leads to a self-fulfilling prophecy of failure for women and for their employers. When employers don't provide flexibility and women don't assert their need for it, the attitudes, behaviors, policies, and practices of employers remain unanalyzed, unchallenged, and unchanged. Then women find they can't handle the cumulative pressures of motherhood and a career. They grow disenchanted with their company's rigidity. Their productivity lags, or they drop out to go to other employers—often competitors of their previous employer.

Employers do not see women's defection as an indication that the policies of the company are at fault. Instead it serves to confirm their preconception that women were never committed to their careers in the first place. Thereafter employers extrapolate that one experience to all the other women they bring in. They anticipate that women will lack "what it takes" in the long run, rather than consider the impact of inflexible policies. The whole syndrome only intensifies after a woman has had one child and is already perceived as lacking in commitment.

Whether we talk about it or not, everyone knows about and thinks about babies and maternity. If we continue to make the subject taboo, continue to choose our maternity dresses with great care, continue to pretend that all women can return to work full-time, with the same intensity as before, six weeks after the baby is born, we'll continue to shortchange women. We'll go on treating maternity as a short-term disability and not the legitimate, lifetime commitment it is in reality. We'll also shortchange business, because when you deny the reality of maternity you can't plan for it. When you don't plan, the chances are slim that you can deal with it cost-effectively.

THE MACRO EFFECT OF BEING A PARENT

When the responsibility for nurturing children was seen as women's full-time job and contained within the home, the experience of being a parent was revered. Now women have joined men in the work force, and it is less clear whose responsibility it is to nurture children. The enormity of the parenting experience seems to have faded into the background. Just as with maternity, discussion of the experience of being a parent has been relegated to the purgatory of the inappropriate. To do otherwise would be to suggest that the ground rules of business have to change—a reality that must be denied at all costs.

We don't talk about the huge impact a child's arrival has on the lives of working parents. From the moment you bring your child into your home, a whole new way of life begins. Until that child is an adult, you can never any longer do anything without thinking, What about my child? You can't just up and go to a movie. You can't eat dinner yourself without first knowing that you've given dinner to the child. You can't have any social interaction without knowing what you're going to do with the child. You can't come home knowing that you're going to have some free time. You can't go to bed knowing you're going to sleep through the night.

Parenting is one of life's greatest experiences. But combining parenthood with career responsibilities is unquestionably demanding and diverting, even for those who can afford some form of child care assistance. Spend some time at the offices of any company in the dead of winter and you'll soon identify the parents of young children—no matter how career-absorbed, fathers and mothers can't help but catch the five colds that started in the schoolyard. At any time of year you'll find the new parents muffling their yawns at meetings, having been up with hungry or scared or colicky babies the previous night.

Well-meaning advocates for workplace family supports often arm themselves with statistics drawn from studies of the impact of parenting. Sometimes they cite research that has been done into rates of absenteeism or lateness for working parents. Sometimes they explore employees' own perceptions of how parenting responsibilities affect their work performance. The purpose of using these statistics is to convince employers of the toll parenting takes on work performance and, therefore, the necessity for policies and practices that will support working parents.

Studies such as these depict the impact of parenthood in excruciating detail. Yet it seems to me that the end result is to minimize its huge effects. Researchers trivialize parenthood with a statistic that talks about "one day more per month of absenteeism on the part of women than men." They fail to capture the magnitude of this experience that is, for the most part, one no longer of mothers at home, but of parents at work.

All you need to do is trust your own experience as a parent to recognize that having a child changes every aspect of your life. No statistic can begin to suggest the enormous need of the mother and father both to bond with their child. No figure can begin to show the anguish that goes way beyond "feelings of distraction" at work when parents cannot find or afford quality child care. And today, when most mothers are no longer at home, men are as worried and distracted as women by concern for the child's well-being. Statistics can't nearly describe the additional pressures that ensue when a two-career couple decides to have a second child. This is usually when the delicate balancing act created for the first child can get thrown almost impossibly out of kilter.

The truth is that we're fooling ourselves by pretending that being a parent can be broken down into a series of finite figures. We're fooling ourselves when we expect women to bend to fit the rules of when they should return from having babies. We're shortchanging business when we pretend that new parents can operate on all eight cylinders all the time. We're just wrong when we penalize working mothers because they can't do the impossible.

It's not that employers have to take a loss when they employ new parents. But, unlike the past, companies do have to expect that employees will bring the responsibilities of parenting into the workplace. With both parents working, children are a workplace issue today. The experience of parenting is inseparable from the workplace experience. And we haven't yet dealt with the implications of that fact.

THE SEPARATE SHIFTS OF MEN AND WOMEN

Men have begun to do household chores, and women have embarked on careers. But the redistribution of *responsibility* for life's work in a more profound sense has not taken place. Women, for the most part, still take primary responsibility for the work of the home, and men take primary responsibility for the financial well-being of the family.

Women are afraid to ask men to take more domestic responsibility. Before marriage women will not talk with men about to what extent they someday hope to divide their homemaking and child-rearing responsibilities. Once married, they won't talk about their desire for men to take a bigger role at home. The reason, at least in part: They are frightened at the prospect of a failed marriage, being reduced to poverty and isolation. But there's nothing in marriage that can be more destructive than the anger generated by feeling exploited and not being able to talk about it.

Sensing the danger inherent in bringing up the issue, women talk about their double burden vehemently, but only in the most careful, guarded way. Hence the assertion by some women that their husbands "pitch in" enough at home. In one poll of married women, for example, 61 percent described their husband's efforts as a "fair share" of the domestic burden—even while the same poll found that the women did the lion's share of the shopping, cooking, cleaning, bill paying, and child care.[8] In *The Second Shift*, the book in which she describes the division of household responsibilities in two-paycheck marriages, Arlie Hochschild gives a poignant profile of a couple in which the woman insists her husband is pulling as much weight around the house as she, when in fact all he's doing is taking care of the family dog. The wife feels anxious and doesn't want it to seem as if she's making waves. After all, he's doing *something*. That's better than nothing. So she not only goes along with it, she even praises him for it, hoping that with her reinforcement maybe he'll do a little more.

That men won't share in women's traditional domestic responsibilities is only part of the story. There is a counterpoint to women's "second shift" that gets expressed even less often. It's another burden, one traditionally shouldered by men—the responsibility to support the family financially. Both men and women feel at a very deep level that it is natural for the man to be the provider. It is in part a mind/feeling split for women who are committed to their careers but who were raised by mothers who expected to be "taken care of." It's so highly charged a subject that it's difficult to confront—more difficult even than women's second shift—so we seldom talk about the inexorable pressure on men to support the family. This part of the domestic role division won't bear examination or challenge.

I asked a well-off young couple I know to list how they divide their domestic responsibilities. On her side of the balance sheet was supervising all house maintenance, gift purchasing, watering the plants, taking the children to doctors, arranging play dates, and coordinating any entertaining they might do. His side included getting the kids up, dressed, and fed in the morning, taking out the garbage, planning vacations, and all financial investments. They alternated putting the children to bed. I talked with them about the list and found that they consider their responsibilities equal or tipping toward the wife carrying a heavier burden.

Tellingly, in our conversation they gave short shrift to one item that did not even appear on their list: all responsibility for the financial support of the family. Although both of them have paying jobs, the husband assumes it is his responsibility to support the family. When I raised the issue, the wife was indignant.

Men don't talk about this second shift of their own because their sense of masculinity is so wrapped up in their provider role and because they feel guilty over women's better-publicized second shift. Women don't talk about it because they don't want to lose any ground in getting men to take some of the domestic burden. They're afraid that bringing men's disproportionate financial role into the dialogue would render their husbands' nonparticipation at home more acceptable. Further, if men's financial burden was part of the equation, it might lead to women having to assume some additional responsibility that they cannot in all fairness take on.

As it is now, women are so angry because of the schism between their expectations and their experience, and they are so burned out from carrying their domestic burden, that they are unwilling to take on any further financial burden. Men feel such subliminal pressure from carrying the primary financial burden that they can't see taking on anything else. Each is impatient with his or her spouse for not fully understanding the weight of that burden. The irony is that it is in large part the fact that men carry an unacknowledged financial responsibility that makes them unwilling and even unable to share the domestic responsibility with women.

THE CORROSIVE CORPORATE ENVIRONMENT

Corporations are hemorrhaging talent because of their employment policies—or nonpolicies, as the case may be. I've talked privately many times with senior executives who have an uneasy sense that their female managers are hitting barriers male managers aren't facing.

I see employers' reluctance to discuss the barriers women face as a series of levels. At the deepest level, they believe women should be home, or in any case they're not looking for ways to keep women in their world. At the next level, they don't want to know what the problems are because they don't believe they are soluble. Finally, even if they understand the problems, they don't want to address them because they think it's too difficult, too expensive. That's an extra burden. What for? they think. To help this woman who's not really committed to my company anyway?

It's also difficult to get women to concede that there are barriers. They fear that the admission will reflect unfavorably on their toughness or that they will be punished for the breach of company loyalty. They also worry that they will be perceived as different, which translates to "not as good as."

When you go into a company to explore its environment for women, as Catalyst does frequently, you get an avalanche of usually pent-up assessments of the corrosive conditions for women.

I've culled just a few examples from companies that must, for obvious reasons, remain anonymous. These observations give the texture of women's corporate experience—an experience shaped by managers' preconceptions about women, counterproductive male behaviors, the exclusion of women from informal male networks, the absence of mentors and role models, and sexual tension and harassment. The stress and difficulty of the experience increases as women move to higher levels, where, as women, they are more isolated.[9]

> My boss's first response to me [when I asked for a promotion] was, "How can you do this job with your family and wife responsibilities?"

> He [a senior executive] confuses our names. There are a couple of relatively senior women, and he's been here for several years and he can't distinguish us from one another.

Another woman and I went to an important meeting, and we walked into the room and immediately a senior manager at this company said, "Are you sure you *girls* are in the right meeting?"

A few colleagues very directly propositioned me, and that's just sort of how they behave and how their leader behaves. . . . I've never told anyone about that, although after one particular instance I was upset and angry enough that I almost went running to somebody in personnel and said, "You can't let this go on anymore. . . ." But I didn't do it. . . . I felt like I would have been perceived as yet another one of the women who was complaining.

The other day I got very, very angry. So what do women do when they get very angry? Yeah, they cry, which is regarded as a fatal error! I shed a few tears in front of [the director], and the next day he came up to me and do you know what he said to me in front of all my colleagues? "How are you holding up?" I thought I would die!

My manager plainly refused to assign me to emergency duty. He said it was too dangerous for me and wouldn't let me go even though he knew legally he was supposed to. It wasn't because he didn't care. He cared about me; he was concerned, but it wasn't his place to make that decision for me. . . . I wanted to go.

At grade fifteen level, women have to be "unobtrusively female." They have to fit in with the guys. . . . Men have to be comfortable with you and like your company. Communication is very, very important at this level. . . . The way you express your ideas . . . the timing with which you insert your wisdom, is very important for a woman. Men have fragile egos and don't want to hear all your news and views. If the timing is off, it can be a disaster.

There aren't many women here, and there's strength in numbers. Women are still excluded from the male networks. At an off-site meeting, men go into the men's room and talk, and you're alone in the women's room.

[Successful women are] not perceived as nice. . . . [They're] aggressive, which intimidates men.

Management is high on her as long as they're helping her, but not when they're dealing with her as a peer.

A male manager: Because the company doesn't provide support, I won't hire women with babies or single men with kids because they may not always be available.

A male senior manager: Despite the progress we've made, there arc still biases in male managers. At the top, which is predominantly male, there are still people who don't feel as comfortable having a woman on their direct staff. Still, most people have never worked for a woman. Some of them still feel, "She's not going to be as dedicated. . . . She won't be there when I need her. . . ." It's hard to say what kinds [of biases exist]. We never talk about it . . . but the sexual issue exists. I'm not sure how comfortable my wife would be if I mentored an attractive young woman. It's an issue, and it will take time.

A male senior manager: Recently at teamwork day . . . a high-level prospective customer was there with one of my center managers, and they met another center manager who's a woman. The customer said, "Gee, if she came along with the package, I would definitely buy. . . ." followed by laughs and jokes.

THE DISPROPORTIONATE ATTRITION OF WOMEN

All the forces described in this chapter—corporate inflexibility about maternity, the macro effect of parenting, corrosive conditions, and the separate shifts of men and women—combine to drive toward one inevitable outcome: there is a higher rate of turnover among women than among men in corporate America. Yet few people want to admit that women's attrition is higher than that of men. Male executives don't because they know it would draw negative attention to the policies and practices within their companies that are contributing to the tendency for women to leave in midcareer. They don't want to risk bad publicity, let alone litigation. Women don't because they are afraid that awareness of the high rate of turnover will reinforce management's preconceptions about women's lack of commitment. Both policymakers and women do their best to keep data about turnover rates concealed, rationalizing that it's too difficult to track, irrelevant, minor, or an inaccurate reflection of reality.

These rationalizations are wrong—and, worse, harmful. Turnover is the most obvious, and costly, manifestation of a crisis of critical proportions.

Neither women nor men, of course, tend any longer to stay with one employer throughout their professional lives. But there are two causes of attrition that are unique to women. One, the corporate environment is more difficult and stressful for women than it is for men. Second is the absence of flexibility that forces many women to be overwhelmed after the birth of a child. There may be other reasons women leave their jobs, but none is so profound as maternity—especially in combination with the barriers to women's advancement that are so pervasive in the corporate environment.

Once again we see a vicious cycle. Women are expected to quit. The suspicion is not talked about. The reasons that might cause them to leave are never dealt with. The climate becomes impossibly stressful. Finally women have no choice but to move their careers to another company.

Before we look at evidence of the turnover, it's instructive to examine the forms the denial of women's higher attrition takes.

First, the corporate side of the equation. Although it is standard procedure in many of the larger companies to collect a massive array of data about their work force, employers aren't keeping records in a way that would illuminate the reasons women in their companies succeed or fail. They're not analyzing where women are clustered, how career paths differ for men and for women, attrition following the birth of one or two or three children, or the barriers women are experiencing that men do not.

Employers rarely keep records, for example, on the gender ratio of managers in staff versus line positions. They don't identify the performance patterns of women in relation to men in sales. They don't even keep records of disability by category—that is, they don't want to indicate on the record that a disability is for childbirth because they may be accused of tracking women who go on leave. The only gender-related numbers companies are willing to look at, and this they do infrequently, are the number of women at the very senior levels. And this is information that doesn't really tell them very much.

They are afraid to track patterns that might illuminate why women are having a hard time advancing in their companies. What scares them is that taking note of these patterns might be construed as finding excuses to keep women down or force them out. They might be accused of red-dotting women for lack of commitment and condemning them to failure.

I spent a half hour recently with the vice-president of human resources at a financial services company. For a good fifteen minutes he described what an excellent year they had had financially, the last in a string of ten to twelve good years. He was quick to point out that the firm had increased its total of female managing directors from 0 to somewhere about 7 out of a total of 184. The firm's record was at least as good, he said, as any other financial firm in the city. It seemed clear to me that although the company did not yet see women as a business imperative, it had a slowly dawning awareness that there might be some few good women out there.

When we discussed next steps for his firm, the human resources executive agreed to take a new cut on his quarterly printouts of employee turnover—he would separate the figures by gender, which *had never before been done.* I found this absolutely amazing.

Let's say one of the best and brightest managers decides to leave her company. Wouldn't it help to prevent future losses if her employer had a clue as to why she left? Yet there usually isn't any indication of her reasons for departure in her personnel file. Her company often has no idea if she left for a better career opportunity at a company whose climate is more conducive to women's career advancement. Neither does her employer know whether it was the inflexibility of the company's maternity leave policy or the behavior of one less-than-sensitive boss that caused her to give up and go. All these are problems that can be remedied, but not if they remain invisible.

When women dispute the idea of a higher rate of turnover for female employees, one argument I've heard is explicit. It's simply too dangerous, women have told me, to draw management's attention to it. But other arguments are called into service as well. One asserts that women's and men's lifetime rates of turnover are about equivalent. Hence, women would have it, women's turnover during the childbearing years doesn't warrant discussion. Another rationale is that men suffer disproportionately from heart disease and alcoholism, both of which raise their attrition rates.

I think women who minimize the importance of attrition are missing the point.

It is in the crucial framework of the childbearing years that an employee who has potential begins to prove herself in a way that could put her on the fast track toward top management. It's also the time when a company's investment in training an employee begins to pay off. You could say that this is exactly the worst time for a promising employee to leave the company, both for individuals and for employers. So although it may be true that men also have reason to leave their jobs in disproportionate numbers in other seasons of life, it's important to note that the impact of a job termination in one's late twenties or early thirties is more of—and much more frequent—a loss on both sides, given current conditions.

The size of the loss, once you look beneath all the denial, is really quite large. I find it especially ironic that the extent to which companies are losing women comes through perhaps most clearly in studies that purport to demonstrate how many women return to their jobs after maternity leave. Implicit in these results is the huge proportion of women who do not return to their jobs.

I remember a study by the National Council of Jewish Women that documented the impact of employers' responsiveness on working mothers' performance and tenure. An article described the results:

> Women working in highly accommodating settings reported higher job satisfaction and appeared to show a greater sense of responsibility. They missed fewer days from work, were in better health overall, spent more time at home on job-related work without pay, and worked later in pregnancy. Follow-up interviews found that *78 percent of women in highly accommodating workplaces returned to the same employers after childbirth, as against 50 percent of those working for unaccommodating bosses.* [Italics mine.][10]

Certainly it's cause for encouragement that companies can do much to maintain the productivity of pregnant workers. Why, though, isn't there a greater outcry about the 22 percent (or 50 percent!) of women who don't return to their jobs? Are our expectations about women's capacity for consistent job tenure so low?

I challenge you to imagine what would be the reaction if one-quarter, or fully half, of male employees who had left the workplace for six weeks for any reason chose at the end of that period not to return to their jobs. We'd acknowledge the huge cost for the company that had employed them, and surely serious steps would be taken to upgrade retention levels in the future. Certainly we would not accept the results with equanimity.

I heard a hint of that equanimity in the response from Frances Stancill, vice-president of Affirmative Action at Corestates Financial Corporation, when I asked her what had been the company's experience with maternity. "Seventy-five percent of the women return," she said with some pride. She added that this was only a snapshot look, but the bank felt it was "doing very well."

This is a company whose youthful chairman, president, and chief executive officer, Terrance Larsen, is the driving force behind what I think is a very significant effort to respond to the needs of women and minorities. So far the company had sponsored thirty-two focus groups run by a consulting firm and designed to expose problems within the company, particularly in the areas of development and retention. They'd even held three follow-up sessions to discuss what actions would be taken.

Nonetheless, it would appear to be acceptable for this better-than-average company to lose one-quarter of its women in the normal course of maternity.

Recent Bureau of Labor Statistics findings provide further proof that substantial numbers of women are not returning to their jobs, regardless of whether or not they receive medical disability or other employee benefits, although benefits do make a huge difference. Researchers correlated the likelihood of women returning to their jobs after maternity leave with the type of benefits and length of leave they received. The analysis shows that from 1981 to 1985, 70 percent of women with paid leave or other benefits returned to work within six months of childbearing, while only 44 percent of those women without benefits did so.[11]

An important factor in women's higher turnover is that women continue to want to take sufficient time for motherhood, at least while their children are young. A Catalyst study of parental leave takers in major corporations showed that a majority of women would prefer not to leave their jobs entirely but to work on part-time schedules for a period following childbirth.[12] For most that option doesn't exist. Given the scant flexibility provided under current corporate conditions, the only alternative for women who want sufficient time to care for their babies is to drop out entirely for a period.

You can see members of the next generation building a hiatus for child rearing into their plans. The business students I spoke with recently exemplify their attitude. They're not terribly realistic. They don't want it to jeopardize their career growth, but they are determined to take the time they need for family. They aren't aware of the sacrifices they might have to make. Here are just a few of their observations:

> I want to be the one to stay at home. It's just something that I want to do. I want to be there with my kids for those first two years.

> At thirty-five, I would like to have two children. I would also like to spend the bulk of my efforts taking care of the children, I think. I'll be out after business school for maybe two or three years, two if I could plan it exactly as I'd like to, and then I want to have kids. And then I'd like to take off a significant amount of time. Something like a three-or four- or five-year period. And then go back [to work] at a point where I could say, "All right, my kids are standing up and going to school."

> I think we're underestimating how much women want to stay home. I mean, if your husband said, "Hey, I'm happy to quit my job and hang out with the kid," you'd be, like, "Well, no!" I think there are women, myself included, who could definitely see giving up [a career] for a while.

Study findings reinforce the idea that young women embarking on professional careers intend to take the time they need to raise their children. A 1990 study of how undergraduate women planned to juggle career and family, for example, found that 97 percent of the women it surveyed intend to resume work after having a baby. But while 44 percent of the women plan to resume work shortly afterward,

53 percent want to wait to go back to work until their children are older—perhaps school age.[13]

What does all this add up to? Not, I think, an excuse for not trying to develop and retain women. Turnover is as costly for companies as it is harmful for women's careers. Allowing it to continue unacknowledged or underestimated saps the confidence of women and destroys their employers' trust in them. Both have an uneasy sense of failure, but no hard data to back it up and no legitimized avenues for talking about the issues. Once again we must face the reality of turnover in order to take the necessary steps to minimize it.

There have been some few instances where a company has tracked its turnover experience in terms of men and women and in so doing showed that the benefits outweighed the dangers of doing so. Corning Glass Works, for example, conducted a study of its attrition rates between 1980 and 1987 for different employee groups—white males, minorities, and women. It found that about one in thirteen white male employees left the company each year. For minorities and women the rates were much higher—during the same period, about one in seven black professional employees left, as did one in eight professional women. The reason most often given in exit interviews: lack of career opportunities.

The result of Corning's total look at its internal demographics was a comprehensive plan to fully integrate women and minorities into the mainstream of its business.

In the last few years I have seen other employers begin to consider undertaking similar research. I remember meeting with some of the executives at Liz Claiborne, Inc., for example, a thirteen-year-old company whose record with women struck me as fairly impressive. Women represented 65 percent of employees, at all levels, except for the top four or five members of the policy committee, who were all male. The environment was known to be tremendously fast-paced, upbeat, and unusually caring.

When I spoke with Kathryn Connors, vice-president of human resources, she told me of her observation that women in critical positions who have had children are being torn in all directions. As a result, the company had examined its data and found that fully 34 percent of women who go on maternity leave were not returning. The analysis persuaded the top managers that they had a problem they had to address. A work and family policy is in the draft stage. They are moving toward managing maternity.

Despite the positive efforts made by a few companies, the problems I've discussed are not going to vanish as long as we refuse to talk about them. Perhaps if we look at where we've been, and see how far we've come, we'll start to develop an understanding of where we need to go from here.

CHAPTER FOUR

Public Progress, Private Pain

*T*here are two stories here. One is the tremendous empowerment of women over a very brief time span. It's a familiar story, one that has grabbed headlines for thirty years. Consider the multiple sources of women's empowerment that can move them forward in the workplace.

Increased Variety in Life Patterns

Until quite recently, women's lives were ordained by tradition, not personal choice. Convention dictated moving from one cloistered, isolated arrangement to another. Women went straight from their parents' home to their husbands' home, with perhaps a stop out for college in between. A wife's responsibility was to her husband and children. She stayed at home until her children went off to college. Only then might she pursue work outside the home.

That sequence is no longer a given. For one, women marry later. Consider that in 1963 the rate of married to unmarried twenty-three-year-old women was three to one. By 1982 a woman of the same age who was not married was almost as typical as one who had married.[1] In 1988 the mean age of first marriage reached 25.9 for men and 23.6

for women—for women, later than they ever had married in the history of the country.[2]

Women are now able to experiment with different life-styles before and between marriages, rather than simply adopting the values and behaviors of their parents. In my generation premarital sexual relationships were unusual and not discussed. Then the divorce rate soared, and cohabitation became accepted either before or instead of marriage—in 1960 there were 439,000 couples living together; in 1983, 1.9 million.[3] Women are free to leave marriages that aren't working, to remarry, or to remain single.

Not only has the order of a woman's life changed, there has also been a switch from one role at a time to multiple roles concurrently. Marriage and education, or marriage and work, or work and raising children—these are now simultaneous options in the life course. Accordingly, the number of married women in the labor force rose from 20 percent in 1947 to over 50 percent in 1982, to 59 percent in 1991.[4] It is now typical for mothers of young children to hold paying jobs, which is an even more radical departure from past norms; since 1950 the labor force participation rate of women with preschool-age children has more than quadrupled.[5] In 1990, 55.3 percent of mothers with children under the age of one were in the labor force, up from 31 percent in 1975.[6] Motherhood is clearly no longer a bar to career commitment.

Rising Educational Attainment

Fifty-two percent of all undergraduate diplomas are awarded to women.[7] The rise in women's college participation, though, has been gradual over the course of the century. More empowering is the explosion of women's participation in graduate and professional education. Of all master's degrees in 1989, 51 percent went to women, up from 31.6 percent in 1960.[8]

There are two great outcomes of this dramatic increase. One is that women represent an ever-increasing proportion of the total educated population from which business receives its workers. As the number of female participants in educational programs expands, the proportion of male students shrinks. Between 1972 and 1981, for example, total college enrollment grew by 34 percent. Male enrollment rose by 14 percent and female enrollment by 61 percent.[9] There was a 12 percent decrease in the number of male Ph.D.'s between 1977 and 1987.[10]

Companies, of course, compete to stock their incoming management ranks with the very best college students they can attract. It's how they build their future leadership group. Today college recruiters simply cannot bypass women, because they are among the best candidates. The only alternative for those shortsighted enough to insist on hiring only men with leadership potential is to take on men with weaker academic credentials. Thus women's success in school sets them up for equal acceptance in the workplace.

Another outcome of women's rising educational attainment is that they are positioned to surge ahead in those fields that are traditionally male-dominated. We haven't yet seen many women at senior levels (let alone at the helm) of industrial or heavy manufacturing companies, for example, but they are entering the pipeline that goes to the top by virtue of their educational preparation. For example, the proportion of BAs in business earned by women grew from 8 percent in 1965, to 33.7 percent in 1980, to 46.7 percent in 1990.[11] Similarly, in 1965, .4 percent of engineering BAs went to women, a figure that jumped to 13.6 percent in 1990.[12] Women earned 2.6 percent of all MBAs in 1965 and 33.6 percent in 1990. They earned 5.5 percent of MAs in accounting in 1965 and 43.7 percent in 1990. Women's law degrees rose from 2.5 percent in 1960 to 40.8 percent in 1990.[13]

Sexual Freedom

Everybody knows about the sexual revolution. But what relevance does it have for women and their careers? Simply this: The sexual revolution took the mystique away from relationships between women and men.

Before women's sexuality was openly discussed and accepted and before premarital intercourse was condoned, sex was acceptable only within the narrow confines of monogamous, lifetime marriage, and everything in a woman's adolescence was geared toward finding and preserving that ultimate romantic bond. The entire premarital relationship of women and men was a romantic courtship that was a prelude to a sexual union, to be achieved within the state of matrimony.

When I was an undergraduate, male and female students were seldom friends because friendship is based on common goals and shared experience. The goals of men and women were polarized: women dreamed of and planned for marriage, men for careers. Their focus in high school and college differed, their experiences in pursuit of their separate goals differed, their perceptions of one another differed.

Then several trends converged. As greater latitude in sexual interaction grew to be accepted, the mystique of the relationship between women and men diminished. The sexual revolution freed men and women to explore different kinds of relationships. It gave women and men a *choice* about whether to be involved romantically.

At the same time, and as women began to think about and plan for careers, men and women began to share more of life's interests as peers. In going through school together, studying together, worrying together about what they were going to do with their lives, in taking part in activities as friends, young men and women gained mutual understanding and respect. The ultimate consequence is that women and men are growing increasingly relaxed with one another as work colleagues. Tension still exists, but among younger people in business there is certainly a higher comfort level than ever before.

Fewer Children, Later Childbearing

Perhaps most significant, most empowering for women in terms of opening up their career options, has been a set of trends regarding childbearing decisions. At the height of the baby boom of 1946 through 1964, women averaged 3.7 births.[14] The advent of safe, effective birth control in the 1960s facilitated women's decision to limit the size of their families.

Something else changed, as well: the use of contraception was seen as morally acceptable. We tend to forget that in the earlier part of this century even some women shunned the idea of controlling their fertility. Many felt that making contraception freely available could only encourage men to indulge their bestial natures and so exacerbate the exploitation of women. However, even in my generation, when women welcomed the power to control the *timing* of their fertility, a big family was still the cultural ideal. It was generally thought that if you chose not to have children, you were selfish.

That gradually changed. There evolved a consciousness that the large family was leading to a "population explosion," and women were exhorted to have fewer children. The size of the ideal family shrank. The result of all these trends: The total fertility rate dropped to an average of 1.8 births per woman in 1975 and has remained at about that level through the present.[15] Women today want children as much as ever, but the norm is now one or two children rather than three or four.

Further, women have begun to postpone the age at which they begin having children until, on average for college graduates, thirty-one. This behavior has a huge payoff for women in the workplace.

When I started Catalyst in 1962, women were thought of not only as full-time but as lifetime wives and mothers. To make the case for employing women, I often used a bar graph that showed the shape of women's lives and the shape of men's lives. (See figure 4.1.) The graph for men showed that from age twenty-two to sixty-five virtually all of them worked full-time. The graph for women showed that they were at home from age twenty-two to thirty-five, raising their children and supporting their husbands' careers. From age thirty-five to forty-five they were free to work outside the home half-time because their children were in school. From forty-five to sixty-five they could work full-time. I used these graphs to show that women really did have time for careers and that it was worthwhile for employers to view them as a resource.

My graphic representation of the life of a typical American woman would look different today. (See figure 4.2.) Now it is more common than not for the serious career woman to enter management at age twenty-two and work full-time until the birth of the first of her two children at age thirty-one. Before she has a baby, today's woman has chosen her career, trained for it, gained substantial experience, and given her employer ample time to assess the quality of her performance. By that time, if she's good and seriously motivated, she is a highly valued, seasoned professional in whom the company has made a substantial investment—as much as $90,000, for example, at IBM.

She's a great business resource with a fount of firm-specific knowledge. If the company were to ignore her needs and watch her leave the company, the statistical likelihood is it would replace her with another female employee, who would also have a child at some point in her career. But this new recruit would be inexperienced, untrained, and untested. Thus, to amortize the investment the company has

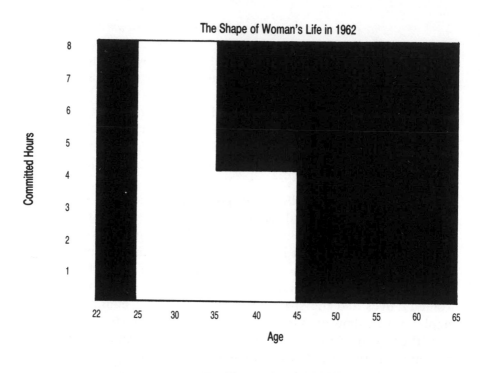

The Shape of Woman's Life in 1962

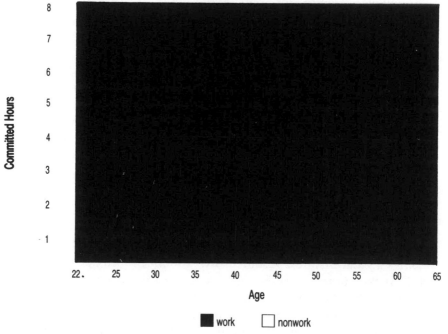

The Shape of Man's Life in 1962

■ work   □ nonwork

FIGURE 4-1: The Shape of a Woman's Life and a Man's Life in 1962

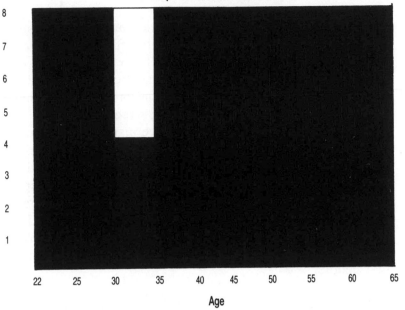

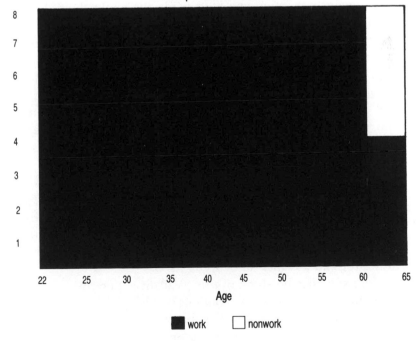

FIGURE 4-2: The Shape of a Woman's Life and a Man's Life in 1992

already made in the training and development of the seasoned manager who has a baby, it is motivated to offer longer leaves, flexible hours, and other policies that will help her balance her career and family responsibilities. The fact is that the cost of these initiatives pales beside the cost of losing her. And it will become increasingly costly as the competition for able employees intensifies.

Even if she takes off five years, the company will benefit. Consider how my graph would look then. The woman would work full-time from age twenty-two to thirty-one and then from age thirty-six to sixty-five. A total of thirty-eight years as opposed to the typical man's forty-three, the last five of which may well be part-time. And I'd wager that most women would be willing to work part-time during that five-year period, given the opportunity. Their employers would be rewarded for this responsiveness by the higher retention of their best people.

Changing Attitudes

Until recently women who held paid jobs while their children were young were viewed as pariahs in their communities, their mothers excoriated them for their irresponsibility, and their husbands tended to resent the loss of the status symbol and support system that their wives had provided. Today the common expectation is that the majority of women, including mothers, will pursue employment.

A complementary change is that women are accepted as intelligent and capable. That sounds pretty basic, but in my generation the pervasive attitude among leaders in business and the professions (and even among women themselves) was that women were not smart enough, or at least not analytical or quantitative enough, to be professionals, managers, or leaders. Today, although corporate leaders harbor doubts about women's career commitment, their willingness to take risks or to close a deal, there is no doubt in their minds that women are as intelligent as men, that they have the ability required to master and advance in every field.

More specifically, think of this. A scant generation ago the prevailing belief was that women "couldn't do math." Today, as I've pointed out, over half of accounting graduates are female, and they are well represented in the top of their classes.

Women now see careers as a right (if not a responsibility), just as men do. Little girls are raised with a more androgynous message. As a result women are beginning to assume that they must be able to support themselves (if not their families). Some women even build their families around their careers, as men have traditionally done, rather than building their careers around their families.

All these changes are leading to what will be probably the most significant attitudinal development. As employers begin to see women as a business imperative rather than superfluous to their staffing needs, they will see that they can't afford to let women remain in subordinate or ancillary positions in their companies. It will become clear they must remove the barriers to women's advancement. They will also see that family issues *are* workplace issues, and they will respond by providing family supports that enhance employees' productivity and commitment.

THE GENERATIONS OF WOMEN

There is an underside to this story of women's empowerment. It concerns everyday lives, specifically those of the successive waves of women as they entered the workplace. And although this second story also shows forward movement, it is permeated with a sense of the personal struggle corporate women have faced in an environment created by men. For thirty years corporate leaders haven't seen much applicability of women's increasing autonomy, education, and skills to their bottom line. In this environment their successes have essentially gone unnoticed and unrewarded.

Though women have all along drawn pride from their triumphs in the arena of paid work, equally dominant in their vision is a deep pessimism, a product of the hardship of entering this essentially closed world. And as women have been increasingly integrated into the workplace, their experience has in some respects grown more difficult. The reason: Women's empowerment is undeniable, inexorable, yet the situation remains essentially static. Women remain outsiders. Even today, when corporate leaders have a growing awareness that it will serve their business interests to remove the obstacles to women's productivity and advancement, corporate practices are still governed largely not by this bottom-line reality, but by traditional values and attitudes.

I think a good way to understand this more complex story is to think of the women entering the workplace since the middle of this century as a series of generations. Mine is not an academic or political understanding of each successive generation's evolving role in the home and at work. Instead I've been an active participant from the very beginning in the changes that have taken place.

My experience at Catalyst aside, at a very personal level I have lived in the center of four generations' experience—my parents, my peers, my children, and my grandchildren. So I have seen and felt at close range the different patterns of our lives: from my mother's unquestioned center of gravity in her home to my preteen granddaughter's solid, freely chosen sense of self.

Women are clearly a resource to business as never before. Yet they are a resource that is still for the most part underutilized. With each generation of women entering the workplace, forward movement has therefore been matched by frustration.

MY MOTHER'S GENERATION

I can't recall women of my mother's generation talking about the confinement of the home.

In that era, the era of the 1920s, highly polarized roles for men and women were embraced with little question at virtually every income level, throughout American society. In fact, my mother's peers seemed not only to accept the roles delineated by society, but to thrive on them. After an early marriage, soon out of high school or college, the typical couple settled down to raise a large family. The husband's pride in supporting his stay-at-home wife was matched by her sense of dignity and purpose.

The challenges of mothering back then included greater infant mortality, few packaged goods, no wash-and-wear, no prepared formula or baby food, no diaper service or disposable diapers, primitive washing machines and dryers, and later school entry for young children. By today's standards this is nearly incomprehensible. The homemaker role was a consuming one, and succeeding at this difficult task must have yielded rewards in kind. Homemakers were respected and appreciated. In addition, women of that era found fulfillment in religion, in community activities, and in "meaningful" volunteer work, particularly as their children grew less dependent on them.

In my parents' day, "until death do us part" was a reality as well as a ritual vow. There's no reason to believe that couples were more happily married in that era. But divorce was so traumatic, both difficult to obtain and socially unacceptable, that husbands and wives stayed in marriages that were far less than perfect. And because women counted on moving directly from the home of their father to that of their husband, there was no practical incentive for them to earn money. Throughout their lives they could trust the truthfulness of a little voice inside that had always said, "Someone will take care of you."

This is not to say that even in my parents' time there weren't women who held paying jobs. There have always been women who worked. For the most part it was the highly educated woman (help was readily available at home) and the woman in the low-income family. If you were to look at a census from early in the century, you'd find women performing jobs that were surprisingly diverse—in the 1900 U.S. census, for example, women could be found in 295 of the 303 listed occupations.[16] But until after World War II, it was unmarried women for the most part who entered the work force. Though their highest ambition was to find a husband, other reasons for working might include moral improvement, lessening the tedium of their lives, or bringing superior feminine moral traits into society. Only if a family otherwise faced destitution would a woman who was married, especially if she had children, seek work outside the home. Whatever their motivation, most women saw their work force participation as temporary. Their true place in society was at home, rearing children, ironing shirts, and fixing supper.

The archetype of breadwinner husband and stay-at-home wife, the one we summon up when we talk about the "traditional" family, is largely believed to have existed since time immemorial. In fact, the polarized work and family roles of my parents' era were the product of specific and fairly recent historical forces. Until our century, men and women worked more or less side by side in rural communities. Most families worked their own small farms, and all hands were needed to get the work done, regardless of gender. Some division of roles was natural, of course. Women may have shouldered the job of nurturing young children, but men shared responsibility for their upbringing and education. At the same time, while men's greater physical strength was needed for heavy manual labor, women produced goods needed to survive, from candles to clothing.

The Industrial Revolution moved the production of goods to outside the home and so split the one world encompassing work and family into two spheres. Now men went out to a central workplace to earn wages. Still, the system of men's world of work and women's world of home and family was not yet a cultural given. That came to be the case, according to many historians, because of Americans' desire to replicate the life of the European nobility on American soil. Surplus production allowed husbands in more affluent families to indulge in the status symbol of keeping a stay-at-home wife. As society in general grew wealthier, the model of breadwinner husband and stay-at-home wife trickled down to the lower economic levels. More important, the practice became institutionalized as an ideal.

By my calculation, if the separate worlds of men and women became crystallized at the end of the nineteenth century, my parents' generation would have been the first to accept their polarized roles as preordained. One function the women of this generation embraced was passing on the values of their gender to their daughters and the wives of their sons. They were so entrenched in this heritage that it never occurred to them their daughters might not be similarly rewarded.

THE CLASS OF 1945

It was this generation that produced the women of the college class of 1945, the women who were to become the feminists of the 1960s. The roles they would ultimately reject were those they had learned at their mothers' knee.

Why did my generation not accept the roles that were handed down, especially since our mothers seemed to have found such fulfillment? I think there are a couple of reasons. One, not only did we get the message of separate roles for men and women from our parents, we were beamed a singularly strong and unequivocal message by a society that had been immersed in war for five years. For five years we hadn't produced consumer goods (refrigerators, cars, houses) or babies. The message to men was "Go to work and produce goods." The message to women was "Go home and produce babies." Our roles were not only passed down to us by our parents, they were imposed on us by society.

Then, too, the wartime era had allowed women a certain amount of freedom—to work and be autonomous, apart from the men who had left for the front. These two elements set us up to feel later the narrow confines of the home, after we were already ensconced there. The combination of the message we had been raised with and the freedom we experienced was a combustible mixture, and later on it turned my generation into natural revolutionaries.

I entered college in 1942, exhilarated at the prospect of the intellectual climate, the opportunity to learn. But, like my classmates, I had been socialized for a purely domestic future. We spent those World War II years waiting for our men to return. We dreamed of marriage and homemaking, never doubting our delight in visions of full-time mothering, running up curtains for our suburban homes, preparing gourmet meals, participating in community affairs, and being at all times attractive to our husbands and happy and radiant, loving our lot.

One of the things I recall was my senior class hoop rolling contest, held on commencement day on one of the college's long green lawns. Victory designated the winner—what else?—to be the first married. In caps and gowns, six hundred members of the class of 1945 applied themselves to rolling those hoops with sticks as we had for four years to more intellectual pursuits. Guess who won? (Actually I was the second to the altar.) Today a science center occupies that lawn, for me a symbol of the changes that have taken place in the forty-seven years since my graduation.

Socialized by our mothers to tend the hearth and raise the children, even the most independent-minded women of my generation counted on traditional roles in marriage as the ticket to spiritual fulfillment. "Togetherness" was the ideal. It seemed that everyone got married. After all, married couples occupied four out of five American households.[17] In 1957, 2,400 American couples were asked about the character of a person who chose not to marry as part of a study about the work, parent, and spouse roles. Four-fifths of respondents said that such a person must be either selfish or neurotic.[18]

In those days the vocation of homemaker was one we took entirely seriously. That's why the women who did not marry immediately after college took only a "little job" to fill the one- or two-year gap until they did. Upon getting married, the woman's "real" job would begin—to manage the home, rear the children, and support her husband's career needs.

One right after the other, the typical couple had its children. Caring for them was less consuming than in my mother's era. The women of my generation had mechanized kitchens and laundries, packaged foods. They formed a community, a network. The suburban streets were filled with children at play. Bursting with energy, these young mothers devoted themselves to creating an environment that supported the family's needs. They arranged car pools and covered for each other when necessary. The infrastructure that women built for their roles as full-time homemakers was constructed for that purpose. And it was solid. In fact, there was an economy of scale in having children. All the systems were in place. A mother at home full-time could as easily raise three or four children as the first.

This was in large part a function of life sequence. For women family came first, and the infrastructure was built to support that one huge commitment. After that phase of fifteen to twenty years, she might go on to a job or, for some, a career—and a second, new infrastructure would support these plans. Each was manageable because they were separate.

In that era, as in that of my parents, most families depended on the man as the single wage earner. His acceptance of this role maximized his commitment to compete with his peers for promotion and salary increases by working late and on weekends and traveling; his time and his role at home were thus minimized. At the same time this limited his freedom to take risks at work, to change careers or employers, to make demands, or to voice dissatisfaction. In this climate his company was free to foster competition among men at every level and expect that men would focus all their energies on work, knowing that their wives would take care of things at home.

Married women with jobs were viewed as unfortunate. A Gallup poll taken in 1938, for example, asked what respondents thought of a married woman earning money in business or industry if she had a husband capable of supporting her; 75 percent of women and 81 percent of men disapproved.[19]

The postwar graduate started her adult life in the same mold as her mother. But the culture was rapidly changing. Suddenly she wanted more freedom, autonomy, purpose, and participation in the world outside the home. The divorce rate was escalating; some women were choosing not to marry, and the voice that said "Someone will take care of you" was no longer telling the whole truth.

The feminist revolution of the early 1960s was ignited by the frustration of this elite, highly educated group then entering early middle age. It legitimized their anger, and it gave voice to the unarticulated idea that life could be more fulfilling. Women felt defiant that their needs for intellectual stimulation weren't being met by PTA work and carpooling kids to swim meets. They were determined, not yet to pursue a career, but at least to do something useful, when they reached their late thirties and their kids went off to college.

It was this generation of women to whom Catalyst addressed its early career counseling programs. The average age of the women who came to Catalyst in the early days was thirty-eight. So far in her life, she'd done what she was supposed to do. She'd gotten a college degree. She'd taken a job after college. She'd gotten married soon thereafter. She'd raised her children. Educated and highly motivated, she was ready for a job. She hoped to find something interesting to do with the rest of her life. The only drawback: it had to be a part-time job. And business for the most part had no use for part-time, middle-aged women workers.

I think of the years spanning 1962 and 1977 as the period of awakening and ambivalence. *How to Go to Work When Your Husband Is Against It, Your Children Aren't Old Enough, and There's Nothing You Can Do Anyhow* was the title we gave Catalyst's first published book, in 1972. The title makes us chuckle now. But in those days we saw many talented women so lacking in confidence that they hid behind excuses like those in that title, even when they sincerely wanted to go out into the world of work. Given the reception women received in the workplace and the lack of support they were given by their families, it is not surprising that they were plagued by guilt and insecure about their abilities.

"These are women's high prerogatives—to make and inspire the home—to aid mankind in its upward struggles—to enable and adorn life's work, however humble." So go the words inscribed on a stone rotunda at what was the Margaret Morrison College for Women at Carnegie Mellon University. In 1964 Catalyst organized its first conference at that site. We were committed to changing the reality expressed in the motto that was carved in stone high above our heads. Though at that time I didn't notice the inscription overhead, the still prevailing assumption of society stared down at us as if mocking the idea that the world as we knew it could change. I saw that inscription again recently and felt a flicker of pride and amazement that a quarter of a century ago we challenged the assumptions that were so deeply engraved in the minds and hearts of previous generations and of our peers.

An essential conflict, one that would recur throughout the saga of women's entry into the workplace. Women were ready for the change, albeit not yet on a full-time career basis. But society was not. At Catalyst we chose our every word with great care for fear of provoking the guilt of women or the hostility of employers. I remember making the corporate rounds for contributions with a Catalyst board member, Barney Barnes, then in top management at Time, Inc. Together we worked to persuade employers of the need for educated women working part-time in the public sector. But he would have objected if there were any reference to the rights of women to pursue full-time, lifelong careers—or to do "men's work."

We saw opportunities for the returning woman in the public sector, where there was a situation of terrible inertia in the face of huge needs. In public welfare, for example, there was barely one applicant for each vacancy. For two years we petitioned virtually every public welfare office in the country to consider hiring caseworkers on a part-time basis. Finally, in 1963, the Boston Department of Public Welfare took the lead. The commissioner's office agreed to provide twenty-five full-time jobs and let us fill them with fifty half-time caseworkers. We put out the word about these fifty jobs through public service radio announcements and the press. Sixteen hundred women applied for fifty half-time positions.

Contrary to the expectations of welfare officials at that time, these women were not less committed, or less able to perform their jobs, because they came to the work force late. The truth was quite the opposite. An evaluation conducted by an outside consultant after two years reported that on average, these half-time workers were 89 percent as productive as full-time employees—and that the turnover rate was 14 rather than 40 percent. In other words, they worked half the time and produced nine-tenths of the work. After twenty years of confinement to the home, to children, and to community work, these intelligent, mature, highly motivated women made their quite extraordinary mark.

That was an exception, though. I recall going to speak with managers at the Equitable Life Assurance Company in 1968 to raise the issue of part-time professional jobs for returning women. I made my case in a letter, saying:

> There are 4½ million women college graduates and 13½ million women with some college training between the ages of twenty-two and sixty-five. It is estimated that nine million college-educated women have meaningful, constructive jobs today, but there are another nine million women with equally well-trained minds who, despite their interest and qualifications, are lost to teaching—social work—business. Most of these women have families, but at an average age of thirty-five their children are in school and they are eager to put their education to work. They seldom get the chance to make a contribution commensurate with their abilities. Usually for no better reason than that family responsibilities prevent them from working a conventional eight-hour day or a five-day week.[20]

The response was less than enthusiastic. "Neither the Underwriting Department nor the Methods Research Department felt that it would be worthwhile for them to train college graduates . . . for part-time employment. The extensive training required would take too long on a half-day or part-time basis to make it beneficial to their activities."[21]

This is not to say that these people couldn't see the value of women working. It was just a very limited vision. One Equitable manager I met with shared with me a speech he'd given on one college's Founder's Day to a group of "young ladies." It's almost comical now to read his words, which were meant to inspire women to participate more fully in society but were bound by his conventional view of women's place. On the one hand he told his audience: "Today's college-educated woman will not work just to fill in for a few years before marriage and retirement, but will usually spend a big share of her adult life in a job outside the home" so "she will have new decisions to make—decisions for which there are few precedents." On the other hand:

> Raising good children and maintaining a good home still is the most important contribution the vast majority of women are going to make to the welfare of our nation.

Some, yes, will make important discoveries in laboratories, become bank presidents or chief copywriters. Many, if not most, will play lesser—perhaps auxiliary—roles in the fields they enter after college and reenter later if they retire to raise a family.

While women may not have to *confine* themselves to the duties nature has prepared them for, it must be admitted that they are important duties and that no other way than the traditional one of accomplishing them appears even remotely possible. I doubt if you would have it otherwise.[22]

With so many cards stacked against them, it's amazing how many women went on to satisfying, successful careers. The era had exhilarating moments for some women. One of the few female economists in 1973, Mary P. Rowe, Ph.D., gave a speech at the Massachusetts Institute of Technology in which she described accepting an invitation to a New England Conference of Women Economists "with delight, full of curiosity." She thought, "She and I will have a lovely evening together." In fact there were forty-seven present at the meeting, a number she reported to a fellow economist the next day at work. His response: "I hadn't known it was to be a world conference."[23]

A sometimes-overlooked casualty of that era was the husband of the woman who found a second career after their children had grown up. After all, these men had been satisfied with the traditional arrangement. They'd married women who were going to manage their homes, rear their children, and support their careers. These women would be ready to relocate if their husband got transferred to another location; they'd entertain their husband's friends, have supper ready and the children bathed when he walked in the door after a long day on the job.

Now these women's frustration had been legitimized, and they were expressing it. And their liberation didn't have many perks for their husbands, least of all any promise of relieving them of the financial responsibility they felt. Wives were no longer managing the home full-time, and they weren't earning enough to buy services. Instead they were beginning to make demands on their husbands. Even the woman who did not go back to work and had discretionary time expected her husband to do the dishes.

Also, watching their wives hinted at other possibilities these men had never before imagined. After all, men had walked a sort of plank, under pressure, into careers, so that they could do what society expected and support their future families. They had little time to think and to plan, to consider alternatives, to fail and try again. And once they started to work, they experienced incredible pressure to climb to the next rung of the corporate ladder. In those days men almost always followed a straight and narrow path. Straight out of school to a job, then on to more job responsibility, to a bigger paycheck. But a straight and narrow path does not necessarily lead to satisfaction. Many of these men, in fact, found less and less excitement in their work. Very few of them relished the sound of their alarm clock at five or six o'clock in the morning. After all, they had chosen their careers with an eye not to fulfillment, but to keeping the wolf from the door.

And, of course, men were also locked out of the domestic rewards their wives experienced. Their wives, despite their earlier frustrations, now in many instances had the time to explore their options, to make choices, and to pursue work that they loved. Indeed, the anger and frustration these women had experienced earlier with an overdose of mothering gave many of them the strength to break out of their traditional roles, to define their own identities, and to add a new dimension to their lives.

The life cycles of husbands and wives in that era were thrown out of sync. Men had spent their productive energies, for the most part, earlier in their careers. Now, just as they were getting ready to wind down and relax, women were gearing up, ready to make their professional contribution. The lives of many couples began to move in opposite directions. The husband's career tapered off as that of his wife began to flourish. The result, in many marriages, was discord, even divorce.

THE JOB SEEKERS

The feminist revolution was a powerful motivator for the women of the class of 1945. But the revolution would have come to naught had it not been for another historical force, which began to shift the balance in the status of women as the sixties turned into the seventies—the force of economic necessity. The elite first generation of feminists were joined by women driven to work by the need to support their families as single parents or to make ends meet in two-paycheck families.

Inflation and the breakdown of the traditional family created a strong economic incentive for a new, more broad-based cohort of women to seek full-time, lifelong employment. Within marriages the cost of living and the rising standard of living required, or seemed to require, two incomes. At the same time there were increasing numbers of households headed by women—from the beginning to the end of the seventies, the number of female-maintained families increased by 52 percent.[24] Further, women no longer could count on a husband's lifelong support. So the entry of women into the world of work became a populist movement.

There was an irony: the women's movement brought a good measure of freedom from dependency, including no-fault divorce laws that were passed in forty-three states in order to allow women easier escape from unhappy marriages. Those same laws, however, eliminated alimony as a given and often forced the sale of the family home. Women, who typically retained custody of the children, often suffered a substantial drop in their standard of living after a divorce, while the ex-husband's living standard jumped.

We can see today that the entry of huge numbers of women into the work force represented a surge forward. It was a mark of women's grit that they persevered despite the obstacles, a quality that would actually stand them in good stead in their careers. But in the micro sense, in women's private experience, the situation was more difficult than ever.

Because women were superfluous to the needs of business but could be counted on to seek employment—because it was quintessentially a buyer's market for the employer—there was little business incentive in the late 1970s to identify and nurture female talent, to remove obstacles to women's upward mobility, or to provide flexibility to those women who wanted to combine career and family. And because women were superfluous to the mainstream, there arose EEO initiatives and affirmative action plans to force business to accept women. These were necessary, but they further strained an already adversarial relationship between employers and women.

One 1971 study of corporate executives reported that a majority of respondents felt that women had less motivation than men; that women did not provide as much return for investment in educational and training dollars as men; that while men had careers, women had only jobs, because women didn't take any deep interest in a career.[25] Nonetheless, begrudgingly, spurred by affirmative action goals, companies began to make room for women. Despite the lukewarm reception they received, the job seekers were determined. (To help them, in 1973 Catalyst established a national network of carefully evaluated career resource centers to provide information and support services. It began with 83 centers, serving 56,000 women, and expanded by 1982 to 240 affiliates serving 200,000 women annually.)

As they gained entry to men's world of work and began to achieve in their careers, women's self-image gradually shifted. Some became less guilt-ridden, more confident of their strengths. Some began to prepare for traditionally male fields, but so sparsely that in 1974 we felt it was critical to develop a series of publications for female undergraduates, focusing on traditionally male fields such as engineering, banking, and industrial management. Women also began to enter management. In 1970 one in six managers was female, up from one in ten in 1940 and one in twenty-five in 1900.[26]

This period of transition, as women inadvertently violated the traditional all-male corporate order, was pain- and conflict-ridden for men. I remember a terrible meeting I had with the CEO of a huge pharmaceutical firm. I explained the business advantages of promoting women's leadership. He responded to me with anger. He said, "You want all women to work in corporations and to devote themselves to moving up. Women who don't need to work don't want to leave their children." He continued, "Why would any woman prefer to be a chief financial officer rather than a full-time mother?"

Now here was a successful man. His wife had raised their children. It had all worked for him. His anger had a big component of fear that the values and traditions he cherished were disappearing. And in all fairness, his outrage was interspersed with recognition that individuals needed options, and they needed freedom and support to pursue those they chose. It was an exhausting hour for both of us. As he walked out to the elevator with me, he slipped away and returned with a bottle of a new, lavish perfume they were marketing. "This is for you," he said. "I guess you're a woman."

THE CAREER QUESTERS

In the late 1970s I began to see a third generation of women coexist with the returning women and the job seekers. These women, the career questers, viewed work not as a lesser part of life, but as central to their identity.

Women's life goals reflected the change. One poll, conducted in 1983, asked women how they regarded work and family and compared the results with statistics from a 1970 poll. In 1970, 53 percent of women cited motherhood as one of the best parts of being a woman. In the new poll, 26 percent did. Perhaps most tellingly, 58 percent of working women said they would rather work than stay home even if they could afford not to work—and so did 31 percent of nonworking women.[27]

A "tipping point." That's how sociologist Jessie Bernard described the moment when the sheer prevalence of a cultural pattern leads to the reformulation of the social norm.[28] Certainly one of these moments occurred in the late seventies, early eighties. Suddenly more positive attitudes toward working women took hold. No longer were working mothers seen as pariahs. Men began to see their wives' work as important. In 1981, Catalyst conducted a study of two-career couples (so new a phenomenon that we had to advertise for two-career couples because there were no existing lists we could buy) and found that nearly three-quarters of both wives and husbands agreed that their careers took equal precedence. But, of course, they were the pioneers, the believers.[29]

The chief executive officer in his late fifties began to experience an awakening to women's talent because he had seen more highly capable women participating in his company. Not only that. He was seeing his children, now in college or just out, who were turning out to be remarkably different from him and his peers. He watched them confronting some of the same questions as the younger members of his company. I always felt encouraged when I entered a CEO's office to see pictures of daughters in their early twenties on his desk. I knew then that he probably had already thought about many of the questions I was there to discuss with him.

A symbol of the change that had taken place was in front of my eyes. At Catalyst, Thomas C. Mendenhall, president of Smith College, turned over the chairmanship of our board of directors to Donald

V. Seibert, chairman and CEO of J. C. Penney, consolidating the transition from a board that had been composed in 1962 exclusively of college presidents to one that reflected the new corporate awareness of women. Its members were beginning to see the employment and development of women as good business practice.

The happy implication of the evolution that has begun to take place is that the continuing progress of women does not depend on a full, 180-degree turn in the attitudes of male corporate leaders. The change has taken place a little at a time, and the shifts in attitudes are accelerating as we move from one generation to the next.

Yet despite the attitudinal changes, despite the progress that had been achieved thus far, the overall experience of these women, the career questers, was probably worse than that of the previous generations, the returning women and the job seekers. The late 1970s was an era of an exploding work force, an expanding economy, and an abundant, homogeneous supply of able males ready to be recruited from high schools, colleges, and graduate schools. It was from this large pool that corporate leaders could choose the most talented men for management and leadership positions.

And here was an essential irony of this generational shift. The class of 1945, the women who returned after raising their children to part-time jobs, had earlier on produced a huge generation of baby boomers. The sons of the women of the class of 1945 made their daughters superfluous to the needs of business.

CAREER OR FAMILY?

The pessimism of the career questers crystallized around one particular aspect of their entry into men's world of work: the difficulty of combining a meaningful career with family involvement. I became acutely aware of this dilemma at a YWCA "Salute to Corporate Women" in the late 1970s. I knew most of the fifty women, all in their early thirties, seated on the dais of a large hotel ballroom. I suddenly realized that almost none of them had children.

I recall that prior to serving on the board of the GM Institute, a five-year engineering school, I visited its campus in 1980. A decade before, its female enrollment had been .1 percent. When I visited, one-third of the students were women, and they were moving toward half female enrollment.

I was guided by eight seniors—attractive, intelligent women, all comfortable with themselves as engineers. We were joined at lunch by several faculty members and GM executives. My host invited me to lead the discussion.

I asked how many of the young women were planning to have children. The response: Not one. They all assumed that having children would jeopardize their careers. The GM executives confirmed their assumptions, saying, "We believe that once you step out of the work force, the shelf life of your engineering expertise is about six months."

I think that toward the end of the luncheon, we were all aware that these policies and practices forced women to make an untenable choice. If they decided to have children and to cut back for a period of time, they would lose their jobs and GM would lose not only their much needed talent and training, but the $25,000 cost of their education.

At Catalyst we formed the Career and Family Center to investigate ways that employers could enable women to combine family and work. I told the audience at Catalyst's 1979 awards dinner:

> Today women are pursuing careers in every field in far larger numbers than most of us foresaw a decade ago. But, a great many career women are choosing not to have children. We seem to have come full circle—to have simply traded one option for another. In spite of all that has taken place, women are still forced to choose between family and career.[30]

Catalyst was founded to open career options for family women—now, fifteen years later, it began to appear as though career women wouldn't have family options.

How had this happened? It seemed to me that this first generation of career-centered women had put their personal lives on the back burner in order to concentrate on their work.

Some of these women wanted career success so badly that they were willing to forgo children to do it. A 1986 study reported that the typical corporate woman was married and childless and believed that high-achieving women must forgo having children to stay on the fast track. For 64.5 percent, "work affords above average pleasure," and for another 10.7 percent, "work and pleasure are one." In that study 53.7 percent of respondents were childless. Half said that work affected their decision to remain unmarried. Of the participants in the study, 19.4 percent had never married, 21.3 percent were separated or divorced, while 82.6 percent had never interrupted their careers for family or homemaking.[31]

Sadly, some of these women had waited too long. Suddenly they heard their biological clocks ticking. By this time they were already in their late thirties or early forties. Either they found it impossible to meet a mate—a 1982 Korn/Ferry survey of senior-level men and women found that although 27.6 percent of the women had never married, that was true of only .9 percent of the male executives[32]—or else they had married, but by the time they were ready to have a baby, it was too late to conceive.

At the same time, because business was still glutted with male managers and rife with barriers to women's advancement, most of these women couldn't realize their ambitions of making it to the highest levels. Four-fifths of the respondents in a 1984 study said that being a woman in business could be a disadvantage. Of the group surveyed, all of whom had titles of vice-president or above, 61 percent said they had been mistaken for a secretary during a business meeting, 70 percent felt they were paid less than men of equal ability, and 60 percent felt cut off from male social activities and conversations of male colleagues. Less than half had children.[33] It's no wonder that in the 1982 Korn/Ferry study, 117 out of 300 high-level women felt that simply being female was the single greatest obstacle to their success.[34]

During this period I was asked to speak at the meeting of a Philadelphia group of women from finance and banking. About 125 women qualified for membership by virtue of earning $35,000 or more. Throughout the cocktail hour and the luncheon I heard talk of gloom and doom, discrimination, lack of opportunity, standing in place, or even backsliding. When I got up to speak, I commented on the pessimistic mood and asked why the group hadn't been organized five years earlier. The immediate response from a chorus of voices: "We couldn't. There were only a handful of women earning enough to qualify five years ago." There was a self-conscious silence.

With this generation, women embraced an idea of themselves as career primary. They were willing to make whatever sacrifices seemed necessary—forgoing family. Yet business still had no real need for them. Women as a group were still viewed as less committed, less suited to business concerns, and less able to perform consistently as well as men. As a result, though women were moving, it was not as fast and not as far as they thought they should—and not as far or as fast as the men they saw all around them.

The women of the class of 1945 returned to the workplace. Then, large numbers of women were driven by economic necessity to follow. Still, senior management remained unaware of women as a business resource. Upper-level male executives had been comfortable with the roles played by their traditional wives and secretaries. Now some corporate executives were aware of high-level, high-performing women in their own companies. One indication that CEOs' perceptions of women were changing was a shift in the kind of experience they sought in appointing female corporate board directors. In the past they tended to appoint publicly visible women who had achieved outside the arena of business. Increasingly they saw it was in their interest to seek women with substantial business experience, who could contribute to the bottom-line concerns of the board.

Yet the shift of recognition that drove CEOs to find women board members had not yet taken place on a broad-scale level within the corporate community.

As a result, the dominant mood of working women was not optimism, but dismay and distrust. The *Harvard Business Review* conducted a survey of opinions about executive women, a reprise of an earlier survey. Hearteningly, the percentage of male executives who felt either strongly or mildly unfavorable toward women executives dropped from 41 percent in 1965 to 5 percent in 1985, while the number of male executives believing that "the business community will never wholly accept women executives" had declined from 61 percent in 1965 to 47 percent in 1985. However, in that same period the number of women *agreeing* with the statement doubled, from 20 to 40 percent.[35]

THE CURRENT SCENE: WANTING IT ALL

As word got out about the disillusionment of these women, the fourth generation got the sense that martyrdom to one's career was not the ticket. A 1985 poll of American women found that 63 percent of women wanted to combine work, marriage, and children—up from 52 percent in 1974.[36]

Some women of this microgeneration are succeeding. Yet barriers still exist. They are subtler than the discrimination of an earlier time, but just as pervasive and just as damaging for women.

At the same time, corporate women still shoulder the bulk of responsibility for the daily care of children and the upkeep of the home. And the time sequence has changed as well. Now, as we've seen, women are starting families later in their lives. That has the positive outcome of increasing their value to their employers. However, it means many women, for a considerable period, will have responsibility for both career and family.

Earlier generations of women, having built a solid infrastructure to support family, had seen an economy of scale in having multiple children. Today, for the woman who starts her adult life with a serious career for which she has constructed an infrastructure, and then has a child, the family becomes something she supports on an outrigger. I think of the relationship as a sort of central derrick, with an extended arm on which is balanced the child; when a second child is added, it's loading down that rather fragile arm.

To compensate, women who combine career and family develop an incredible efficiency. They sweep up things on the way to getting something at home, they think actively about a problem or a decision or a report they have to write while doing mentally undemanding chores. There is an incredible streamlining of priorities. But it takes great determination. Women in this situation tend also to be isolated from other women. A sense of competition coupled with lack of time prevents them from joining forces with their peers at work or even developing close, supportive emotional bonds with each other.

Add to this the element of psychic drain that results from a woman's isolation at the higher corporate levels. It's the discouragement that comes of watching four male colleagues be promoted when you know that you were really the most qualified. The higher up a woman moves, the tougher it gets.

Reaching even the tenth percentile level makes some difference in the degree of comfort. But think of the experience of a woman who is the first to reach the top floor of a bank like Chemical. If you have only one woman at the top, she is really considered an intruder on the environment.

Because you are the only woman at your level, you're often looked to as a showpiece, for advice and catharsis, as an outlet for anger. It's what I call the over-the-transom phenomenon. You're assigned duties that seem appropriate for you to do in large part because you happen to be there and you're a woman. There are so few women in the company's upper precincts—as a result, you are called upon to attend every public event, to sit on the dais at a hundred time-consuming, energy-draining chicken dinners every year.

Many women of the current generation dream of freedom from guilt and pressures, of time for themselves and with their husbands, of being at home when their children return from school. Yet their careers are central to their lives. The result is ambivalence, guilt, and anger at their employers.

My generation proved that men who were career-focused because they were sole providers often did not know their children and deeply regretted it later. We also found that most women could not with equanimity be full-time mothers. But those lessons are too far in the past to have much impact on young women today. Suffering from the cumulative fatigue induced by the demands of a career, the stress experienced as a woman in management, and the fact that they have considerably more than half the responsibility for home and children, women often find appealing the alternative of dropping out of the work force for a time.

A recent issue of *Wharton Alumni Magazine* reported on changes in the last decade in the attitudes and goals of ten female graduates of the class of 1979. Five years ago all of them were working full-time. Now half of them have either stopped working or have part-time positions in order to have a family. Most predict that five years hence they will again be working full-time.[37] Their experiences corroborate information from the 1987 "Current Population Survey" report published by the Census Bureau. According to that survey, one in three women who stopped working in 1986 did so to devote more time to home and children, compared with one in a hundred men.[38]

Women are disillusioned. They look at the generation just ahead of them and recognize that they can't "have it all." They realize much more clearly than men that "all" includes real involvement in family life. And they don't want to settle for either-or.

We are now in the midst of a period of transition from the stability of defined roles for men and women toward a time in which individuals will be able to determine the balance of work and family responsibilities they prefer independent of gender. During this transition, many women are experiencing work overload, loneliness, guilt, anger, a sense of inadequacy, even despair.

Perhaps this is why one national poll found virtually no change between 1970 and 1987 in the number of women—just about half—who responded "No" when asked if a woman with the same ability as a man has as good a chance to become the executive of a company. In the same period, though, the number of men who thought women's chances were just as good went up, from 39 to 50 percent.[39]

The life we are leading is filled with contradictions. On the one hand women are more empowered than ever before. I was struck by a 1989 survey of women attorneys. A third of respondents earned more than $100,000. All but 13 percent said that they felt their salary and bonuses were comparable to their male peers. Yet most of the women surveyed said that their careers exacted a toll on their personal lives, and 90 percent said they "believed that even if their firm offered part-time or flexible work schedules, women who used those arrangements would be slowed or blocked in their quest for partnership." Fully 43 percent said that taking advantage of a normal maternity leave would hurt their career.[40]

Women's gains are no longer free floating. Employers are beginning to be aware of women's value as a business resource. Yet they still don't know how to fully utilize their talent or to stem the flow of women out of their companies. Companies don't have a plan for changing the environment for women, so they throw out one ad hoc response after the next, responses that won't be effective because they are not subjected to the rigors of strategic planning and they are not comprehensive. So still women face barriers, and still there is pain.

These are some of the unresolved issues of today. Although women are better positioned than ever before, they are also more disillusioned. It's a volatile mixture.

And I got caught in the explosion.

CHAPTER FIVE

The "Mommy Track": Anatomy of a Reaction

*E*veryone told me I shouldn't write this chapter. It's too self-absorbed, they said, too much an exercise in navel gazing. "Never apologize, never explain," runs the old adage. And I had my own reasons for not wanting to revisit an experience that did, after all, have many painful moments.

But I think there is something to be learned from the brouhaha that ensued when, without fully intending to, I defied the conspiracy of silence. Here is a cultural phenomenon worth broader consideration—an essay about women and business published in a somewhat parochial academic journal triggered an avalanche of public interest and debate. Why did it happen? Why did an essay I wrote for the *Harvard Business Review* capture the public imagination as it did? Why did my views become the lightning rod for a controversy that was extreme even by the standards of an age that coined the phrase *media event*?

I don't know that hindsight can ever be completely accurate. Analysis of an event in the past always runs the danger of being too formulaic. I grew aware of this in looking through the boxes of paper—clippings, letters, phone memos, transcripts of meetings, drafts of speeches, notes to myself—that filled my office by the end of the brouhaha. Those records show that real life is messy, while any interpretation I attempt will be unnaturally neat. For what it's worth, however, I'll try to set down as clearly as I can what happened, my conclusions about why it happened, and their application to the larger question of where women stand in business today and how we can best move forward from here.

THE NEW FACTS OF LIFE

It all started back in January 1989 when I published what seemed a fairly straightforward essay in the *Harvard Business Review*. "Management Women and the New Facts of Life" was written for an audience of corporate leaders and policymakers—a population that is for the most part homogeneous, insular, conservative, and male.

I saw the essay as a call to action to these corporate leaders. It pointed out that women managers still face substantial barriers to their productivity and advancement and urged employers to recognize a new business payoff for removing these barriers. It did not contain the phrase *mommy track*.

In writing the *Harvard Business Review* article, I recall being driven by the feeling that we had reached a critical turning point. It seemed clear to me that women in the work force were about to find themselves in a seller's rather than a buyer's market—that their full integration into the world of work was about to be swept forward by a set of powerful historical forces. Prominent among these forces were some of the demographic factors that are central to this book and examined, at length, in a later chapter.

As I saw it, the confluence of these forces would give individual women unprecedented leverage in expressing the problems they were facing and in articulating their needs. They could be confident in expecting that employers would want to do everything in their power to clear away the barriers and help them succeed, because it was in employers' business interest to do so.

I had a clear outcome in mind as I wrote the piece. I wanted the reader, that top-level, senior executive, to come away from it and say, "Wow. It's costing me much more in attrition and lost productivity to impede women's career growth than I can gain by removing the barriers and giving them flexibility. I can capitalize on this huge, talented, trained resource, particularly as the population shrinks."

Judging from the letters and calls I received from members of the corporate community, women as well as men, in the first nine weeks after the article appeared, my call to action had some of the effect I'd wanted. It had put the issues on the table, and corporate leaders seemed to welcome the opportunity to talk about them.

David Maxwell, chairman and CEO of the Federal National Mortgage Association in Washington, D.C., called it "one of the most thoughtful and balanced pieces about executive women I have seen," in a letter dated January 31, 1989.[1] He continued, "Building on our success these last several years in moving women into the management ranks will require new ideas, resources, and ways of thinking. I appreciate your raising some of the difficult issues."

"It is one of the best analyses that I have seen concerning women in management," wrote Kay Nalbach, president of Hartmarx Corporation's charitable foundation.

"Your *HBR* article represents, I believe, a historical turning point in the discussion of women in business," wrote Richard Lewis, chairman of Corporate Annual Reports. "You looked at the reality of the situation and you didn't blink."

I also received letters from editors at women's magazines. "Having given a number of speeches myself in regard to 'where we are and where we're not'—I couldn't agree more with your views. The piece is superb!" So said Anne Sutherland Fuchs, senior vice-president and publisher at *Elle*. Wrote Geraldine Rhoads, editorial director of the Resource Center at *Woman's Day*, "It's a while since I've read something so important, germane, and well developed—and important for both women and business."

Kate Rand Lloyd, founder and editor at large for *Working Woman*, called to tell me she had read my article on her plane trip to speak at a meeting of the top human resources people at Southwestern Bell. She quoted from the article in her presentation, she said, and was glad she had attributed it correctly because the organizer of the conference had distributed copies in advance to all those who attended.

I heard from individuals in the civic arena. Wrote Mary Schmidt Campbell, commissioner of cultural affairs for New York City, "Sometimes the truth is hard to face; but in order to succeed, necessary to hear. Thanks for writing such a candid piece."

I also heard from business scholars. Demographer Arthur Anderson of Fairfield University wrote to tell me that "the overall thrust of your article is absolutely on target, and the way you make the case is the only realistic, bottom-line way that will move executives beyond tokenism." Frank Macchiarola, former New York commissioner of education and a business professor at Columbia Graduate School of Business in New York City, described the piece as "outstanding and full of 'new' news."

I heard from individual women in that nine-week period, too. "*The best article I have read to date on the topic*," read the letter I received from Alice Galloway, a manager at a small California company. "I found it enlightening, powerful, and quite articulate. I have circulated it to the two other women managers in my organization, as well as to my male supervisor and to our male executive management." She added a P.S.: "I am a high-performing career-and-family woman, a department manager, age thirty-three, was widowed at thirty-one with a five-year-old daughter, now remarried to a co-worker with two children. And now, gulp, I am contemplating having another child."

And Roslyn Rosenblatt, a senior-level manager at Procter & Gamble, wrote on January 17:

> You have articulated the very issues that we have been addressing at P&G, and that I have been telling my daughter and sons about for so many years.
>
> Thank you for stressing flexibility and individuality.

I recall one response in which I took particular pride. The New York Women's Forum is composed of women who are preeminent in their fields. Several times each year the group sponsors evening meetings at members' homes to discuss specific topics. One of these gatherings happened to be scheduled just after the article appeared, and I remember vividly entering the room and how rewarded I felt that the piece seemed to have struck a chord with every one of these nine or ten discerning women.

It's natural to feel some pride in an effort well received. But I felt something else, too, from the positive reactions of both the Women's Forum members and the other business people who had approached me in this nine-week period. Perhaps their reactions confirmed my hunch in publishing the article when I did: it seemed, since those who were in a position to make change were receptive, that the time indeed was ripe to move ahead significantly toward the goal of expanding options for women.

In all of those first nine weeks, the *HBR* article generated only a single media commentary. In her syndicated column, journalist Ellen Goodman delivered a balanced, accurate assessment of the ideas in the piece I had written. She acknowledged the truth of my observation that women in business cost their companies money "because they are more likely to leave, taking the company's investment with them. They are also more likely to drop off the fast track."[2] She succinctly described my arguments that working women are empowered as never before and that the pool of potential employees is shrinking. Finally she got at the conviction that had driven me to write the article in the first place:

> To protect their investments, business should respond to the needs of women and their families: Deal with maternity more openly and flexibly, take an active role in providing family supports and child care and alternative work schedules.[3]

Yet although Goodman's take on my essay was supportive, she somehow was aware that a storm would follow. Listen to her forecast the reaction that was soon to greet my article's opening sentence, "The cost of employing women in management is greater than the cost of employing men":

> Can you hear a collective gasp? This polished analysis from a woman who has spent twenty-seven years working for women and business is sure to stir anxiety among those who remember when those corporate heads were looking for just such a bottom-line reason to exclude women. If her words find a receptive audience, then it represents a wholesale change, a coming-of-age for women in business. What we have talked about as personal needs are also business needs. In the long run they don't increase costs, they cut them. Can flexibility become the new standard of an efficient and effective workplace? Yes, *if* we can all get past that gasp.[4]

Time would tell, of course, that we had not gotten past "that gasp."

THE OPENING OF THE FLOODGATES

The morning of March 8, 1989, found me somewhat fatigued yet energized. Fatigued, because the night before had been Catalyst's Annual Awards Dinner, an event many months in the planning, where three companies are honored for forefront initiatives they've taken to develop, advance, and retain women. Yet I felt energized by the audience's response, both to the award-winning initiatives and to my speech at the dinner, which had addressed the movement toward shared roles for men and women in relationships and in families.

When I arrived at the office, the telephone was already ringing off the hook. It was nine weeks after the *Harvard Business Review* had published my essay. That morning, *The New York Times* had come out with a news story about my article. Cast in a classic "us against them" mode, it purported to describe my views and featured the (mainly negative) comments of various "authoritative" sources. When I saw the article over breakfast, I had thought it so farfetched as to be not worth taking seriously. Later, as I went about my business, I was told that ABC and NBC had clocked in and that numerous papers had requested follow-up stories. Even so, that day I remained but dimly aware of the intensifying buzz of media interest, and I certainly had no notion of what was soon to come. The reason, I think, was that I simply couldn't fathom it.

Yet overnight my life changed utterly. In a matter of two weeks I grew familiar with the green room at the morning and evening news programs of every network. "Donahue" and "Good Morning America" did battle over my availability. In the next two months I gave more than seventy-five interviews with print and broadcast journalists from around the country. A colleague traveling in Singapore sent a clipping about the controversy from a local paper. Strangers began to greet me by name in elevators. A cartoon with my likeness appeared in the *Boston Globe*. By the time the first wave of media attention had ebbed, over five hundred articles had lauded or lampooned my ideas or, more often, someone's misrepresentation of my ideas.

Since then people have often asked how that sudden barrage of interest felt. I have to answer that the experience left me reeling, but not for the reasons you might expect. Celebrity status, first off, was not particularly gratifying, since it was not a condition to which I'd ever aspired. As head of Catalyst and the organization's primary spokesperson, I wasn't a stranger to the media, but I'd always been most comfortable working behind the scenes. It was disconcerting when photographers showed up on a daily basis in order to place me in some photogenic pose, whether they wanted the standard, fairly innocuous shot in front of bookshelves in Catalyst's Information Center or a tableau—attempted by the folks at *People* magazine, who later killed the story anyway—featuring my feet up on the desk, with my *HBR* article, family photos, and a plastic baby bottle strewn artfully in front of me.

On the other side of the ledger, I didn't feel devastated, either, that not everyone agreed with my views. Throughout my life I obviously hadn't ever desired to be universally loved. You couldn't stand in my shoes day after day for close to thirty years—holding out my tambourine, pleading for what I felt was fair and right for women, and encountering rebuff after rebuff—if you needed blanket approval.

It was something besides my classic fifteen minutes of fame, or infamy, another aspect of the brouhaha, that touched me and disturbed me the most. "Totally mission driven": that was the way I'd described myself many times in the past. The mission that had driven me for more than a quarter of a century had been to learn how the process of expanding women's career and family options could be facilitated. Now I watched as a tornado of public opinion began to spin farther and farther from my intention and from my ideas. Over and over again I was challenged for things that I not only did not say, but do not believe and find abhorrent.

My dismay over being misconstrued in a way that might ultimately be damaging for women was something that grew. At the beginning, though, my major reaction was surprise—surprise at being front-page news, surprise due in part to the fact that the article that now was being seen as so inflammatory—it had set off "a furor," said the *Times* headline—was no great departure from ideas I had expressed in the recent past. On earlier occasions I had thought that my ideas might generate attention, I had hoped to break through the conspiracy of silence. But in vain.

Six months before the *HBR* article came out, for example, I had advanced some of the same ideas in a keynote address at a meeting of human resources professionals sponsored by the Conference Board. I remember wanting to get an audience's reaction to some of the themes I planned to stress in my article. I thought there could be a real blast—that I might be blown out of the room by the reaction—

because I was talking about the costs to employers of maternity. Yet nobody seemed perturbed, and there was very little discussion during the question-and-answer period. Later, during the controversy, when I was trying to understand what had happened, I asked about it, and I remember someone's explanation: Well, those women were wearing their corporate hats. At the time, though, I thought, If my analysis hadn't evoked a reaction there, why would it evoke a reaction from women to an article in *HBR*?

Other writers in the field of women's issues had also touched on similar material. Consider a handful of articles that had appeared in the year before my essay came out, articles whose authors mined a similar vein without earning any public disapprobation. A story, for example, by Dana Friedman, a work and family specialist then at the Conference Board, had made the point that women might at times choose to trade career advancement for greater flexibility.

> Somehow women need to accept the inevitability of making trade-offs. Does this mean that women can't have it all? For several years of their careers, they may decide they don't *want* it all.
>
> Perhaps there are self-imposed plateaus. Some women may have reached a level high enough to provide pay and flexibility that is sufficient for them to cope with work and family life. As a consequence, they may refuse promotions that mean longer hours, more travel, and more stress.[5]

Even the magazine that was to print one of the most negative articles, *New York Woman*, had run a piece not four months prior to mine that suggested as definitively as did my essay the price companies are paying by not attending to the needs of their women managers. Wrote contributing editor Maureen Orth:

> Despite years on the job with immeasurable psychic and professional investment, many of the best and brightest women leave the corporate world and never return—they change careers entirely, work part-time, or start their own business. . . .
>
> In a more enlightened world, of course, women wouldn't have to make such wrenching choices. But despite the strength of their numbers in the work force, women have made surpris-

ingly few demands in the workplace, and consequently they've gotten little in return. For the most part, business remains serenely inflexible. . . . Corporate America has barely acknowledged the need to provide adequate child care, and the idea that a woman might want to keep her job but temporarily switch her hours to part-time (while her children are young) instead of having to leave a job where she may already have put in ten years, is practically unheard of.[6]

Somehow, though, even as writers such as these delineated the problems women were facing in business, we were contriving not to confront them in a genuine way—hence the conspiracy of silence. Plenty of people, for example, were talking about maternity leave. The Family and Medical Leave Act was going before Congress for the umpteenth time. We were seeing the release of studies documenting the numbers of women who returned from maternity leave, begging the question of the numbers who were not returning.

Thus, having both heard and articulated similar views in the recent past, I didn't expect the ideas I advanced in my *HBR* article to stop the presses. Yet I did hope that my essay would command attention. I recall my editor's amusement, as we finalized the piece, when I asked, "But will it make change?" That, as always, was my biggest concern. And in my desire to change at least the thinking of corporate leaders, I fashioned my article both to capture their interest and to resonate to their deeply held beliefs. Specifically, in all truth I hoped the first sentence of my essay would ignite a spark.

"The cost of employing women in management is greater than the cost of employing men."[7] That opening, I was well aware, ventured onto turf we usually avoid—I deliberately led with a statement that corporate leaders believe but are not free to enunciate. My aim was to get under the reader's skin to what was truly felt. The CEO for whom I was writing had to know that *I* knew—as a result of always looking at the issue not from the vantage point of women only or of business only, but from both sides—that issues that are often seen as women's problems also present difficulties for their employers. Only then, I thought, would the CEO respond to the second half of the equation, which I presented on the following page:

The greater cost of employing women is not a function of inescapable gender differences. . . . What we need to learn is how to reduce that expense, how to stop throwing away the investments we make in talented women, how to become more responsive to the needs of women whom corporations must employ if they are to have the best and the brightest of all of those now entering the work force.[8]

My first sentence, then, was intended to cause a sort of shock of recognition and relief, which would open the reader to a deeper understanding. Again, I intended to light a spark. But because I had this very specific reader in mind as I wrote, rather than a broad audience, I didn't anticipate the enormity of the reaction that would follow.

As I look back on it now, the controversy took place in several stages, with several dominant players. The media, professional advocates, and individual women all played a part in carrying the debate a step further. This was roughly chronological. The media set it in motion, shaped some of the main contours of the debate, and then passed it to the professional advocates, who used it as a platform for their own agendas. Individual women inherited the controversy from these first two players and brought to it their own anxieties, their shattered expectations, their bitterness.

THE MEDIA

I don't want to fall into the trap here of castigating the media for fanning the flames of controversy. That approach strikes me as better left to communications scholars, who can bring greater objectivity to bear than one who has been personally embroiled in a media circus.

It seems to me, also, that the media, as a business enterprise, must naturally endeavor to turn a profit. It's not surprising or improper that what makes a story interesting and therefore salable is conflict, and that it becomes the job of journalists to play up whatever conflict is inherent in the material they observe. The only problem is that the media is not known for its penetrating analysis—it's hard to bring out the subtleties in a thousand words, on deadline. It's easier to hang the piece on a familiar hook, even if that approach won't necessarily lead to outcomes that are beneficial for any of the participants in the story. The hook might rest on somewhat hackneyed assumptions. Or it might be the product, in large part, of the journalist's private experiences and biases.

However right or wrong the tactics of the media may be, my experience is a case in point of the power it wields, particularly the power of the big guns like *The New York Times*. I watched the brouhaha explode after the *Times* article came out. There can be no doubt that whatever the news value inherent in an event, simply appearing in the *Times* can launch a story into the public arena with a velocity it would not otherwise have had. *The New York Times* sets the news agenda.

That article did something else, too. It packaged my ideas in such a way as to make them both more accessible to the public imagination and more volatile. The *Times* story was to shape and even to dictate the portrayal of my ideas in almost all subsequent stories. The terms used in the *Times* piece attached themselves to my concepts like doppelgängers for the duration of the controversy.

Few people actually read the original article. After all, the *Harvard Business Review* is not available on every newsstand, people are pressed for time, and it wasn't the easiest reading in the world. In addition, if what one veteran news editor told me recently is true, journalists tend to be "timid followers." The result is evident if you compare the vast majority of later reports with *The New York Times* story of March 8: with few exceptions, stories and broadcasts took their cues almost word for word from that piece. Since most people read the *Times* article (it had over one thousand syndications) or the coverage in their local paper of the coverage in the *Times*, or spoke with their friends who had read that coverage, it's not surprising that the doppelgängers were impossible to shake, no matter how many times I might go on the record with my clarifications and my rebuttals.

"Mommy track" is the clearest example. It was astounding to see this pejorative catchphrase headlining an article about my ideas. The term is antithetical to the points I'd made in my article and, in fact, to everything I'd spent my life fighting for: options for women. Not tracks of any kind, but freedom as individuals to choose now and at any time whether and how to combine family and work responsibilities. And although I staunchly back the acceptance of maternity within the context of business, use of the diminutive in "mommy track" surely suggests a nonprofessional, nonserious image for working mothers.

It was also curious to see the phrase affixed to a story concerning me because I had already had one run-in with the *Times* about the term. I knew it had been used by the paper in an article some six months earlier, "Women in the Law Say Path Is Limited by 'Mommy Track.' "9 That article reported on women in law firms who were permanently discounted when they cut back in order to have more time for their families, and thus doomed to lesser functions and status. It described this cul-de-sac as a mommy track.

When that article was published, I had protested the use of the phrase in a letter the newspaper chose not to print. I wrote:

> The traditional criterion for making partner—an intense, uninterrupted career focus—no longer makes sense. Naturally, the partners want to recruit the brightest Ivy League graduates, age twenty-four, to work eighteen-hour days plus weekends, without interruption, for a total of forty-one years. The problem is: graduates are no longer virtually all male.
>
> Just under half are female, and these females constitute at least 50 percent of the top 10 percent of graduates. Firms that rely on those graduates who are male, plus those females who are willing to be childless or to have minimal involvement in their children's lives, will fail to capture the talent of women and of increasing numbers of men. The alternative: permit those who want to cut back to do so—and let them rejoin the partner line five years later, if they choose. They will return refreshed, enriched by the experience of parenting, free of guilt and ready to go full speed for a total of thirty-six years.
>
> And don't call it the "mommy track." It's an alternative track for committed professionals—still predominantly female—who are also committed to being integral to their children's lives and, through them, to the future of the firm and the country.10

It doesn't, of course, indicate malice on the part of Tamar Lewin, who wrote the story about my *HBR* article, that she linked a buzzword to my ideas, or of the *Times* editors that they allowed it to stand. Nonetheless it was a strange quirk of fate. The very label I'd gone out of my way to criticize came back to haunt me.

Even when the catchphrase was originally coined, however, I think it reflected women's fears perhaps more than the reality. It didn't take into account a genuine movement now taking place within the law toward providing flexibility without penalty. Sure, the practice of giving women time off for their families probably originated mainly as a gesture of good faith, one in which the penalty was inevitable yet unspoken. A year after the article came out, however, that had already begun to change. Davis Polk & Wardwell, for example, has initiated a policy through which attorneys may take up to three years off and return to the partner track with compensatory time. That's no mommy track. What we need to do is work to make the alternatives for individuals nonpunitive, not disallow flexibility for anyone because we're still unsure how to institute the practice.

Irrelevant to my ideas as it may have been, "mommy track" served a critical role in the brouhaha. It instantly evoked a highly charged, emotional picture. The debate gained a handle that called to mind whatever each individual chose to make of it and with whatever intensity he or she brought to that interpretation.

I became the "mommy track author" in headlines, photo captions, and television sound bites. If you were against the idea of a mommy track—and who wouldn't be?—and I was identified as the creator of that concept, you'd find it easy to believe I was your enemy.

A convenient, if inflammatory, handle. That was one legacy of the story in the *The New York Times*. A related fallacy, one to which the media would return repeatedly, was that I had said women were either "breeders" or "achievers." The *Times* lead itself hinged on this distortion. Wrote Tamar Lewin:

> Her article argues that employers can make the most of their women in management by identifying two groups early: the "career primary" woman who can be worked long hours, promoted, relocated, and generally treated like a man; and the "career and family" woman, who is valuable to the company for her willingness to accept lower pay and little advancement in return for a flexible schedule that allows her to accommodate family needs.[11]

I don't know if someone who hasn't experienced this kind of misinterpretation can imagine the sensation. I reread my article several times to see what could lead critics to think I was prescribing so rigid a remedy. What, in fact, had I actually written?

There is ample business reason for finding ways to make sure that as many of these women as possible will succeed. The first step in this process is to recognize that women are not all alike. Like men, they are individuals with differing talents, priorities, and motivations. For the sake of simplicity, let me focus on the two women I referred to earlier, on what I call the career-primary and career-and-family woman.[12]

Here, probably, was the answer: my attempt at creating a dichotomy "for the sake of simplicity" was rendered simplistic. But I had two definite reasons for painting such a stark picture. The first: to get the guy at the top of the company to begin to realize that women are not a homogeneous group. Most of my readers, I knew, tended to believe on a subconscious level that all women have babies and therefore are not committed to their careers. When you separate women into two groups, you start to break that link. My intent was to show that women, like men, are individuals.

My second reason for distinguishing two "types" of women was to show policymakers how simple it would be, while each woman situates herself differently on the career-nurturing spectrum, to reach every woman at any point in her life. Employers need only do two things: remove the obstacles that exist for women but not for men, and provide flexibility for those women who need it.

In fact, there is no such thing as a "career primary" woman, and there is no "career and family" woman. There are only individuals who fall at many different points on the spectrum from work to family-oriented. We change positions on that curve continually, throughout the course of our lives. That reality is so much in my blood that I didn't think to spell it out more clearly than I did. I was guilty of shorthand, but not of proposing a system that would circumscribe individuals' options.

Further confusing the matter was Lewin's contention that I had said employers, not women themselves, should determine which "category" an individual woman is in order to keep her there for life. This was another point that was misrepresented in the translation: the need for corporations to identify at an early stage in their careers those women who show real promise. The fact is that "high-potential" employees, at this point mostly men, are red-dotted very early on and have to be, in order to be given the lateral experience needed for general management. Women are not thought of from the beginning as potential leaders, so they miss out on the opportunities that are stepping-stones to the top echelons. Often, managers' preconceptions and stereotypes blind them to a female manager's promise—by the time her talent is duly noted, she's already ten years into her career, and it's late to start playing catch-up. So certainly women should be able to self-select and shoot for the top at any stage of their career, but I wanted to encourage the employers who read my piece to make a greater effort to identify early on more of the women who had high potential, in order to give them a shot at the experiences they needed to rise to the level of their competence. Competence, of course, has nothing to do with whether a woman has a family.

This distortion was carried a step further in the analysis, also originating in the *Times* article and continuing through the debate, that I'd said the top of the pyramid was the sanctuary of the unmarried, or at least the childless, woman. Women with children, according to "my" view, couldn't expect to get to the top. In actuality I think it inexcusable that the current corporate environment makes it so tough for women to have children *and* high-powered careers. I can't recall the number of times I have deplored the findings of one survey that 97 percent of male corporate leaders have children, in contrast with only 39 percent of women at that level.[13] What I did say, and continue to believe, is that the kind of time commitment that is, in reality, required in the very top jobs—the eighteen-hour day, the ten-hour day, or even the chock-full eight-hour day—almost always precludes a concomitant intense involvement in the life of one's children. This holds as true for men as it does for women. I don't believe that one can both be a CEO and regularly pick up the kids after school at four o'clock, or even be home for dinner every night.

"The mommy track." "A two-track system." "Employers should label women." "The top as the province of the childless woman." Though none of these concepts originated with me, the *Times* story identified them as mine. The rest of the media, the timid followers, fell in line. So although the first depiction of my thinking was, I think, misrepresentation, later stories could be described more accurately as rerepresentation. They reported fairly accurately *not* on the text, but on the text about the text. Here are just a few examples.

Time, March 27, 1989:

> Should women have to choose between a career and a family? . . . Workingwomen's resentment of the two-track no-

tion has burst into the open, sparked by a management expert's proposal to introduce a formal basis for such a discriminatory system. . . . The plan suggests relegating most working mothers to a gentle career path, which wags have dubbed the Mommy Track. Only women willing to set aside family considerations would be singled out for the fast lane to the executive suite.[14]

Or *The Baltimore Sun* on March 14, 1989:

See Mommy. See Mommy Run. See Mommy Run in Place.

They call it the Mommy Track. If you simplified the concept and made it a children's story, it would go pretty much like that. Because women at work are being told that there are two tracks—one for single-minded professional women who don't have children and another one, a slower one, for women who do. . . .

Ms. Schwartz, asserting that "the cost of employing women in management is greater than the cost of employing men," urges managers to identify and support two different kinds of women at work: "career primary women," who can work long hours, be relocated and generally treated like men in the workplace, and those in the majority, "career/family women," who are willing to accept lower pay and stalled advancement in return for flexibility at work.[15]

If that last bit, after the cute lead, sounds familiar, it's because it's paraphrased almost word for word from—what else?—Tamar Lewin's *Times* story.

For the mass reading public, those without access to the article I wrote and without any reason to doubt what they saw in their morning paper, in a glossy newsmagazine, or on the evening news, these *were* my ideas. And given that they are all reprehensible ideas, it's understandable that they would be criticized.

In all fairness, though many people read only the press coverage and drew their opinions from it, there were many who did actually read the article itself. By this time the subject was aired everywhere—in companies, of course, but also in the home, at dinner tables, and in classrooms. Even the Bureau of National Affairs saw fit to hurriedly schedule a conference, "The 'Mommy Track' and Beyond: Public Policy? Corporate Reality."

The *Harvard Business Review* gained an unexpected windfall. It sold more than eleven thousand reprints over the course of the debate, at seven dollars a pop. I'm sure there must have been many times that number photocopied and circulated within companies. Often when I arrived someplace to speak, I would discover that the audience had been given copies in advance. Even so, if they had already seen or heard the misrepresentations in the press, the distortions would often have a powerful effect on their interpretation.

Sure, there were some responsible journalists. There were even some writers who disagreed with me but still checked their sources and represented my views fairly. But most followed the pack.

I recently took the saga of the media's response to my *HBR* article to a group of media scholars at the Gannett Center for Media Studies at Columbia University, to get their thoughts on why and how it happened. One of the fellows for 1990 was Jay Rosen, an assistant professor in the Department of Journalism and Mass Communication at New York University. Rosen's interpretation of the reception my article received in that broader context was intriguing. He saw a larger problem at issue here, "a fundamental problem that involves the whole culture of debate."

Within journalism, said Rosen, there are really two traditions. One is the information-gathering and debate function, which Ellen Goodman saw fit to fulfill. This tradition stresses finding out what's happening, gathering facts, accurately representing points of view. The other is a narrative tradition, which involves telling stories, particularly stories that are compelling or controversial, that would provoke an intense reaction.

"In general, a journalist can operate for the entire course of his or her professional life without really ever facing the conflict between these two methods of operating," Rosen told me. "It's very easy for a journalist to talk within the same sentence about gathering facts and evidence, about accuracy, and also about 'the story taking me this way' and 'the story developing that way,' without ever seeing that stories can take you in ways that the facts don't necessarily support."

In the case of my *HBR* article, he said, because of the way the coverage developed, the storytelling function of journalism took over, and a public narrative was created, symbolized by the two words *mommy track*. When I was asked to appear on talk shows, it was not so much as Felice Schwartz, originator of the ideas in the article or president of Catalyst, but as a character in this narrative.

I remember reaching a low point on account of being cast in this role. As I said, I had done seventy-five print and broadcast interviews in the course of nine weeks. It was stressful, day after day of confrontation and distortion.

At that time I had been planning a trip to the Soviet Union, on the invitation of the Soviet Women's Committee, issued to a group of women from the International Women's Forum to tour four cities in the USSR. The day I was leaving, Vivian Todini, Catalyst's director of public relations, came into my office and said, "Okay, this is the last interview you have to do, and then you can go. Just keep your cool one more time." It was a live radio interview that Vivian thought was very important because it reached the whole West Coast. The audience was enormous, she said, and it was a real opportunity.

So I picked up the phone, and the host of the show introduced me and proceeded to ask a series of obviously slanted questions. Still, I kept my cool. Then she said, "We're going to have a commercial, and then we're going to invite calls from the audience." So the commercial took place, and the first call was from someone who said, "How can you ask Felice Schwartz such biased questions? How can you so distort what she said in her article?" I'll never forget that host's reply: "I didn't read it."

And it was one of the most wonderful catharses I've had in my life, because I exploded with a diatribe about the media and their attitudes, and I felt I was just spreading my wings and soaring along the whole West Coast. Even Vivian was not mad at me—although I'm sure that host will never invite me back.

THE PROFESSIONAL ADVOCATES

I went halfway around the world on that trip to the Soviet Union, but I couldn't shake the mommy track controversy. It was a small group that went, and among them were several individuals who styled themselves my arch-opponents. One woman had even been a major presence speaking against me in the press during the previous weeks. The debate was thus carried on, in our little tour bus or over dinner, with all the gusto to which I'd recently grown accustomed.

The enthusiasm of this gang on my tour probably shouldn't have surprised me. By that time the controversy had begun to draw its strength not only from the media distortion, but also from the staking of the battleground by another party—the professional advocates.

The article in *The New York Times*, in addition to shaping the terms of the debate, had set this war in motion. To support the theme of a feminist "catfight," emotionally charged quotes were gathered from Representative Patricia Schroeder ("It's tragic") and from Sylvia Ann Hewlett, author of *A Lesser Life: The Myth of Women's Liberation in America* ("I resent terribly the notion that children are a women's issue").

Journalists eagerly adopted this vision of Felice Schwartz as feminist turncoat. A March 13 *Newsweek* story, for example, began:

> For nearly twenty years, the feminist message to the business world has been loud and clear: men and women are the same and should be treated accordingly. New issues like parental leave, flexible hours, and part-time work have all been put on the bargaining table. But the basic goal has remained unchanged—to make women equal partners in the workplace.
>
> Now a leading expert on career women has challenged that premise—and stirred up a controversy in feminist circles.[16]

Although it is most certainly true that I challenged the premise that "men and women are the same," this article reads as though I don't support initiatives like "parental leave, flexible hours, and part-time work"—all of which, of course, I advocate daily.

After the big guns repeated it, the smaller local papers reflected it back. "At issue is our vision of Supermom, who, it seems, has just been derailed by Felice Schwartz and the Mommy Track, to the abject horror of feminists and the applause of corporate America," wrote one.[17] The *HBR* article "sparked a wave of criticism by feminists and by specialists on work and family issues who charge Schwartz is betraying the women's movement," reported the *Boston Globe*.[18] The *Los Angeles Times* sought out the comment of Betty Friedan, who eagerly complied: "The feminist leader and author of *The Feminine*

Mystique attacked Schwartz's categories, calling them 'dangerous' and a kind of 'retrofeminism.' "[19] *Ms.* published an article by Barbara Ehrenreich and Deirdre English that dismissed my essay as "a tortured muddle of feminist perceptions and sexist assumptions that should never have been taken seriously."[20]

My reputation as an enemy of feminist progress had been solidified when I was roundly chastised on the editorial page of *The New York Times* five days after Tamar Lewin's "mommy track" piece appeared. Predictably, the editorial led with a subject sure to make all good feminists see red: the wage gap.

> Women have always worked outside the home: harvesting fruit, digging ditches, making airplane parts, cleaning houses, selling clothes, teaching children, emptying bedpans, taking down somebody else's letters. Labor for pay, then, is nothing new to them; but *good* pay is, and so, finally, is a sense of entitlement.
>
> American women, in general the most fortunate of the world's females, have only started to achieve income parity with American men. Sexism, like racism, has deprived the United States of the talents and energies of millions.
>
> But if the people who make up America's work force are more diverse than ever before, it's men who are still in charge—and who'll stay that way if they heed Felice Schwartz, who heads Catalyst, a nonprofit organization devoted to advancing women's careers. In an article in the *Harvard Business Review*, she does not, as might be expected, regret that concentration of power. Instead, she reinforces it.[21]

The *Times*'s editor who penned the item followed the lead set by its news article earlier in the week—accusing me of advocating that employers spot and track women. The editorial closed, strangest of all, with an admonition for me to heed one of the great homilies of the 1960s: "If you're not part of the solution, you're part of the problem."

Now, unlike the first *Times* article, the editorial appeared once only. Nonetheless, with it the baton was passed. Right-thinking liberals aligned themselves with this analysis. The professional advocates got some pep in their step. As the weeks went on, even those who had applauded the article at the beginning, when it first appeared, felt compelled to recant in order to remain on the correct side of the debate.

I think of one event as particularly ironic. That was the day I spoke at a luncheon sponsored by the New York Women's Forum, held at a midtown hotel and attended by members, each of whom had invited a younger-generation representative—protégeé or daughter or employee—to join her. By this time I had seen many events such as this degenerate into name calling and unproductive debates. I asked Vivian Todini to double-check the format before I agreed to appear, and the organizers of the event assured her that it would not be adversarial, that I would simply address the group and respond to their questions.

In fact, the "forces" had been lined up in advance, with an "opposing" speaker and a moderator. After we made our remarks, the audience was invited to stand up and speak out. And many key feminists, with Betty Friedan in the forefront, rose to pour out their indignation, to testify against my terrible views. I couldn't help but contrast this event at the height of the brouhaha with that evening not so many weeks earlier, when my article had been so well received by members of that same group.

What could have prompted this about-face? How was it possible that my ideas were perceived earlier as forward thinking, progressive, and later as regressive, dangerous—by the same people? What had happened?

I think there are a couple of reasons why my views were now interpreted by the professional advocates as "politically incorrect." On an explicit level, my critics' assault was premised on the misperception that I had proposed a two-track system for women. That, of course, was nonsense. But there were other wedges between me and them as well, some more subtle.

The first of my cardinal sins was to suggest that women and men are different. The ideologues insisted, rightly, that women were just as good as men. But they carried this further, asserting that women were just like men. I violated the latter, not the former. (As per the *Newsweek* coverage cited a few pages back: "For nearly twenty years, the feminist message to the business world has been loud and clear: *men and women are the same* and should be treated accordingly." (Italics mine.)

I was always conscious of the risk in saying we have to talk about women's need for flexibility, the danger of reinforcing the stereotype of women as solely responsible for the upkeep of home and family. Now that some time has passed, I've given quite a bit of thought to whether we can run that risk. My conclusion is that we can and we must. In the mid-1970s the senior management team at IBM called me in to talk about maternity provisions. My feeling then was similar to what my critics are saying now: We can't talk about it—it would be detrimental to women.

That has changed now. Today the demographics—which have hugely increased business's need for women—make it worth the risk of talking about women's differences from men. In fact, we have to. If we do not, all we can do is consign ourselves to the status quo. I believe that many employers are aware of and support women's need to care for children (some would like more women to do that full-time). This awareness translates to women's need for flexibility, and I think companies are increasingly ready to provide that—certainly to those in the bottom half of the pyramid. We have to continue the dialogue about women's need for flexibility but at the same time start trying to enhance awareness of men's desire for an active involvement in their children's lives. We need to make clear how positive that is for the child. It is also good for the employer in that making parenting interchangeable frees women to be more productive on the job.

Still, a danger exists in differentiating the needs of women from those of men, and it concerns me. But I can't give up the opportunity to capitalize on the corporate readiness now to respond to women. If I were to go into a CEO's office and start talking about flexibility for both men and women, I think it would dilute the message and confuse him. Most senior executives could not relate to that message—with few exceptions, after all, *they* never played a big role in the daily lives of their families. Plus, employers don't *want* men to take more responsibility at home—they want them to devote themselves to their jobs. They may be recalcitrant about giving women flexibility, but at least they grasp the need for it. We need to use that dim awareness, that grudging willingness, as a lever to press change for women, now.

Men themselves don't seem likely to grab those opportunities, either, in the near future. This reminds me of my worry in the mid-seventies, when women first entered business in massive numbers. It's difficult to imagine now, but then I used to wake sometimes in the middle of the night, thinking, What if all the doors were to open suddenly to women? At that time most women did not yet have the educational or professional experience to assume the topmost positions in business. Something similar strikes me now concerning men's family involvement. We can encourage it and provide men who want it with flexibility. But we shouldn't hinge our movement forward on it, because most men are not yet ready to assume that role.

One has only to look at the experience of Sweden for corroboration of the difficulty in changing deeply ingrained male behaviors and socialization. There, over a decade of intensive education and support was geared toward the importance of the parental role for men as well as women. At the birth of a child, either parent could take—combined—twelve months of leave at 90 percent pay. Researchers still found that 22 percent of men took an average of 44 days of parental leave, while 99.7 percent of women took an average of 258 days.[22] (Recently the government has expanded the parental leave entitlement to fifteen months.)

So the professional advocates insisted that we talk about the needs of families rather than women. Another explanation for the speed with which they jumped into the fray might be that advocates rightly seek out a platform, in order to enter the debate and promulgate their views, and they had an excellent opportunity in the mommy track debate. It must have been hard to resist when a journalist requested an interview to use the occasion to push forward a private agenda.

Representative Pat Schroeder, for example, someone who certainly shares my goals, was cast as my primary opponent both on talk shows and in print. She embraced the role enthusiastically, providing a quote for Tamar Lewin's article, a letter to *The New York Times* and a guest editorial that ran in *Newsday*. I couldn't help but feel that her efforts were somewhat self-serving. Schroeder had just published a book, *Champion of the Great American Family*, and was engaged in a promotional tour as the controversy snowballed. Again and again she brought the argument back to the main points of her book.

Schroeder also appeared opposite me on the "MacNeil-Lehrer NewsHour." There we were, in front of thirteen million viewers, and she said something disparaging about the quality of my research. Now she knew as well as anyone could that over the years Catalyst had generated as much research on women and work as any other organization—probably as much as many other organizations put together. I recall that in 1983 we had completed a study of parental leave policies and practices in 384 corporations nationwide, when Schroeder was just beginning to mount her first congressional bill in that area. We gave her a prepublication copy, in fact, and I'm sure it was useful because such data did not exist back then.

Then there was a question of strategy. For many sixties-generation feminists, anger and confrontation are seen as the only appropriate strategies for bringing change on behalf of women: *If men are all powerful, we must wrest control from them.* They are so accustomed to operating in this way that they distrust any other method. On the other hand, I am not only stating the problem, but actively seeking solutions. My approach, as a facilitator rather than a fist banger, affronted many.

Then, some of the adverse reaction stemmed from a perception that my interests are too close to those of business. And in fact, I do have feet in several camps—women's issues, feminism, and the corporate community, which is largely male and resistant to change. It is also true that I am seen as credible by corporate leaders. I'm respected because I call it as I see it, not because I curry favor with CEOs. But I think it was assumed by many that I was on "their" side, that I was telling corporate people what they wanted to hear.

Thus the assault on my character by Gail Collins in *New York Woman*. "Feel free to have some doubts about Schwartz's analysis," she wrote, "since the corporations whom she wants to influence are the same ones with whom she wants to consult and collect donations."[23] Collins had spent considerable time interviewing me and finding out about Catalyst—she had also attended a meeting to which I had invited representatives of the major women's magazines to try to find out from them what strategies, if not the ones I had proposed, they believed we should adopt to move forward.

Why didn't Collins acknowledge our shared goals and write, at worst, about what she perceived as the negative impact of my strategy? In fact she inaccurately described the role of Catalyst, which is not a consulting group, but a not-for-profit, tax-exempt educational organization. And Catalyst has been entirely forthcoming about the inadequacies of business. That's why we exist—to change the policies of business vis-à-vis women. I assume that Collins knew this.

Inherent in the reproaches of the feminists, of the liberals, of the advocates, was the legacy of the conspiracy of silence. Repeatedly I was warned that telling the truth about women was dangerous, that it was antithetical to progress. Their conviction was firm that discussing the needs of women in public would reinforce the biases that corporate leaders still hold. The net result would be to keep women down.

I organized a meeting, for example, with editors of women's magazines, in order to discuss their thoughts on the controversy and how we could make use of this opportunity to move forward. These women, from *Savvy, Working Mother, Working Woman, Executive Female, New York Woman*, had already squared their views with each other. The message they gave me was strong: It may be true what you're saying, but we just cannot discuss these things at this point.

Finally it grew to be a question of ideology apart from substance. In the quiet of their own surroundings, individuals like the magazine editors or the Women's Forum members might read the article and recognize the truth of what I said, even if they disagreed with some specific point I made. But in public the threat of breaking the conspiracy of silence was clearer, especially as it began to mean breaking rank. Maybe this was because the most adamant objectors were prominent feminists and when these women who had applauded me recognized that, they joined the chorus for fear of being in the unsophisticated minority or on the side of the enemy (that is, the employer—or men).

Over and over again I would have discussions with people who ostensibly "disagreed" with me and yet repeated all of my own arguments as if they didn't hear me. What impelled them more than the logic of the argument was the idea that it was politically correct not to be on my side. The feminists circled their wagons, and it was understandable that people would want to be inside the protective ring rather than out in the cold with me.

"A deeply structured silence": that was the way Jay Rosen, a media critic and journalism teacher at New York University, described the situation that my article challenged. The silence does not exist, as one might assume, because nobody's talking about these issues; rather, "it's the reverse: nobody is talking about these issues *because* of the structured silence." He described it as "a kind of fault line in a political and media system where nothing's happening for a lot of different reasons, which come together around the silence."

Part of the structure, said Rosen, is created "from the left, in the ideological community of people who want to monopolize discussion of gender differences, and get upset when anyone other than they try to discuss these kinds of issues." The structure also comes from the right, where "you have the hypocrisy of profamily Republicans who don't want to countenance the fact that corporations can be highly antifamily themselves, because the Republican party represents both family interests and business." Add to these two factors the reluctance of the media "to do the kind of work you're doing," he told me, "which is actually very journalistic. The kind of work and research that provokes debate is exactly what good media organizations ought to be doing. They would rather Felice Schwartz do it, and take the heat for the controversy it provokes, then come out as *Time* magazine or *The New York Times* saying, 'Look, this problem exists.' " When someone like myself enters this structured silence, he explained, what happens is "all the reasons for the silence in the first place collapse on you, causing distortion, character defamation, and what have you."

Understanding something of the power of all these motivations causes me to reread the letters to the editor published in the wake of my article by the *Harvard Business Review* more dispassionately— because the *Harvard Business Review* itself participated in this effort to polarize the discussion. I'm not faulting the impulse of the magazine's editors to stimulate controversy, to enlarge the debate, because controversy makes people think. That's a legitimate goal.

On the other hand, there are times when a debate seems to assume a life of its own. I read an item in *The New Yorker* that captured this tendency well. It described a formal debate between liberals and conservatives concerning whether free-market competitiveness is best for America. The problem was, the debaters essentially agreed with each other. The result was a certain amount of absurdity or direction- lessness throughout the evening. The writer concludes:

> Agreement can be confusing. Antagonism, on the other hand, often creates structure. It can provide the antagonists with an identity, a role, a sense of purpose, a place in the scheme of things, and a motivating belief in their own rightness. In a way, it aids communication, by sharply defin- ing the terms of debate.[24]

There is a kind of security in the old structures and the old struggles, even when they are no longer viable or even appropriate. The profes- sional advocates who sent the letters to the editor at the *Harvard Business Review* shared this impulse.

What happened was this. After the controversy had begun, I received a call from the editors. They told me that they were going to run a series of letters they had received in response to the article. They asked if I would write a short follow-up essay to print in conjunction with the letters, saying I could feel free to answer any of the points made by the letter writers.

When I saw the letters, which were faxed to Catalyst thirty-six hours before the deadline, I was stunned. They had solicited the letters from a short list of advocacy and liberal groups that had already jumped on the bandwagon of negativity. They had given these groups time to prepare careful analyses and critiques of my article. They'd even taken down the rough words of some experts who were short of time and crafted them into more elegantly worded letters. I, however, was being asked to prepare a rebuttal practically overnight.

How could they do this? I thought. So I picked up the phone and got through right away to the editor. I said, "You're not really going to publish twenty negative letters selected only from advocacy groups? That wouldn't be honest, or fair, would it?"

"You're absolutely right," he said. "I'll tell you what—any letters that support your point of view that you can arrange to get, we'll publish."

Of course, the people who could really validate my point of view are very hard to reach. And to have the CEO of a major company sit down to write a letter in that period of time is terribly difficult.

When the May/June issue came out, people kept asking me why virtually all of the thoughtful people who wrote letters were stirring up the controversy further. It naturally appeared to them as if the letters had materialized in a more organic way, not that they had been solicited and shaped by the editors.

So I called the editor again. I said, "Gee, you know, I'm beginning to get an awful lot of people who are saying there must be a real feeling out there that there was something wrong about this piece."

"You're right," the editor said immediately. "I'll print an apology."

And he did, but of course the damage could never be undone. This unbalanced presentation of the controversy legitimized the sense of readers that there was a correct and an incorrect side to this debate.[25]

INDIVIDUAL WOMEN

It would be wrong to suggest that the only reason for the escalation of the brouhaha was that my views had been distorted by the media or that I'd been made an ideological straw man by the professional advocates. The whole controversy might have remained an insular, esoteric debate had it not been for the deep pessimism of individual women—a product of their experience in the corporation in the all-too-recent era when women were viewed by employers as superfluous to their staffing needs. To date most women have simply not experienced sensitivity and responsiveness from their employers. They have not had the sense that they are valued, much less needed, as a business resource.[26]

Women *did* hear some of what I said. In effect I broke the conspiracy of silence by uttering things that were true but that nobody wanted to hear.

After all, in the 1980s the banner waving and consciousness raising, the rallies, demonstrations, and protests, had subsided. The decade had been a relatively quiescent period for women. Though, as I've tried to demonstrate, they'd met with obstacles at every step of their entry into the ranks of business, women's anger and resentment were submerged, replaced by a grudging acknowledgment that progress was being made, if slowly. Commonplace now was the feeling among women that if they didn't talk about them, perhaps the impediments they faced would magically disappear.

I didn't invent the fact that women have babies. But in the response to my article, you would think that I did. I dared to suggest that women are different from men and that women have needs that men do not at present have. And while the big-name feminists resented my statement of what seemed to me to be the obvious on an ideological basis, individual women feared the admission on grounds that were closer to home. They were certain that if their employers were reminded that they weren't just the same as men, they'd lose their already tenuous standing in their companies.

Certainly, I wrote, women differ physiologically: women anticipate birth, their biological clocks tick for a finite period, they carry, deliver, nurse, bond with, and are the primary caretakers of newborns. Another factor is tradition, which maintains that women, not men, have primary responsibility for the rearing and socialization of children. This encourages women to be nurturing, supportive, responsive. Although these aspects of tradition and socialization are in the process of change, they still permeate our culture.

What often happens when women's biology, tradition, and socialization meet with the typically male structures and conventions of business? We've all seen it, though when my article came out, few wanted to admit it. Women have babies, tradition argues that they more than men are encumbered by family responsibilities, and socialization causes them to deal with this double burden in the most "acceptable" way: by cutting back at work or dropping out for a time to raise their children. It was my articulation of these ideas that triggered women's latent insecurities and anxieties.

The media framed the idea that I had proposed a two-track system. But why was that idea so broadly picked up and run with by individuals? Because women themselves felt they had to choose one or the other track in life. They sensed that once off the fast track, they could never get back. The inflation of this distortion so that it dominated all discussion of my ideas was fueled by women's disbelief that they could have it all. Their long-submerged anger over not being able to have it all surfaced, and instead of being directed at employers—because that would still be too dangerous—it was directed at me, as employers' factotum.

Exposed in the mommy track debate was a serious perception gap between employers and the many women who feel, as Ellen Goodman predicted, that differentiating women's needs from men's needs would give employers the excuse they'd been waiting for to discount women. Some women claimed that, indeed, men in their companies felt that I had legitimized their feelings that an investment in women was a much higher risk with a much smaller return than an investment in men. As a result they were behaving differently toward women.

I could understand women's pessimism, their cynicism. After all, I had spent twenty-five years in the field. And although enormous progress had been made, I knew that many employers were motivated only by the law, or by a sense of fairness, of "doing the right thing" in the most minimal sense. Some companies, though, knew that women were here to stay, that this was just the beginning. These companies put in elaborate equal employment opportunity (EEO) recording systems and mounted comprehensive affirmative action plans as a result of government pressures, and they maintained them even in the Reagan era. But rarely did even these companies recognize the new demographic realities, that women would soon become a critical business resource.

So women had reason to distrust the intentions of their employers. Yet the experience that women knew as the truth wasn't the whole story. I felt that policymakers were on the cusp of an understanding and that they could be pushed forward. Many individuals based their opinions on the two or three companies they had worked for and on an experience that had been quintessentially negative, with few signs of improving and with no window to the future. I had an advantage. I was visiting companies constantly, talking with the top leadership and studying the progress of the demographics.

I knew that business leaders appreciated having discussion of the down side of "women's issues" sanctioned in order to move toward addressing these issues. True, the vast majority of companies are not yet aggressively committed to finding ways to develop and retain women. But more and more employers are without a doubt aware of the price they pay when they allow talented women to fail.

Despite my confidence that the risk was not too great to discuss women's needs, and regardless of my understanding why women found it hard to make that leap of faith, it wasn't easy to experience their rage. I remember when the extent of women's anger dawned on me. Throughout the first nine weeks of the brouhaha, I didn't have time to catch my breath. At some level I knew that I was perceived by a lot of women as the enemy, but I think I insulated myself from really absorbing the reality emotionally. Then, after I had returned from the Soviet Union and I had some distance from the maelstrom that had engulfed my life, I remember I took a walk in Central Park. I hadn't planned for it, but I somehow knew I was taking the walk to face this reality. And that was the first time I really digested the idea that women, who had been my concern for a quarter of a century, felt the way they did.

I realized then that there was a deeper level, too, in women's reactions to my article. In addition to this insistence on maintaining the conspiracy of silence, because of their basic doubt of employers' motives, women projected onto me their own vulnerabilities and angers, their frustrations, their sense of inadequacy. It took some time to sort out why and how, and I don't know that I have it even now. But here are some thoughts on the complexity of the reaction.

I touched a nerve in women's feelings about themselves. Women themselves feel conflicted about whether they do indeed have the commitment to make it to "the top," whatever that entails. It was more palatable for them to blame me or business for having to make trade-offs than to admit to themselves the necessity for doing so.

The woman, for example, who is dedicated to her career and is willing to have other people care for her children, who internally remains ambivalent about her choices, doesn't want to be reminded that she is not actively participating in her children's lives because that means to her that she's not a "good" mother. I saw this in a phone conversation I had with a woman who called me in a rage. She told me she had for many years admired me and applauded Catalyst's work, but she hated me now and was deeply resentful of my position. I had accused her, she said, of not caring for her child, of not being a mother to her daughter. She had both a high-powered career and a two-year-old child. I can only assume that my reference to women with children who choose to pursue their careers intensely and are willing to delegate the primary care of their children to surrogates had triggered in her feelings of dissatisfaction and guilt. My surmise from her reaction is that either she had not processed clearly the degree of her desire to participate in her child's life or that traditional values—which define motherhood in absolute terms, as a full-time commitment, and which are now anachronistic—had imbued her with guilt.

During a recent interview, I talked with an intelligent, thoughtful young reporter about women who are primary players in their children's lives. Later in the interview she referred to my having said that it's "good" for women to be home with their children. I had said no such thing. She, like others, was influenced by traditional values, by what others think, and confused my reference to what one might choose to do with what it's "good" to do.

Others didn't want to be associated with maternity at all. The woman who really wants to make it to the highest level and is ready to give her all (to remain single or to marry and have children but have them raised by surrogates), to build her family around her career, doesn't want to be associated with the career-and-family woman. Quite rightly she wants her career commitment to be differentiated. Because the media picked up only on the career-and-family aspect of the discussion, on the "mommy track," she felt my article made corporate leaders think all women are career-and-family-oriented.

The woman who wants to "have it all"—to rear her children and to have a high-achieving career—worries that it is not possible, so she'd rather not see it discussed. And this was a pity, that those who are truly committed to career and family, who want to have significant careers, did not see the importance of exposing their problems in combining the two.

Every woman had spleen to vent on me except for one group, who actively applauded my article. These were the married women with children—those who want to pursue careers but are not looking for high career achievement. Many of them feel overburdened and seek a less demanding alternate career track. These women were ready to face the reality of trade-offs, to accept lesser rewards in return for greater flexibility.

This brings me to a point that still puzzles me. In all the discussion of women and the media, the entire focus was on the career-and-family woman. It's as though I hadn't mentioned the career-primary woman. One reason could be that the needs of the career-and-family woman are more complex, another that I discussed them at greater length. Another answer might be that the woman who is really ready to give her all is much more confident that she'll be recognized.

Even more significant, I think, is that the career-and-family conflict is central to women, emotional, threatening, and both guilt- and anxiety-provoking. It also raises issues of women's anger at men for what is perceived to be their easier or better life, their freedom from the second shift, their position of "superiority" in the world, which implies the flip side, the potent feeling of women that they are still second class.

EPILOGUE

The adversarial aspect of the controversy had "legs." Fourteen months after my article was published, Betty Friedan continued to go on the record with her views about me. "Her article was a very dangerous retrogression and acquiescence to sex discrimination," she told an AP reporter. Time may heal some wounds, but not this rift: "I have not changed one iota in my outrage at Felice Schwartz," she insisted. "She is simply not a feminist, not committed to equality. She has an employer mentality."[27]

An article in the October 1990 *Working Woman* also carried on the assault. The profile it ran was perhaps not as outspokenly damning as some had been during the brouhaha. But the cover line—key in any magazine's sales strategy and traditionally the responsibility of its most senior editors—was pretty harsh. "MOMMY TRACK" DEAREST? THE CONTROVERSIAL WOMAN BEHIND THE THEORY, it read.[28]

For some people, then, I—or the cultural cartoon, Felice Schwartz, Mommy Track Author—might still be perceived as the enemy. But that was really the less significant outcome, it now seems clear. No matter how trying the reaction was at some moments, the great resounding outcome was that the controversy *got the discussion going*.

About nine months after the debate began, I began to have the feeling when speaking to audiences that the tide had started to shift. I think it really hit home when I visited Minneapolis in order to speak with three groups there—a group of financial women, a small group of CEOs, and a larger audience at 3M. Shortly before, a producer at ABC had called to get my impressions in the wake of the controversy.

As part of the ABC segment, a television crew came out to Minneapolis to follow up on people's response to the debate. The TV crew attended my presentation to the women's financial group. So there I was, with the cameras and the bright lights all around. Sure enough, the very first question was from the head of a major company.

"I really enjoyed your talk," he said. "I learned a lot from it, it pinpointed the critical issues. Tell me, if I could do one thing in my company, what should it be?"

It was like a plant in the audience—because that was the very question I most wanted CEOs to ask. "Create a climate of trust," I answered, "an environment that makes it clear that women are needed and valued. Change your environment so that we can break through the conspiracy of silence."

Then the second and third and fourth questions were from women, saying, "What should I do to move things forward?"

To me this was the turning point. By the two-year mark I wasn't asked anymore to clarify, to rebut, to defend the positions in my article. Everyone had moved on in their thinking to the next step: Where do we go from here? And how do we get there?

PART II

Springboard for Change

CHAPTER SIX

The Demographic Imperative

*B*efore we can discuss how to improve the situation of women in business, it's helpful to understand the motivation for making the necessary efforts. There is no reason for people to change unless they have a motivation to do so. And there's no reason for people in business, specifically, to change unless they are driven by a business motivation.

That is why, when Catalyst conducted a 1990 survey of Fortune 1,000 chief executives to gauge the status of women in their companies, we thought it was important to find out what motivates them to increase the numbers of women in management. Answers were multiple choice, and CEOs could choose more than one. Over 75 percent of our respondents were driven by "increased presence of talented women," while 62 percent cited the "need to use the most talented human resources," and 20 percent said "corporate social responsibility."

One of the answers we listed, at my insistence, was "shortage of qualified males." To my surprise and dismay, this response was chosen by not one CEO.

To understand my reaction, you have to know that for many years I had built my analysis that companies must respond to women on what I saw as a rock-solid foundation. It seemed clear to me that the

127

future would bring slower growth in the overall pool of workers and, as a result, a greater dependence on women (and minorities). The result would be a reduction in the percentage of managerial employees companies had long depended on, white males. Employers would have a bottom-line need to seek out new sources of talent, not only at entry levels, but throughout their enterprises.

Now it seemed that although CEOs *were* motivated to develop and retain women managers, sensitivity to demographic realities was not the reason why. Some may wonder why I cared what the motivation was—as long as corporate leaders feel compelled to bring more women into management, surely it makes no difference what compels them.

I think it makes a great deal of difference. Awareness that women are talented, desire to get the best human resources, even corporate social responsibility, all have their place in stimulating change that will benefit women and business. But none, I think, leads so directly to substantive and enduring efforts as a realization that business conditions mandate the change.

When not one CEO in Catalyst's study acknowledged a shortage of qualified males as a motivation for upping the representation of women in management, I had to do some serious thinking. I saw two possible explanations. Either I had overemphasized the demographic impetus that would push women forward in business—or else I was correct and CEOs were somehow unaware of it. If the latter was true, it was tremendously important that they be made aware of this.

So I challenged myself to look with fresh eyes at the reality of the labor force changes, to sort out demographic fact from fiction, and to gauge the level of urgency with which the facts had to be addressed. I went back to the literature. I reviewed census data and government projections. I took specific questions to individual demographers, who were generous with their insights.

This crash course in demographics confirmed my sense that numerical changes in the size of the population and the labor pool are indeed critical to the unfolding story of women in corporate America. But that is only one of a number of developments that will transform the American labor force to the benefit of women and their employers. A spectrum of interlinked trends will gradually become more and more visible. It will make working women irresistible to employers as a business resource. I also found some clues that begin to explain why CEOs don't yet feel the wolf at the door—though without a doubt they will, and sooner rather than later.

I began my self-elected minicourse, then, with a hunch and two basic questions. The hunch was that demographic forces would propel women forward in the work force. Answers to these questions would prove or invalidate that premise: What is going to be the labor supply available to American employers relative to their needs in the future? What role will women play within that overall supply? I think I figured out how to answer those questions in a way that is clear and uncluttered, and that won't take inordinate energy or a degree in sociology or economics to fathom.

THE FERTILITY–WORK FORCE CONNECTION

To understand the major changes that will transform our country's supply of labor, it helps to start at the beginning. Rather than examining the size of the population or the size of the work force then, now, or in the future, it's simpler to start by looking at the number of babies American women on average—all women, of all ages—produce in a given year. The name demographers give that useful snapshot of population patterns in the making is the "total fertility rate." It was the dramatic rise, drop, then leveling in the total fertility rate over the last several generations that brought alive for me the relevance of demographic changes for women in business.[1]

Take a look at figure 6.1. At the peak of the baby boom, in 1957, the total fertility rate was 3.7 births per woman. This is a number I found very manageable and easy to visualize. I could relate to it from my own childbearing years, when my peers and I were for the most part each producing three or four children.

The graph also shows the gradual decline in average births per woman until 1975, when the TFR dropped to 1.8. I could also understand that number from the personal vantage point of seeing that my children and their peers were, with rare exceptions, having much smaller families of one or two children.

The total fertility rate has hovered there, at around 1.8, up to the present. True, in the last couple of years the number of actual live births has exceeded the expectations of demographers, a surge that can probably be attributed to delayed childbearing patterns of baby boom women. However, we still have little reason to believe that that

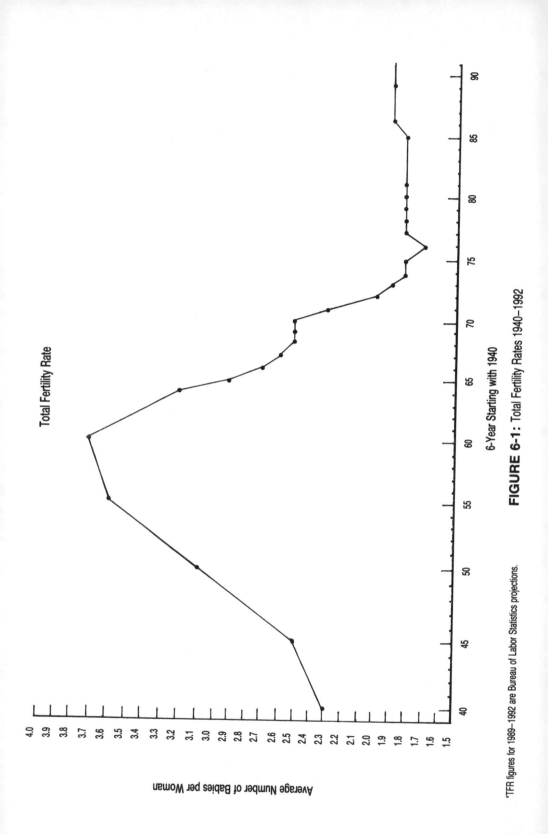

Total Fertility Rate

6-Year Starting with 1940

FIGURE 6-1: Total Fertility Rates 1940–1992

*TFR figures for 1989–1992 are Bureau of Labor Statistics projections.

1.8 average is going to increase significantly in the future, for a number of reasons. It is so expensive to have children, for one. Infant mortality has declined drastically, reducing the need to bear several children in order to guarantee that one or more survive to adulthood. Underscoring these practical concerns is the social message not to further overpopulate the earth. Finally, women are finding fulfillment in activities in addition to child rearing, and they are starting their families later in life. There could be changes in the total fertility rate in the future, but they're apt to be relatively minor. For example, the family patterns of some immigrant populations that tend to have more children can alter the total fertility rate—but not significantly.

Now, it's important to remember that the drop in total fertility from 3.7 to 1.8 didn't take place overnight. Almost no demographic phenomenon does. Everybody knows about the explosion in births that took place in our country immediately after World War II. A boom in births is not unusual following a war, when men and women have been separated and the normal functions of society, producing goods and babies, have been put on hold. The surprising thing about the American baby boom after World War II was its duration—it lasted eighteen years, until 1964.

During that period, however, the fertility rate didn't remain at a static high level. It began higher than it had been before the war ended, at 2.5, zoomed upward over the course of the next decade, peaked at 3.7 in 1957, then gradually went down again. The baby boom per se ended in 1964, when the total fertility rate was 2.9. But the TFR continued to decline until 1975. For nearly twenty years, since 1975, women on average have produced half the number of children that were produced at the peak of the baby boom.

The number of babies the average woman has is only one factor in determining population shifts. The other is the number of women having babies. And the most important thing for this analysis is to remember that even though women are having half as many babies on average now, there is a larger generation of women who are having them—because the women having babies between 1974 and today are a product of the baby boom.

Demography deals in geometric rather than arithmetic effects. I think that staple premise of the field is important to take into account in understanding the impact of the total fertility rate on the growth of the American population. In other words, demography relies on multiplication rather than addition. As a result trends can be explosive, in the degree to which the numbers can both expand and diminish.

Let's apply that premise to this situation. When two parents have four children, as they did during the baby boom, and those four children, with their spouses, each have four children, you wind up with sixteen children in the next generation: from two to four to sixteen.

Conversely, when two parents have two children, as is true of people on average today, and those two children, with their spouses, each have two children, you wind up with four children in the next generation: from two to two to four.

Had the baby boom continued at the same rate, we would have seen the first scenario, with a second generation of four children per family and a third generation of sixteen children. Instead we are experiencing a combination of the two scenarios. Each set of parents in the baby boom generation produced, on average, four children. When those four children grew up, each produced, on average, two children. In either case, initially, the population continues to grow, but in the latter case, if the TFR remains constant, four represents the high point. Beyond that point the population diminishes as opposed to the geometric growth that continues in the former case.

The effect was not a doubling in the next generation. Instead the size of the upcoming generation has virtually stabilized, because twice as many women, produced in the baby boom, were in turn producing half as many children.

Let's look at the real numbers. The total fertility rate dropped from a high of 3.7 in 1957 to a stable low of 1.8 in 1974. Women born during the baby boom are producing half as many babies as their mothers. Since the baby boom generation is twice the size of the generation before, we have had twice the number of women producing half the number of babies. So the size of each maturing generation has until now remained fairly constant.

When these children mature to adulthood and begin to produce children of their own—and they will most likely have an average of just under two children—we will have half the number of women that we had in the baby boom generation producing half the number of babies. The result: we will have a generation that is half the size of the baby boom generation. Again, not a *leveling effect*, as we are already seeing, but a *halving effect*.

Of course, this geometric shrinking of the successive maturing generations will not take place in one burst. As I mentioned, the baby boom itself took place gradually, over the eighteen-year period from 1946 to 1964. In the same way, the baby bust, created in large part by boomers bearing their own children in families that average just under two, will take place gradually. We're just beginning to see the eighteen-year-olds of the first 1.8 generation, born in 1975, enter the work force.

As smaller numbers of babies are produced each year, the growth of the U.S. population is destined gradually to slow. In the 1990s the population is expected to grow less than 1 percent each year. According to projections released by the Census Bureau in 1989, by 2000 we'll begin seeing the births falling off, because these will be the babies born to the baby bust generation. After 2038 the population may actually start to decline.[2] Though the unexpected rise in real births in the last few years has caused some demographers to rethink the *rate* at which population growth will slow, level, and then decline, the downward trend from now until the middle of the next century is inexorable.

Currently business wouldn't be hurt by slower population growth if the economy didn't keep expanding. But it has. One of our best indicators of economic health, the gross national product, grew tenfold between 1960 and 1990 and will in all likelihood continue to expand.[3]

The population overall won't start to decline until well after the turn of the century. But business will begin to feel a contraction in the pool from which it draws its workers a good deal sooner—in fact, companies are already starting to feel the pinch. That is because business is dependent on each entering generation of young people as it matures, on the people born in each successive birth year—and that is precisely where we are already starting to see the leveling off and where we will in the not-too-distant future see a halving effect.

If you take the total fertility rate of each age cohort and project into the future, you get a picture of the size of the microgeneration produced in each birth year that has come of age and is entering and beginning to move through the work force. *Now, in 1992, we have half the number of twenty-year-olds we expected.*

What do I mean by "expected"? It's not that anyone thought the baby boom would go on forever—but in a very real sense the people who ran businesses still operated on the assumption that there would always be enough people to fill all the jobs available. They imagined the same abundant supply of workers would enter the work force each year as did in the baby boom, that there would always be enough male workers. Business executives made plans as if the boom were going to continue. The fast-food outlets, dependent on large numbers of employees as well as consumers, proliferated, along with giant new corporate headquarters that also reflected optimism about the future.

Businesses that rely today on an influx of eighteen-year-old workers—that depend on the generation created during the flattening effect—have already begun to feel shortages relative to their needs. These eighteen-year-olds are in the forefront of the reverse geometric progression (that is, the geometric recession), the current phenomenon whereby twice the number of women are producing half as many children. When the eighteen-year-olds now entering the workplace start to have their children, and those children mature and join the labor force, their numbers will constitute literally half that of their parents' generation. That will not happen until the next century. An approximate date, if you take 1975 as your starting point, would be 2023. That's if a baby bust woman waits until the age of thirty to have a child, who then enters the work force at age eighteen.

So, though the population is growing more slowly in general, it is actually tapering off and will shrink at the younger age levels—the very generations business needs to concern itself with now as these young people reach the age of eighteen or twenty-two. That's why businesses that rely on an entry group of high school graduates are already feeling the pinch, while companies that are heavily dependent on their older management-entry-level supply are not yet as aware of the imminent decline in workers.[4]

The supply of potential employees is also being eroded by another factor: the failure of the American educational system. The United States Department of Education estimates that nearly 13 percent of Americans age twenty and over are totally illiterate, 20 percent lack the basic skills needed to cope well in society, 33 percent lack twelfth-grade equivalence in education, and two to three million each year join the ranks of the functionally illiterate.[5] With the Department of Labor's 1- to 6-point reading-level scale as a guide, the average young adult in America reads at a 2.6 level, while most new jobs require a 3.6.[6]

In the words of David Kearns, former chairman and CEO of Xerox Corporation, speaking in 1989, "The failure of our public education system is imposing enormous costs—and business is footing a good part of the bill. At Xerox, we'll spend about $200 million on training this year alone. Finding and training the right people costs American industry $210 billion a year for formal and informal on-the-job training."[7]

So we have a labor shortfall whose effects are compounded by educational problems, along with a steady overall expansion in companies' labor needs. According to R. Scott Fosler, vice-president and director of government studies for the Committee for Economic Development, "The long-term trend of economic growth increasing more rapidly than labor force growth is likely to create a generally favorable market for qualified workers and a labor squeeze for business."[8]

Recently I spoke on the same platform as Robert Winter, the CEO of Prudential of America. His topic was public elementary and secondary education. It was obvious from the start that his speech was from the heart, not a text prepared for him that he had scanned only briefly. The reason for his passion: Prudential hires thousands of high school students each year for its huge clerical level. In the past the firm could depend on an ample supply from which it could hire the most qualified applicants.

Those days are clearly over. Now there is a real shortage of high school students—those born in 1975, when the TFR was 1.8. Suddenly the competition for able young people has become intense. Since 1978 the number of workers from the age of sixteen to nineteen has dropped by 20 percent.[9] Not only are there half the number senior executives had anticipated, but 20 percent of that pool are functionally illiterate. Additionally, huge numbers have grown up in circumstances that have not bred the values of responsibility, commitment, or belief in a system that has served them so poorly.

Businesses are going to great lengths to recruit and train young workers. Aetna reportedly saw a 44 percent drop in job applicants in 1988, with the sharpest decline apparent in entry-level positions. In response the company started a program called Hire and Train, which focuses on underqualified yet motivated recruits for entry-level spots such as that of claims processor. Says an administrator at Aetna: "We aren't being magnanimous. We're doing it because we've seen the numbers."[10]

Projected labor shortages in the food service industry—the number of jobs is expected to grow by 36 percent in the 1990s—is leading companies like the Chicago-based Hyatt Hotels Corporation to direct intervention. Hyatt is training 350 students a year for work in the industry. To do that they're spending $280,000 to build a kitchen in a Chicago high school, develop a curriculum, and provide Hyatt chefs to train students.[11]

This is ground level, of course. The neighborhood McDonald's is not the corporate boardroom. But it's the start of an ineluctable movement. "Where we're feeling it right now is at the bottom of the pyramid, but in the coming decade, as you have more difficulty getting people in at the bottom, you will have a smaller total pool and therefore fewer candidates to move up through the ranks—it's a 'trickle up' theory. That pyramid eventually will feel it at all levels." So says Marilyn Block, executive vice-president at the Naisbitt Group, a research and consulting firm specializing in trend analysis, forecasting, and strategic planning.[12]

You can also see the beginning of shortages in technical fields. The number of BS degrees in science and engineering is expected to fall short by 450,000 in 1996 and by 700,000 in 2010.[13] Dick Morrow, former CEO and chairman of Amoco, told me, "We have great difficulty in getting skilled people at every level. Increasingly, we have to provide in-house training." At a senior management meeting last year, he said, an emphatic point was made of the need to retain women engineers, to provide whatever family supports are necessary to capture their talent. Energy companies that depend on engineers and geologists were until very recently male bastions with no interest at all in women. Today, companies like Tenneco, Exxon, Mobil, and Amoco are in the forefront of responsiveness to women.

According to an update of the 1987 *Workforce 2000* report, which surveyed a number of larger corporations: "Fifty-three percent of the group currently report some difficulty hiring for professional jobs, while 10 percent are experiencing great difficulty. Forty-four percent report some difficulty hiring secretaries and clerical workers at present, and 11 percent find it very difficult to do so."[14] Technical and professional employees—known as "knowledge workers" or "gold collar" employees—are the most difficult to recruit. The "demand for them is expected to be so great that they will be able to name their own salaries and the conditions of their employment."

There are, of course additional factors that affect population size and, hence, labor supply. What about the impact of people leaving or entering the country? It is estimated that we will receive 560,000 immigrants each year over the coming decade.[15] That number will serve only to maintain replacement levels, and it will not be large enough to compensate for the inevitable decline in births that is just ahead.

The upshot is a projection of shortages that will at first be relative to the needs of business and in the long term absolute. The areas that will be hardest hit at the beginning are the lower levels, technical areas, and fields requiring advanced education. Eventually, however, no field and no specialty area or job will be immune from the effects of a shrinking labor pool.

A WOMAN'S PLACE IS IN THE WORK FORCE

It's all very well that the labor pool available to employers is gradually constricting. Where do women stand within that pool?

First, a numerical sketch. The labor force is made up of the total number of people ages sixteen or older who are working or willing to work. As of 1991, 75 percent of all men were counted as labor force participants, compared with 57 percent of all women. The rate of male labor force participation won't change more than a hair by the year 2000, while the percentage of women who are working or willing to work will rise to 62.9 percent. As of May 1991, 45 percent of the work force was female, a proportion that will rise to 47 percent by the year 2000.[16]

Not only that, but those women who are in the labor pool are a better resource than ever before. In an earlier chapter I discussed a number of sources of women's empowerment, including their increased sense of autonomy, a pattern of later childbearing, and increased educational preparation. There is one element of this empowerment that merits further elaboration here. Incredible as it may seem to some people, women are actually beginning to displace men in institutions of higher education.

Over the past decade there has been a much more rapid increase in the numbers of women college graduates than in the total number of graduates. Between 1980 and 1990 the number of men receiving BA degrees actually declined, from 473,611 to 438,097. At the same time, the number of women BA recipients climbed from 455,806 to

534,570. In that decade the number of men receiving MA degrees decreased from 150,749 to 148,982—but the number of women MAs increased, from 147,332 to 160,780.[17]

How about in the more specialized academic arena of advanced business education, which sends most high-caliber managers into American corporations? The Department of Education says that between 1980 and 1986 the number of men earning MBAs increased by 8.3 percent, while the number of women MBA recipients increased by 69.7 percent.[18]

There is yet another dimension to the rapidly growing dependence on women graduates from the best graduate schools of law and accounting. The prestigious law and accounting firms draw their leadership from the top 10 percent of these classes. But the total enrollment at these schools does not expand. Therefore the top 10 percent that was solidly male is now virtually half female. These firms will have to either recruit both men and women for their future leaders or dip down to the twentieth percentile for men. The same holds true for business, where almost one-third of the men have been displaced by women.

Women are increasingly likely to consider their jobs a central, lifelong commitment. A 1990 study found that 45 percent of women think of their work as a career, up from 41 percent in 1985. That can be compared with men's career orientation: 57 percent of men regard their work as a career, with no significant shift from 1985.[19]

Now, it can be asserted that despite their increasing educational attainment, and despite their expanding job commitment, women are less solid a resource to business because of their work patterns. Fewer women than men work full-time, and fewer work throughout their careers without interruption. Both observations are true. Of all labor force participants, 25 percent of women and 10 percent of men work part-time. At the management level, 9 percent of women and 4 percent of men work part-time. Of professionals, 22 percent of women and 8 percent of men work part-time.[20]

Regardless of these patterns, it's clear that because of slower population growth in general and labor force shrinkage in the long term, business is going to need women. Simply put, those men born after 1975 cannot possibly fill all the entry-level jobs vacated by advancing baby boomers or the millions of new jobs business creates every year.

Impending personnel shortages seem inconceivable now, when the common corporate experience reflects a labor glut. Looking at the changes in the total fertility rate helps explain why it is that managers today are facing such intense competition and helps to predict the reversal that the not-too-distant future will bring.

Let's say people at the middle-management level are around age thirty-five. In 1985 those thirty-five-year-olds were born in 1950, when the TFR was 3.1. In 1995 we will see that managers of the same age were born in 1960, when the TFR was 3.7. Now think ahead a decade, to the competition thirty-five-year-old managers might face in 2005. They will have been born in 1970, when the TFR bottomed out at 2.0. There will be fewer candidates, more opportunities.

With fertility trends as a guide, I even see how a woman born in 1960 could benefit from cutting back to part-time for a period—let's be audacious and say five years or even, with a three-year spacing between kids, eight years—until her children are settled in school. She can return full-time to the workplace in a period when entering generations are so small that employers will compete for her talents.

The labor shortages of the future will be compounded by educational deterioration—but they will be ameliorated at least in part by the availability of qualified, committed women. Dean Donald Jacobs of J. L. Kellogg Graduate School of Management, put the idea succinctly: "We're a competitive enough society so that business can't afford to play bias games."[21]

In spite of all I have just said, I can hear the ubiquitous voices of senior managers—and particularly of CEOs who have perhaps five years to go until retirement—saying: "This is not relevant to me or to my company or firm in the short term."

They're about to have a big surprise, unless they reconsider that judgment. Why? Because unless they start *right now* to develop women at the lower rungs of their companies, they will not have a significant mass of women at senior management levels when graduating classes start to shrink and the competition for the best job candidates intensifies. As a result, the best and brightest women graduates will count the number of women at the senior management and partner level and turn away. They will go to companies where the numbers are significant. Given the demographics, half of all recruits will continue to be female. However, these companies will have to settle for second-tier women. Thus their competitive position in their industries and the world economy will be greatly damaged.

OTHER TRENDS GOING FOR WOMEN

As I looked into the demographic impetus for changing the corporate workplace, I came to see that a number of other social and economic trends will strengthen employers' motivation to clear the way for women.

The first is the shift from a manufacturing to a service- and information-based economy. There is currently a forty to sixty industrial-service ratio within the Fortune 500. Over the past fifteen years 5 percent of new jobs created were in manufacturing, compared with 90 percent in the services and information sector. Nearly 90 percent of the jobs created through 1995 will be in the information service sector.[22]

I see a number of positive implications for women in this shift. For one, it means that we're moving from the need to be on one site, where the machines are located, to a much more decentralized workplace. Then, too, we're moving from muscle power to brain power, from a moderately skilled work force to one composed of large numbers of unskilled workers in the service sector, on the one hand, and highly educated people in the information sector. The latter dovetails well with women's educational attainment.

"Women and the information society—which celebrates brain over brawn—are a partnership made in heaven." So write John Naisbitt and Patricia Aburdene in *Megatrends 2000*. What they are referring to is another change that is already under way, from the command-and-control leadership style of men to what some observers have described as the facilitating, orchestrating leadership style of women. They suggest that "the organizing principle of business has shifted from management to leadership, opening doors to women."[23]

The manufacturing to service switch will also mean smaller enterprises. Some 85 to 90 percent of the labor force will work for companies that employ less than two hundred people, and businesses employing fewer than one hundred workers will generate up to half of all new jobs in the next decade.[24] Often, smaller means greater flexibility and locations closer to the people they serve, a boon for working parents.

The larger, urban-based companies are facing increasing pressures that will force them to provide alternative work arrangements such as flextime, nonuniform schedules, and telecommuting. Commutes are getting longer, as real estate values force people to move farther from the cities where they work. That increases congestion and pollution and requires innovations such as carpooling, which mandates regular hours.

I remember visiting Farmers Insurance Group in Los Angeles a couple of years ago, when the state had just passed legislation mandating a higher ratio of employees to cars. I was greeted at the door by the two people with whom I was meeting. Those who violate air quality measures would incur a $25,000 fine, a fairly strong incentive for compliance. They informed me that our conversation would have to be brief because they both had to leave promptly at four to join their car pools. The implications of this trend for working parents are immense—when the norm is to join one's car pool at precisely four, working parents who want to leave the office on time in order to spend time with their kids after work aren't exceptional.

Continuous training will be needed for this more sophisticated information economy. According to one futurist, "The jobs performed are changing so rapidly that 50 percent of the jobs being done in 1987 did not exist twenty years earlier, and by 2007 essentially all of the work will be new." The sheer amount of all information available, this writer contends, has begun to double every 2½ years. The result: "In the future, everyone we hire will have to be retrained three or four times during a normal employment period. The alternative, of course, is constant turnover, replacing the work force every five years or so."[25]

How will the necessity for retraining enhance the positioning of women? It reduces the cost of creating alternative career paths for those who want to take time for their families. If everyone has to be retrained anyway after a certain period, it will be routine to retrain women who have taken time off to raise children.

The compression of the corporate pyramid is a trend that became well-known in the 1980s—not so well understood, however, are the benefits it may bring for women.

The American Management Association, which has tracked downsizing activity of major corporations since 1986, reports that the trend toward staff trimming continues unabated.[26] The typical corporate structure is leaner, with fewer levels of hierarchy. A good example of the trend comes from General Electric's 1989 annual report: "We began the 1980s with a bureaucracy of as many as nine management layers in some businesses. Today, all our businesses have significantly reduced layers, some as few as four, and now we move a lot faster—

not yet with the speed of the best small companies, but with that goal always in our sights and closer every day."[27]

The outcome, I usually hear, is a curtailing of upward mobility for aspiring managers. It is potentially damaging for those who have traditionally been outsiders to business—the "last hired, first fired" syndrome. So the popular assumption is that the flattening of the pyramid is detrimental to women.

I don't understand it in that way. As competition increases, the trend in layoffs more and more is to be selective, to make them merit-based. In addition, the reduction of management opportunities is causing companies to search for alternative rewards for managers in order to preserve their morale, their productivity, and their loyalty. This willingness to offer new rewards can result in development of policies that will assist women. One boon might be greater flexibility, so that the employee has more control over her or his time. Another is lateral mobility, which has traditionally been denied to women because they weren't seen as in the running for leadership positions that required a breadth of experience. Another advantage to women of the compression of the pyramid is that those employees who are talented and yet willing to remain at lower levels for whatever reason will be more valued by employers.

One casualty of the rampant mergers and acquisitions, layer trimming, and technological advancement that have recently characterized the corporate sector is the traditional "psychological contract" between employee and employer, which was characterized by cradle-to-grave security in exchange for lifelong loyalty and acceptable job performance. Endless advancement was never a given, but security was. Now employees legitimately see commitment to one firm as a risky proposition, and employers are moving more and more toward lean core staffs and a variety of add-ons in the form, for example, of contract workers.

The result: loyalty to one's own career has taken precedence over commitment to one job or one company. Employees who suddenly find themselves unemployed are using their acquired skills as a springboard to seek higher salaries or greater autonomy elsewhere. And as employees become scarcer and more in demand, they are less likely to stick around if their job is imperfect. Currently, it has been estimated, individuals change careers three times in an average lifetime and change jobs as many as ten times.[28]

As a result of the decline in employee loyalty, companies are beginning to recognize that they must earn and build the motivated commitment of their work force. It doesn't come ready-made. The challenge is to devise new strategies to keep morale and productivity high. The answer, here as with the flattening of the pyramid, is to provide more meaningful rewards. And the lowest-cost reward is one that is meaningful to parents: time and greater flexibility.

Declining employee loyalty means that now, instead of men being lifetime employees and women jeopardizing their careers by dropping out of the work force for a period to raise their children, we have a new paradigm of normalcy. Everyone, male and female, moves from one job to the next. Companies are more motivated to keep their employees. Yet companies are no longer looking to hold on to employees for life. The norm is no longer lifetime employment; therefore, if employers can get high productivity and morale at any time, they feel fortunate.

Many observers have noted the emergence of what has been termed the "new breed" worker. "For this emerging group," writes one sociologist, "the meaning and priority of work has changed, alongside other priorities. The New Breed worker places high value on opportunities for self-expression, and work takes its place alongside other life goals and interests."[29]

"Social change, driven by demography, education, and prosperity, begets value change," writes another observer. "The baby boomers and women bring new values and attitudes about work, family life, and society to politics and business. The new value shift centers around time, quality, self-fulfillment, children, and general satisfaction with life. Americans are increasingly assertive of their rights in and out of the workplace."[30]

Florence Skelly, president of Telematics, Inc., and vice-chairman and director of the Yankelovitch Group, predicts a greater focus on nonmaterial rewards from work and home life.[31]

The waning of the work ethic means that men are not as career driven as they used to be. Even if they are not yet thinking about sharing parenting, they're not as driven at work, and they are beginning to think about broader lives.

The outcome of these trends is more autonomy for workers, more potential for work at home, and more of a motivation for business to respond to the needs of women and to create a climate of flexibility— all of which will enable women to combine career and family and men to share in parenting, while leaving ample opportunity for men and

women who are career driven and ready to enter the competition for
the highest levels.

REASON TO BELIEVE

Several years ago Catalyst sponsored a roundtable discussion with
twelve or so corporate leaders to disuss the implications of the new
two-gender work force for corporate policy. I found one comment,
made by Robert Beck, executive vice-president at Bank of America,
especially to the point. "We have seen that our society has very good
correcting mechanisms for our problems," he declared. "Our various
energy problems are good examples: in the 1950s everyone wanted
cars, so we built a massive highway system. Now we have to go back
to mass transit. It's costing us dearly, but we're doing it. Our society
is able to adapt to change. I think that the only issue is how long
we're willing to wait for each solution and what we're willing to give
up to get it." Then Beck paused and said with a shock of sudden
recognition, "It really didn't hit me until today—with all those women
working, where are those kids?" His conclusion: "Now it's a matter
of how long we want to wait before we put in the systems to take care
of the problem."[32] Incidentally it was Bank of America, driven by Bob
Beck, that subsequently established a child care network on the West
Coast.

Also participating in that roundtable was Gordon McGovern, at that
time president and chief executive officer of Campbell Soup Co. "If
everyone participates in all our economic activities—both men and
women—and we agree we're underutilizing our assets and abilities,
and if we can get all that moving, I think that would restore a whole
new momentum to the economic scene. We have great potential, and
women are just one piece of that. What's beginning to dawn on me
is that it's not a social abstract. If we don't do this, we're going to get
wiped out."[33]

I think we're destined to see a broader awareness dawn quite soon,
partly because of a new compression of social issues. These issues are
closing in on us, moving from the long range and abstract (for example,
the discontent of women) to the short range, the personally affecting
("I need the best people I can get to do a specific job"). The problem

of who will rear the children, in the longer range, relates to the future of our society. In the shorter range, it is an issue to be grappled with by individual employers, because the children of today will tomorrow be business's new employees.

Yet in responding to Catalyst's survey, which I referred to at the start of this chapter, no CEO seemed aware of the enormous changes in the offing. Why was this? As I considered the trends that would inevitably shape the future of business, I found several plausible explanations.

First, the average CEO is surrounded by a generation of top executives that is solidly male—these senior-level men are mainly thirty-five- to forty-five-years-olds, born in the baby boom years of 1945 to 1955. It is simply unbelievable to him that that reality is going to change any time soon. Second, in an environment where most companies are actively shedding middle managers, it's difficult to imagine a climate where shortages will have a direct, company-specific impact. Third, a CEO's pride as well as his experience tell him that he can always buy all the talent he needs—and he can choose the qualifications that accompany that talent. If he wants to continue to employ only the smartest men, he is convinced he will be able do so even as the percentage of men in management decreases.

In addition, the research I did showed me that it's easy to misrepresent the demographics or even to misunderstand them when they are presented accurately.

We often hear bandied about a figure of 85 percent, as in "85 percent of the work force in the 1990s will be women, minorities, and immigrants." The implication here is that the percentage of white males in the labor force this decade will dwindle to 15 percent. Policymakers think to themselves, "Whoa, wait a minute, that simply cannot be. I see the composition of my work force now, and I see a growing number of women and minorities and immigrants there, and I see them gradually moving up. But there are still white males as far as the eye can see. That sounds like some kind of alarmist routine, patently unbelievable."

They're correct, at least in part. The specter of an immediate, drastic change is wrong, plain and simple. Unfortunately it clouds the picture and makes it difficult for a rational person to grasp—and therefore to take seriously—the real trends taking place.

Part of the problem is the frequent omission of a crucial adjective: "net." It is true that 85 percent of the net new entrants to the work force in each year between now and 2000 are projected by the Bureau of Labor Statistics to be women, minorities, and immigrants. But you really have to break down that statement to understand its meaning.

A net change is a function not only of the people who enter the work force, but of those workers who retire. In fact, non-Hispanic white males will constitute one-third of work force entrants between 1988 and 2000—but they will account for half of those leaving in the same period in large part because they've been there for the longest time. Another reason the net change in this area is so great is that men are retiring at a younger age. In 1950, 44 percent of all men age sixty-five and over were still actively employed, in contrast with only 16 percent of men in that age group in 1990.[34]

Another point of confusion: When demographers refer to entrants, they're talking about the people who enter the work force in a single given year, say, 1992 or 1995 or 1999. Naturally these entrants change the profile of the work force in an incremental sense. But it's only after, say, forty years that diversity permeates the work force. The change is neither immediate nor total.

There's another factor at work here. Whether it's a characteristic of business or whether it's human nature, we have a tendency to operate from the small shell of our immediate circumstance. We find it difficult to project ahead even five years into the future. In this case the tendency might be our ultimate competitive undoing.

A little over a year ago I participated in a panel discussion about women at the Japan Society. I recall raising my hand and asking why no one was mentioning the demographics. I knew that forty years ago the Japanese total fertility rate had plummeted to below replacement level. Nobody on the panel seemed very interested in the question.

At the end of my crash course in demographic trends, I opened *The New York Times* to find a center front-page article headlined IN CROWDED JAPAN, A BONUS FOR BABIES ANGERS WOMEN.[35] The article went on to say that the government had announced a reward of 5,000 yen, or $38, per month to be given to mothers for each child of preschool age and twice as much for a third child. The bonus was the centerpiece of a broad campaign to combat the falling birth rate, and it was inspired by officials' concern that Japan's population is beginning to decline, causing labor shortages, sluggish economic growth, and higher tax burdens to support social services for the elderly.

Now Japan realizes it has a problem. That demographic trends haven't been felt more pointedly until now is due, I believe, to the fact that the Japanese work force hasn't been depleted, as has ours. That's because they have zero illiteracy, and crime is virtually nonexistent. They do not suffer losses from those who are killed and maimed by criminals or jailed for crimes committed. Theirs is a homogeneous work force. That's why it took them forty years to feel the pinch that we are beginning to feel here twenty years after the drop in the TFR from 3.7 to 1.8.

The only solution, as the Japanese now see it, is to send women home to have more babies—which has caused an uproar among Japanese women. On the other hand, these women don't want to follow in the workaholic footsteps of the men they see. They don't want to remain at home, but they don't see career commitment as a viable substitute.

This could be one important competitive edge American business has in relation to Japan: we can utilize women. American women are not only qualified, experienced, and proven, they are committed to being a part of the world of work at a time when that sector has never been more in need of them.

So in terms of feeling the urgency, the upshot is that you can wait or you can move now. It's your choice. Sure, you can always bring in some mediocre men, but women are there as a resource.

You can quibble about numbers or percentages or the exact year you'll feel the pinch. Nonetheless, the inevitable thing is that the shortages will take place. You *will* feel them. Your response is up to you.

I remember an image with which I described the coming labor shortages in a film produced in the early 1980s by the Bureau of National Affairs. The new demographic realities appeared as a tidal wave that I could see rising up behind corporate leaders while they were standing on the beach with their backs to the ocean. The business leaders who didn't turn around quickly to face the changes would wash away under the force of the water.

It may not happen like the tidal wave I spoke about then. It may instead be more as if you're facing the ocean, say, having a picnic on the beach. You watch the waves creep up gradually. Somehow you think they're never going to reach your blanket. You wait until the last possible moment to move.

Of course then, suddenly, the water is there. It takes you by surprise, washes up, and you're soaked. It's not too late. You can still move. But the force of the water starts immediately to erode the infrastructure of sand on which you were seated so comfortably just moments before. And you have to run pretty fast to stay dry. By the time you do, others have got the good spots on the high ground.

This metaphor refers to the broad picture. The macro forces of population shifts and other trends will prompt a rising business motivation to use women more effectively. If you're still not convinced, it might help to consider the same issue from a somewhat narrower vantage point—that of profit and loss within an individual company. This is the aim of the chapters that follow.

PART III
Women as a Business Imperative

CHAPTER SEVEN

The Cost of Burying Women's Talent

As president of Catalyst I am always out in the field, talking with corporate leaders about the women they employ. I don't come into their offices wielding an adding machine or a club—to count heads or to take people to task—but instead to explore how companies can become more profitable by responding to women more effectively. As a result, the people I meet with are fairly open about the problems they're experiencing and also about the things they feel good about. More often than not I hear them say, "Yes, we have some problems. Maybe we need to do more. Maybe we need to learn what are the best things to do more of. Still, we're basically moving in the right direction."

But it's not working. The vast resource of female talent is not being mined.

This chapter has three messages, all addressed to corporate executives (but not without relevance for any woman or man trying to make sense of the mess we're in). One, you're losing more money than you know because of women's positioning in your company. Two, you can't solve this problem with incremental changes.

The final point is perhaps the most important. If you are to make the radical change in your view of women that I suggest is critical, you can virtually eliminate the costs of employing women—and you can ensure a huge return for your business.

THE RANGE OF EMPLOYER RESPONSES TO WOMEN

Although my conviction is that no company is moving in the right direction in its response to women, I don't want to suggest that all companies today are in exactly the same place. We're in a transition period, and employers are at different levels of awareness. It's instructive, before we go back to talking about companies in a larger sense, to look at some of the differences. So let me share my sense of the patterns companies fall into in terms of their motivation to develop women, because the question of motivation is critical.

In the course of my work I have developed a sort of thumbnail assessment of where companies stand with respect to their response to women. Mine is not a clear-cut ranking. It isn't realistic to assign stars on the basis of issues so complex, so subtle, as those with which we are concerned here. There's no specific way to do it. You can't rate a company on whether it has two women on the board or six women in senior management or a fantastic parental leave policy. Counting heads can be deceptive—you could have a high percentage of women at the top and nobody in the pipeline. And it's entirely possible to have a great program in a company that is far from being imbued with any sense of the value of women. In fact, good policies don't ensure good practices unless they are broadly promulgated and "sold" to managers.

As I travel and observe companies, however, I find it interesting to think of where they might fall along a spectrum that indicates their level of motivation and from what it derives.

Let's say the spectrum goes from 0 to 5. On the low end are those companies that have not yet begun to appreciate the benefit they could gain by developing women. They're the 0's. When I visit I cannot feel even a pulse of interest—they are simply dead to this issue. They pay little attention to the number or quality of women entering their companies or to helping them succeed.

Next along the spectrum, at around 1, are those employers who just want to keep ahead of the law to the minimal extent possible. They track numbers and fill out the forms required for Equal Employment Opportunity Commission (EEOC) compliance but do not take the initiative in responding to women's needs.

At 2 are companies that have a desire to do what is fair and right. They have formulated two or three specific policies, which are usually not broadly implemented or promulgated—say, a child care resource and referral service, part-time jobs at the clerical level, and a limited informal arrangement with some unpaid maternity leave. These employers do have a growing sense of what women can bring to their company. But their feeling is that women will not and should not be part of the real action, that it's a man's world.

There are still only a few employers who can say, "We're really doing well by women," even in an incremental sense. These would be the companies I place at 3 on the spectrum from 0 to 5—Gannett, say, where there is a passion to develop women, or the Federal National Mortgage Association (Fannie Mae), which increased the number of women from 4 percent in 1981 to 32 percent today, or IBM, which was built on Watson's "respect for the individual," or companies like Corning, which devised a carefully orchestrated plan for achieving real change. There are companies also that are starting to do what has always been thought of as "soft" stuff in a harder, more acceptable way—"sensitivity training," for example, undertaken to help men and women recognize talent in its every guise and to accept cultural differences between employees. These companies are really making a comprehensive effort to implement programs and policies.

The 4 marker is where some of these companies are trying to move, to a level playing field for the women they employ. This is some distance away, but I hope to show in the next chapter that to begin to do so is not as difficult as anyone might think.

I think 5 is off the charts as far as anyone is thinking today. This exemplary valuation is the ultimate achievement and will yield the ultimate payoff—it requires the radical change in mind-set I've already referred to. Later in this book I will propose strategies that can take you there.

For now, though, the vast majority of companies stand at the 1 or 2 mark. Those in the 2 category consider themselves better than average and genuinely think they're doing okay "on the woman issue." They may not be exemplary, but in a way that's more to their liking—they're where most companies want to be, toward the front of the pack but not at the cutting edge.

In this chapter I want to discuss why these vast numbers of 2's, the better-than-average employers, are in greater danger than they realize. Not that any company is exempt—the 0's are in worse trouble, and the 3's are only a little better off. No matter where a company falls along the spectrum, it is not going far enough. Unless a company moves beyond the 4 marker all the way to 5, it is wasting a resource that could provide a huge competitive advantage in its industry and in the world economy.

ONE COMPANY'S EXPERIENCE

Let me introduce you to the CEO of one better-than-average company. I've changed his name and all the other identifying details that follow, but his is a real story. Except for minor details it is prototypical of the experience of CEOs in many of the companies I've visited over the last couple of years.

Peter Anderson is chairman, president, and CEO at Top Form Corporation, a top 1000 company recently relocated from New York City to a smaller city in the tri-state area. I spent an hour in his office in the fall of 1990, and I was impressed with his obvious sensitivity, his intelligence and integrity. Anderson clearly had a sense that women could pull their weight in his business. He had also thought about his responsibility to the concerns of those women in his employ.

Anderson conveyed his specific knowledge of where women are located in his company. His work force is 55 percent female overall, with 60 percent women at the exempt level and a group of vice-presidents that is 7 percent female—a proportion that compares favorably with the national average.

During our meeting he described the various policies he has spearheaded to respond to a more diverse work force. Anderson believes he's doing a lot. He is justifiably proud of his company's recently instituted flexible benefits program, which allows employees to select those benefits that best suit their individual needs. He has even supported the adoption of part-time work schedules in some isolated instances.

Though Anderson is motivated to make some responses to women, I did not get the sense that he recognizes women as a bottom-line resource, much less as a business imperative. Perhaps this was because of a recent experience he'd had. It seemed to have suggested to him that his desire to develop and advance women might not be worth the effort.

Reporting to him, he told me, was a very talented woman—I'll call her Elaine Norton—who had been with the company for a number of years. She would have been the first woman in his company to enter senior management, and she was on the threshold of doing just that.

Then she quit. She had four children, ranging in age from eight to fourteen. She said she left to spend more time with them. Her decision was absolutely unexpected.

Norton's departure left Anderson baffled. Here was a woman he had been eager to promote. He had given her every opportunity he would give a man, because it was obvious she was worth it. Not only was she entirely qualified, she would be the first woman in his inner circle, a milestone. He genuinely had her pegged for the highest level—which she knew—and had consequently gone out of his way to develop her. So her defection in itself was a mystery.

Then there was its timing. Anderson understood that Norton was torn between the demands of her family and her work. But she had already weathered her children's preschool years, which he thought surely would be more difficult, even overwhelming, when combined with her job responsibilities. Her choice to leave now, when she was on the verge of unprecedented success, might have been triggered by a crisis with one of her kids. But if so, why hadn't she named it? Why hadn't she asked for help? Why not confide in him, rather than suddenly letting him and his company down? Why not put the problem—whatever it was—squarely on the table for discussion?

"The corporate environment has a corrosive impact on women," I suggested.

Anderson seemed taken aback. "I think that's an overstatement," he said.

I believe that on some profound level, seeing his company's highest-achieving woman leave had shaken his confidence in the commit-

ment of women in general. I had a strong sense that he felt betrayed—
that it didn't occur to him that he may have been the source of the
problem rather than the victim. As I've said, it even caused Anderson
to wonder if his efforts to respond to women's needs would ever pay
off. On the surface, however, he was able to tell himself that her
departure didn't indicate a serious problem for his company. He interpreted her decision as a personal choice. Maybe in the long run this
was a choice that most women who were mothers might make. If so,
so be it. He couldn't fathom my suggestion that the environment in
his own company might have a continuously undermining effect or
my implication that that environment could be improved. It might be
true in some "bad" company (a company we might identify as a 0),
but definitely not in his.

In talking with Anderson, it struck me that although he has some
recognition that the climate in his company is more difficult for women
than it is for men, he doesn't understand just how cumulatively destructive conditions are. He is not aware of all that happens to undermine women as they move up the corporate ladder—how damaging
are the preconceptions about what they can and cannot achieve, how
exclusive the male networks through which deals are cemented and
careers gradually built, how commonplace the sexual innuendos and
casual sexist remarks.

Anderson doesn't see women's suffering because he is shielded
from it by the conspiracy of silence. Women don't speak up because
they are afraid of jeopardizing their jobs or at least creating a barrier
to their growth. They think that talking about the problems they face
will put them in an adversarial position. They do not believe, or even
recognize the possibility, that their boss might appreciate knowing
about the problems they face because they are costly in lowered
productivity and higher turnover and he can only address them if he
knows they exist.

All Anderson sees is the outcome, an outcome he can then attribute
to subjective choice rather than barriers he could remove.

There isn't a CEO anywhere along my spectrum who couldn't tell
a war story about a female star who he thought was superb, in whom
he had invested a lot and then, somehow, lost. I've met some with a
long list of disappointments. In most cases the CEO really doesn't
understand what happened. But it is the cumulative effect of these
defections that feeds his belief that women are not committed, that
he cannot rely on them.

Anderson *did* see problems for women in his company. He was trying to solve them the best way he knew how. Still, his earnest efforts didn't make it possible for him to hold on to this exceptionally able, exceptionally talented woman. And why not? Because his responses to the women he employs tend to be reactive rather than proactive. As such he can never do what is necessary to stem the attrition of his highest-achieving women. There's a crucial element lacking in Anderson's story: the question of his basic motivation.

Anderson does not see what an enormous contribution women could make to *the quality of his company's leadership*—far beyond that of Elaine Norton or any other specific individual he grooms for senior management, good as they are. He does feel some incentive to make use of women's abilities—enough to hand-pick one or another terrific female manager out of the ranks and take great pains to let that individual prove herself in positions of increasing responsibility. But he does not see that pulling out all the stops to change his company's environment could serve his bottom-line interests much more satisfactorily. Not only could he stem the attrition and upgrade the productivity of some of his most talented people, he could make his company a beacon to high-potential and high-performing women.

Here again we see a self-fulfilling prophecy of failure. It seemed worthwhile to Anderson to make changes as needed. His company's record could be deemed a success given a moderate expectation level. But he saw no reason to go back to square one, to reassess the place of women in his company and how it had changed over the past thirty years. He saw no need to question what would be the soundest business strategy to adopt in relation to women. He could not conceive of making the radical shift that is called for now.

And so, women such as Elaine Norton will continue to "betray" him and cost him untold dollars by leaving his company, when they could be flourishing and relishing the challenge, committed to making the company thrive and grow.

WHY CORPORATE LEADERS MISS THE POINT

If you are a senior executive, I could almost guarantee that your reaction would be similar to that of Anderson when I told him the environment in his company was corrosive for women. If you are alone as you read, and in a contemplative frame of mind, you might recognize yourself in his story, but you would be as taken aback as Anderson by the adjective *corrosive*. Yet that continuously undermining environment, and the loss that results for Anderson's company, Top Form, is present to a considerable degree in all but a handful of companies today.

I could name a hundred companies like his, companies where I've had the same kind of conversation with the CEO—where he felt his company was "doing well," where the experience for women is grueling, day after day, and where year upon year it forces disproportionate numbers of the best female executives to plateau in their careers or leave in search of more opportunity elsewhere.

I can understand why even someone like Anderson, a well-meaning guy in a better-than-average company, doesn't see the urgency of radically stepping up his approach to issues pertaining to women in his work force—why his motivation and his response is stuck at the 2 level. The history of how women entered the corporation and how employers have dealt with their entry plays an important part.

Think of the revolution in work and family that has taken place over the past thirty years from the vantage point of corporate management. It started in a way that was barely noticeable. A CEO might have been vaguely aware of the rising voices of women and have seen more women entering the workplace, but to him it was still personally irrelevant, a phenomenon mainly of the lower levels, and even there the numbers of women were comparatively small. How many miles away those first women at the entry level must have seemed from his perspective! He could barely see them, let alone appreciate their abilities.

This distance was accentuated by male executives' long-held ideas about the roles of men and women. They simply could not comprehend the motives of the women who were trying to enter their world. It was not as if they didn't understand women, but what they'd understood about them all their lives, as they'd matured, now was turned on its head. The change was a source of regret, because men of this generation had truly valued women in their conventional roles as homemakers and nurturers. And if the truth be known, they believed that women's interest in pursuing careers was a fad—that they would go home again.

Consider, also, women's approach to their careers in those early years. Women themselves had mixed emotions about entering the workplace. They felt ambivalence and a humility born both of guilt about leaving the home and a sense of inadequacy due to their inexperience. Quite frankly, with rare exceptions, women didn't march into the corporation and perform as stars. They were not supported as were men by a history, an upbringing, and a set of conventions regarding career preparation and achievement. They were further undermined by their day-to-day reception in a hostile world, one in which they were essentially superfluous from the practical standpoint of personnel needs.

Corporate leaders' failure to see women as a business imperative was also forged in the approach taken by women's issues advocates in that early period. The early militant feminists chose to attack and confront—to demand equality for women. Their strategy was designed to make employers conscious of women's resentment about their confinement to the home, of their determination to enter the workplace, and of the need for legislation to ensure they would have equal opportunity. This was, I believe, necessary and effective, but it did not build an awareness of the added value that women could bring to their employers.

It strikes me that even in the period when women were superfluous to the needs of business, greater progress could have taken place if we had made more of the few exceptional women who were already positioned at the highest levels. Then we could have made a telling point: there might be problems to deal with in assimilating women into the fabric of the workplace, but for those companies that did so successfully, there would be a sizable bottom-line reward.

Of course, that did not happen. Instead the relationship of corporate leaders to the women they employed grew from bafflement, and ambivalence, and pressures. As the pressures grew too great to resist, management began to respond.

THE CURRENT IMPACT OF THESE BEGINNINGS

The stance taken by chief executives of companies—anywhere along the spectrum I've described—reflects this history. Many are trying to be responsive to employees' family needs, whether that means instituting a resource and referral service for child care or allowing a period of unpaid leave beyond disability for new mothers. Others are trying to move women up through the pipelines and to increase the numbers of women at senior levels. Some few are even establishing goals for advancing women and holding their managers accountable via financial rewards or penalties.

It would be inaccurate to say that the situation for women is *no good* now. In the context of women as outsiders coming into men's world and being accommodated in that world—perceived initially as super-fluous and then as a source of problems and legislative pressure— we've made stunning progress. In fact, from my observation this is true: there is nothing that could be done for women that is not being done someplace. All the models are there.

But these responses have been instituted on an ad hoc basis. They are initiated after someone demands something. Management's incentive may include a desire to do what is fair and right, reinforced by a fear of violating the law or of a class action suit. Then the company polls employees on what they want or brings in a consultant to assess the situation. Usually the policymakers survey other companies, particularly those in their industry or regional competitors, to decide which of two or three circumscribed programs to undertake without the undue expense of going too far ahead of the pack or the risk of lagging too far behind. Studies are undertaken, task forces formed, reams of paper passed, policies formulated. Funds are then earmarked from some department's budget—sometimes human resources, sometimes contributions. And management implements whatever modifications will satisfy the immediate pressures.

Occasionally some progress is even made as a result of top-down dicta. From my observation such initiatives often move rapidly but lack the infrastructure required to support the change. I'll give one example.

I met with a senior human resources person at a major automobile manufacturing corporation that had made a concerted effort to increase the number of minorities at the senior management level. When it was reported at a board meeting that there were now sixteen black men in senior management, an influential woman who sat on the board raised the question of the company's progress regarding women, and it was recognized that there were only one or two women in senior management. At this point the CEO, in all good faith, commanded, "A year from now we must have sixteen women at senior levels. And they must be fully qualified." In response management promoted some women internally, identified others to hire, and ended up a year later with sixteen truly solid executives. But a business plan had not been made, an infrastructure was not in place, and the process of filling the pipelines from the bottom up was never begun. There was no second generation of female executives to follow the first.

In the meantime, as ad hoc changes are put in place, corporate leaders are preoccupied with other, more pressing concerns. As our competitive position in the global marketplace has waned, the rampage of mergers, leveraged buy-outs, and hostile takeovers has forced business leaders to focus intensely on the short term. They are so caught up in questions of the moment—What are we going to earn next quarter? Who's going to buy me out? How am I going to overcome the competition?—that "women's issues" don't seem urgent.

And corporate executives certainly would never think of turning to one problem to deal with another problem. As the economy tightens, as competitive pressures increase, there is a peeling away of layers of management. It is critical to employers' survival to choose from a still abundant pool those who are not only the most able, but the most likely to succeed. And their sense is that women, although just as intelligent as men, are not as tough or as committed. They quite naturally, given their experience, do not think of women as the white knights who will save them.

In the meantime, women are not moving up in any real numbers. Some of the best are leaving, either to become entrepreneurs or to raise families or to take jobs with more flexible employers.

What most puzzles the policymakers I speak with is this lack of progress. One year, it seems to them, you get an award for some response you've made. The next they bring a class action suit against you. The next year you push for what seems a great policy improvement, and it's lauded, yet it doesn't seem to make that much difference.

This is often the point when I meet with senior executives. They see their experience with the women they employ as basically frustrating. I hear them say, "Well, I know it's important, and I suppose I have to. . . . But why?" There is still an undertone of skepticism about the importance of women to their enterprise. Not the bafflement of thirty years ago, when women first entered the workplace in large numbers. But now, having lived through a period when the family as they knew it has fallen apart, there is a muffled voice from within that asks, "Who's taking care of our children?"

So although a great deal of progress has been made, it's been made incrementally, from a zero point—taking one small step at a time, without a big picture, without linear movement toward a defined goal, without a strategic plan for achieving that goal. And suddenly we're at a point where, despite the progress made by women in a larger sense, it's really not working within individual companies. Moreover, each step employers take now has a component of failure, in that it stimulates expectations and doesn't solve the basic problems.

Companies that undertake these initiatives are doing things right. But still something is lacking.

Warren Bennis, former president of the University of Cincinnati, made a comment that relates to our predicament here in describing the difference between managers and leaders. Managers do things right, he said. Leaders do the right things.

That is what is happening in corporate America. Business executives are doing things right. They are bringing in or developing a few women for senior management, letting individual women cut back their schedules, permitting working mothers to take maternity leave. But they are not filling the pipelines, not institutionalizing flexible work arrangements, not enabling new mothers to return to the fast track, not encouraging men to share parenting responsibilities with their wives. They are not doing the right things. And why not? Because, like Anderson, they do not yet recognize a business motivation to do so. Even with the best companies, there's not yet fire in the belly.

If we, along with Anderson, conclude that the assimilation of women into the corporate workplace is a challenge, yes, but low priority, not central to the concerns of business, not a *business imperative*—a challenge that can be addressed with careful, gradual responses—we miss the point. It's not a question of doing more, or of doing more things right. Doing more of the same, moving in the same direction, without first analyzing the underlying motivation will lead only to failure. The right things will come from an entirely different frame of mind.

What is called for is a basic rethinking and retooling in the way we deal with women and men and work. Incremental steps won't work. The change must be radical.

Say somebody showed up on your doorstep and said, "I've got an innovation that will make a fortune for you. In order to avail yourself of it, though, you'll have to make a turnaround in the way you run your business." The innovation could be a technical one—mass computerization, say. Or it could be a packaging brainstorm, such as the Coca-Cola bottle. It could be a product, even one as offbeat as the Cabbage Patch doll. Wouldn't you make any change necessary to capture that profit?

In this case the innovation is an unplanned-for, underestimated influx of talent. Here is what you do. First you must see women as a business imperative. Only then can you make the change required. Then you will capture that profit.

I'll come later to the changes you need to make. But first let us see why addressing the issue of integrating women into the mainstream and developing them is, in a very concrete, company-specific sense, a business imperative. To do that we must take a fresh look at where women are in your company and just what their positioning is costing you.

PICTURING THE PYRAMID OF THE PAST

Here I will demonstrate as starkly as I can the business costs associated with women's positioning today in a better-than-average company— in, say, a company like that headed by Anderson, where genuine efforts to develop women are being made in an ad hoc manner. To show these business costs, I will use a simple model: a pyramid that represents the management corps of a better-than-average company.[1]

To make this scenario more meaningful, I ask that for the length of this discussion you put yourself in the shoes of someone like Anderson—that you imagine yourself the chief executive of this better-than-average company.

First I want to give a historical point of reference that will help illuminate the situation for your company now. Let us consider the composition of your management pyramid as it might have appeared thirty years ago, in 1962. The eve of the massive entry of women into the corporate workplace, 1962 was also, not uncoincidentally, the year Catalyst was founded. In that year there were so few women in management, or they were so irrelevant to the leadership of your enterprise, that they do not realistically require depiction in this simple model. Your management group circa 1962 is comprised exclusively of male employees. (See figure 7.1.)

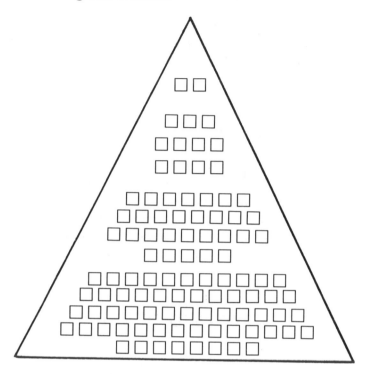

FIGURE 7-1: Your Better-Than-Average Company of Thirty Years Ago

Next I am going to divide your management pyramid into four horizontal slices. (See figure 7.2.) The division here does not refer to grade levels. I have divided the pyramid into fourths in order to convey the concentration of responsibility within the pyramid.

Of course, the naked eye can spot the shrinkage in volumes immediately. What I find even more dramatic is the arithmetic portrayal a math scholar shared with me. In any pyramid, the top quarter contains less than 2 percent of its volume (in this case 1.6 percent), the second quarter almost 11 percent (10.9 percent), the third quarter nearly 30 percent (29.7 percent), and the fourth quarter around 60 percent of the total volume (58 percent). The sum of the third and fourth quarters is 88 percent. These proportions hold for a pyramid of any size. To me they suggest powerfully the sheer difficulty of ascending within a structure formulated along hierarchical lines, which is, of course, the reality for nearly all modern-day corporations.

Let us now inhabit your better-than-average company of 1962 with one hundred managers. We will distribute them throughout the pyramid according to this arithmetic principle of shrinking volumes. (See

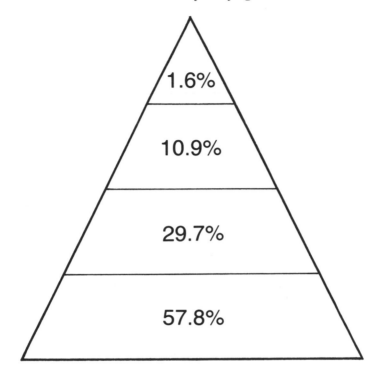

FIGURE 7-2: Concentration of Responsibility Within the Pyramid

figure 7.3.) It's worth remarking how very few men occupy the pyramid's uppermost tier and how large is the number ranged throughout its base.

So far we've seen the overall shape of your management structure—the hierarchical pyramid—and its gender composition—all men. Now let us consider the utilization of talent within the pyramid.

Here are the one hundred men you employ. (See figure 7.4.) Note that each bears a number. I've used consecutive numbering as a rough proxy for something that is nearly impossible to articulate or define. My placement denotes the distribution within the management ranks of those innate qualities that play a vital role in determining an individual's capability and, consequently, in an ideal company, the individual's positioning in the hierarchy.

I have ranked your one hundred managers according to the sum of those traits that are both immutable and distributed at random throughout the population. They might include intelligence, energy, and analytic ability, qualities that cannot be learned but are essential if one is to contribute and advance within any company. The employ-

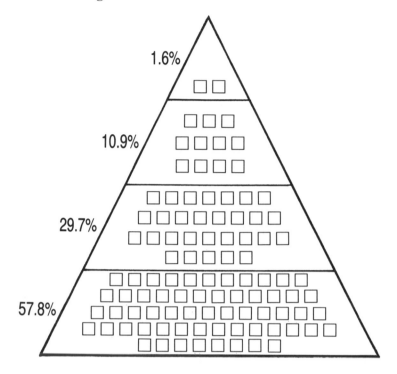

FIGURE 7-3: The One Hundred Male Managers and Where They Are Positioned

ees in your management ranks are thus invested to varying degrees with a combination of those qualities needed to fulfill the requirements of various jobs that drive forward your enterprise. (In the real world, of course, there might be any number of 1's, or 2's, or 35's. I'm trying to keep this model simple.) For this discussion, let's call them the Basics.

To put it another way: You can't make a leader or even a fine manager out of a person who doesn't have a high degree of the Basics. But I strongly believe you can make a leader or a fine manager out of anyone, male or female, who does have the Basics, because everything else is either learned or can be managed through effective policies and practices.

As CEO you recognize immediately that this assessment is incomplete. You know that those traits that can be acquired or taught are critical—from job commitment to confidence to initiative. Here we will call them the Balance. Crucial as they are, for the purposes of discussing your company, I am not including any aspect of the Balance as a variable. We assume that in this better-than-average, all-male

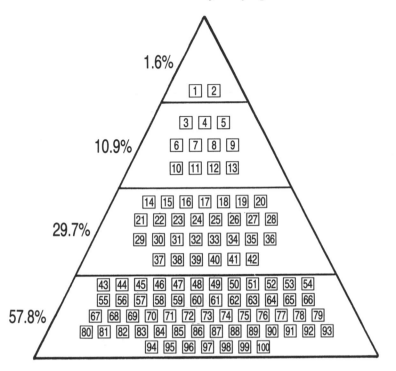

FIGURE 7-4: Distribution of the Basics Throughout a Population of One Hundred Male Managers

organization, every employee is given what he needs to grow and develop in a way that benefits the bottom line.

Because we know that your enterprise is well managed, we can also surmise that you are assiduously heeding one of the cardinal rules of business. That is, you are maintaining the quality of your human resources at every level of your company. To achieve this you have ensured that each of these four tiers is inhabited with those individuals who are most qualified to be there. My premise, in other words, is that you are accurately evaluating the Basics.

As you can see, the numbered employees descend from 1 at the pinnacle to 100 at the bottom of the lowest tier. Those employees with the highest level of the Basics, numbered 1 and 2, occupy the proportionately minuscule top level. The employees at the second level possess less of the Basics than those at the top, but more than those at lower levels. And so on.

One result of this positioning is that each level is inhabited by those people who have that amount of the Basics required to function optimally at their level of responsibility. Another is that those people with less of the Basics report to those with more, all the way up to the top of the pyramid. At its pinnacle sits the leader of the whole enterprise, the individual with the level of the Basics required to run the whole show.

The ultimate outcome: the abilities of the men you employ in management are as well utilized as they could be. Your managers have high morale, high productivity, and high commitment. They are the solid backbone of your profitable enterprise.

CREATING THE PYRAMID OF THE PRESENT

We have seen the composition of your management pyramid as you would have built it in the not-so-distant past. Now suppose that, like Rip Van Winkle, you somehow doze off and thirty years go by. When you awaken it is 1992. You find you still are head of a company that is widely viewed as better than average in its deployment of management resources, including women. . . .

Wait a minute! Women? In your company? In management, no less?

Intrigued, you call in your senior executives, your inner circle. They are the ones who have run your company in your absence. You ask that they brief you on how women came to enter your management ranks. They describe women's entry into your work force. It began gradually, in the mid-1960s, they say, snowballed in the 1970s, and in the 1980s became a fact of your company's life.

Are they any good at my business? you ask. When last you were conscious, women were widely considered not to have a mind for business—they were thought to be "not *quantitative*" and therefore not qualified for jobs in your company. Your policymakers assure you that today women are commonly considered to be as smart as men.

You then ask how many women your management group now encompasses. There are thirty-seven women, approximately one-third of your exempt-level population, they respond with some pride. That proportion mirrors the percentage of women the government stat trackers find employed in the nation's management and professional sector overall.

It's odd, you muse. When I dozed off there looked to be a supply of male talent large enough to supply our staffing needs. True, the economy was in a high-growth phase. Still, we were in the middle of an unprecedented baby boom, and I thought that we would go on forever producing enough men to run our organization.

All that is somewhat different now, you discover. When women first entered corporations, your company did not need any additional personnel. But as the economy soared and your company diversified, and as women educated themselves and took their careers more seriously, they were absorbed into the company's staffing plans.

Not only that, says your senior human resources person, who has done some reading and attended several conferences on the subject of "valuing workplace diversity," demographic projections indicate that the labor pool is gradually shrinking. Women are no longer bearing as many children as they did during the baby boom. The average dropped from almost four children in the late 1950s to not quite two from the mid-1970s through today. That's less than the number required to replace the existing population. We're looking at a new generation of college recruits that is much smaller than we ever expected.

The upshot, says another executive, is that we have thirty-seven women and sixty-three men out of a total of one hundred—that's less men out of the same total as before. But, as we told you, the women are all good. These thirty-seven are absolutely comparable in the Basics to our top thirty-seven men.[2] He adds that you can be confident your company is doing fairly well in making use of the talents of its women managers. There are still some kinks to be ironed out, he says, but basically the company is moving in the right direction.

At this you are pleased. Show me a picture of my management composition today, you say. You are eager to see the new composition of the pyramid you built so carefully thirty years earlier, in which each of the inhabitants occupied a level commensurate with his abilities, so that the whole enterprise ran smoothly, effectively, and profitably. Now, the way you figure it, you have compensated for having half as many men as you expected in your recruitment pool, had the baby boom continued, by drawing equally from the pool of female talent.

Your colleagues bring you a diagram that looks much like this one. (See figure 7.5.)

In this pyramid I have distributed thirty-seven women and sixty-three men as they would likely be positioned in a better-than-average company such as yours today. In the top quarter you see roughly 5 percent women and 95 percent men. This estimate is based on Cata-

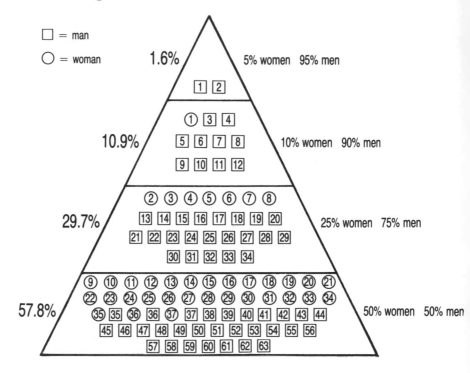

FIGURE 7-5: The Composition of Your Management Pyramid Today

lyst's recently completed study of women in corporate management. In the second quarter you find 10 percent women and 90 percent men. In the third quarter are 25 percent women and 75 percent men. These are my best estimates, based on my own observation and government labor statistics. The lowest quarter, including the entry level, holds approximately half women and half men. This is the well-known ratio in which young managers are now entering your business.

As chief executive of the company whose management is depicted in the pyramid, you knew that you would find fewer women than men. But you notice other features of this new pyramid that surprise you and cause some dismay.

Turning from the diagram to your colleagues, you ask why so many high-ranked employees occupy the lower levels of the pyramid.

We told you there were still kinks to be worked out, they say. Women still face some barriers to their upward mobility. We know that. Our experience is that we cannot count on their commitment. But we're trying to give them what they need. We're doing the best we can for them.

I don't understand, you say. How can the company still be viable if we're being so inefficient in this critical area? When there are all these great people down here, who could be up here? And why are there so many weaker people higher up? Tell me, how are our profits?

Well, times are tough, you are informed. But the senior executives don't see how moving around a few women managers is going to make or break your bottom line.

I don't think you are seeing the big picture, you say. It is obvious that we are not using our best people as effectively as we could be—as we did in the past. In fact, this diagram suggests that what we're doing best is shooting ourselves in the foot.

The senior executives look doubtful.

Listen, you say, to the implications of women's positioning in our company.

1. We're not mobilizing all the best people at the top.

The sine qua non of successful business is a high-quality senior management team. It is, to a significant degree, the quality of those at the top levels on whom the profitability of our company most depends. From what I can see, we could be substantially upgrading the quality at this level.

In our pyramid the number of men has diminished in thirty years from one hundred to sixty-three. The number of women has risen in kind, from zero to thirty-seven. The best of these women, you've told me, match the best men in the Basics. That is, the number 1 woman is just as good as the number 1 man, and the number 37 woman is just as good as the number 37 man. The number 37 woman is better than men numbered 38 through 63. Nonetheless, the top quarter does not contain any women. What this tells me is that we are losing out on an opportunity to stock our leadership cadre with the ablest individuals.

Traditionally, to get the best people at the top, we've drawn from a pretty shallow pool. That is, we've confined our hiring to the top 10 percent of potential management employees. In the past, of course, that has meant drawing our leaders from an exclusively male population, which didn't present a problem since there were enough men in the top 10 percent to satisfy our staffing needs. Today the labor force is expanding at a slower rate than previously, and our leadership needs are growing, both in quantity and, as we move to an information economy, in quality. We need the same number of people at the highest levels, and we need to continue to draw them from the most qualified 10 percent of the population. There are fewer men in the top 10 percent of candidates because there are fewer men in the general population, but, thank goodness, we can maintain the quality of our management by adding women to the pool of those we consider.

Clearly it would be misguided to look only to men to lead our company—we'd be drawing individuals from a much more limited source, one that is predicted in the foreseeable future to decrease as a percentage of the total. We could muster the same quantity of leadership, of course, at least for a while, but it is unlikely we would find the same measure of quality. Inexorably the pool will contain less men and more women, and our need to find qualified personnel for top positions will intensify. To ensure the strongest possible leadership group, we must draw from the entire universe of high-potential individuals, women as well as men.

I see another problem, and that is the number of people at the upper levels of the management pyramid with less of the Basics—innate talent—than it takes to run our enterprise well. This suggests that we have many people who are getting by on the Balance *instead of* the Basics. And they simply do not have the brainpower to do the best possible job at those levels. If we want to build a company that is strong, forward moving, and beautifully managed, people with a high ratio of Balance to Basics are not the ones we need.

2. We're failing to maintain our quality at every level.

We have a bottom-line need to inhabit each level of the management pyramid with the most capable persons. This we are clearly not doing now, as we have highly ranked women at consistently lower levels of the pyramid than men of equivalent innate ability.

Now that there is a significant percentage of women in management, we can enhance the quality of people at each level by introducing the ablest women at each level. Also, now that shortages of able people at each level are imminent, we can avoid the negative impact of the reduction of able males, because there will still be enough women to maintain the quality of our enterprise.

3. We're treating a significant portion of our employees as dead weight.

Our management pyramid would probably reflect women's positioning even more accurately if our female employees were depicted at the sides of the pyramid rather than distributed all the way across. (See figure 7.6.)

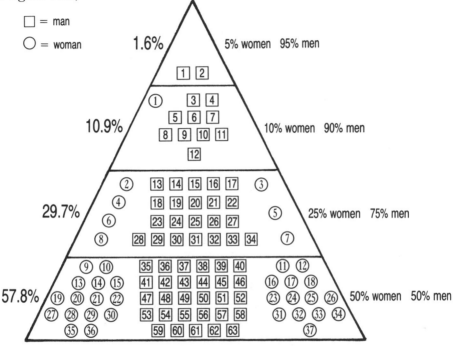

FIGURE 7-6: Women as Adjunct

What I am suggesting is a psychological lag between our decision to employ women and the will to use them. You have accepted the fact that women work in our company. But in your minds women have not yet entered the mainstream of business. Even in a company as forward thinking as ours, management women are ancillary to the corpus of male management. You may not perceive this distinction consciously, and it is seldom acknowledged or discussed. Yet it has enormous significance.

Why is the mainstream still reserved for men? Only because we've inherited the conventions of thirty years ago, when management was an all-male preserve, when the leadership pool was in fact all male, and when those of us who focused only on males could capture the talent of the best and brightest from the entire pool. To some of us, men still represent business, while women represent problems.

The upshot is that we are expending effort to learn how to develop, retain, and advance women only to be sure that women are adequately represented at every level. "Adequate" means enough to quell their restlessness, to avoid their wrath and litigation, to satisfy the corporate conscience, and to develop a few high performers for show.

If nearly half our management is female, and we essentially discount them in this way, we're dragging a heavy anchor. We're investing in the training and experience of people we don't really believe have leadership potential, and we will never amortize that substantial investment.

You may argue that there are legitimate reasons why we cannot treat women, even the best women, as grist for the top. These reasons, you might suggest, have little to do with the Basics and much instead to do with the Balance. In other words, the reason women aren't central is that they lack the acquired traits that serve an equally important function in employees' advancement. And it may well be true that many women have less of the Balance than many of the men in our company, if the Balance is judged to be those qualities that have traditionally been inculcated automatically in men. Long-term commitment, a driving, exclusive focus, and a sense of fit come readily to mind.

I'm not a human resources specialist, and I don't know specifically how you make sure that our women are brought up to speed in whatever areas of the Balance they need to be successful in our company. All I know is that it makes business sense for our company to stop wasting the talent of those we're now treating as dead weight. We have to find a way to identify high-potential individuals regardless of gender and to provide them with whatever support they need to develop. If we want to have the most intelligent, appropriately talented, and committed persons at every level, we must make the same investment in women that we do in men.

4. We're putting a lid on the contribution individual women can make.

We're stifling the talent of women by having them report to men who are less talented. To see what I mean, look again at our pyramid. It is clear that the women within each quarter have a higher Basics rating than the men in that quarter. It stands to reason that many of our female managers report to male supervisors who are less endowed with the Basics than they are.

This situation makes it difficult for women to advance to the level of their capabilities and aspirations. Further, it is entirely possible that many women are unable to fully express their intelligence at the level they are at now. Because the men they report to are not, generally speaking, as talented as they are, too often we have a situation in which the person who has a vision of what can happen is constrained by having to follow a plan made by somebody lacking that vision. So she is working mechanically toward a goal in a job that doesn't give her the ultimate payoff of advancement or even the chance to produce or to grow in the day-to-day. The contribution she can make to our company is defined by the limitations of the men who are at higher levels.

Then consider the bottom-line impact that we suffer when these more talented women at the lower levels are subjected to the indignities of reporting to less talented men, compounded by the effects of men's inadvertent sexist behaviors. These factors affect our business because they undermine the productivity of a significant portion of our best people. The situation does not improve, either, for those stars who move up in the hierarchy. At the upper levels, where there are still very few women, the daily corrosiveness grows more intense. With every step women are further debilitated. And it increases the likelihood of attrition among our highest-potential women.

5. We're discounting high-potential people who want or need to take a role in family care giving.

We are accustomed to thinking of questions of child care and elder care as "women's issues." The result, in our corporation, is that until now family supports have shared the positioning of the women who work here. That is, they have always been off in the fringes, not in the mainstream. As with other initiatives relating to women, they have been instituted incrementally rather than at a pace commensurate with those of bottom-line issues. Women are not assimilated, so child care is not central; women are not a business issue, so flexibility is not a business issue. (See figure 7.7.)

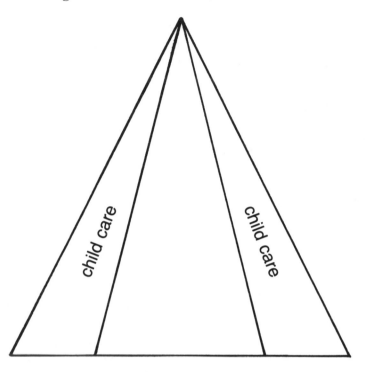

FIGURE 7-7: Family Supports as a Palliative

We now know that failing to mainstream women will result in undue costs for our company. It is also true that allowing family supports to remain on the outskirts of our company policy will have a negative bottom-line impact.

Since women have entered the work force, there is no longer a solid infrastructure, a family support system, at home. According to the Bureau of Labor Statistics, only 16 percent of full-time workers go home to a nonworking spouse.[3] In two-career couples neither parent can expect that the needs of their child will be seen to "automatically" by someone at home. With high-quality, affordable child care still largely unavailable, few working parents are exempt from stress and anxiety about their child care arrangements. And as the population ages, working parents increasingly find themselves responsible for the care of elderly parents or other family members who may be in failing health.

How does this reality affect our business? It's well known that we're beginning to see lowered productivity, for men as well as for women, due to child care and other family concerns while they are at work.

Because high-quality, affordable child care and elder care are not widely available, many people, particularly women, are unwilling or unable to delegate the rearing of their children or their elderly relatives to surrogate care providers. When we don't provide child care and flexibility as a matter of course, we suffer a cost.

We make the mistake of judging employees' potential, especially that of female employees, nearly exclusively on the basis of their commitment to our company, which is seen as the inverse of their commitment to their families. Through relying on this false dichotomy, we force many of the most talented women to leave the company, because given the lack of care-giving options, it isn't possible for them to combine family and career. If we were to make child care and flexibility available, many more would welcome the opportunity to stay in the game. The individuals who leave may well be some of the most responsible employees in the company, because they bring the same standards to their performance in the workplace that they do to the rearing of their children.

6. We're wasting our investment in recruiting and training employees.

We know that college-educated women today are postponing the birth of their first child until they are, on average, thirty-one years old. Say a woman joins our company when she graduates from college. By the time she decides to start a family, we have made a decade-long investment in her training and development.

If she then leaves us, either because the culture prohibits her career growth or because our parental leave provisions or family supports are inadequate, we will fail to amortize our investment in her. It's even more costly if she is leaving to work for a competitor. And the chances are high, given the current demographics, that we will replace her with another female employee. This new recruit will be relatively inexperienced and untrained. We may well find that she doesn't perform on a par with the employee we lost. Unless she has an eight-year prior work experience with another company whose training and development programs are as good as or better than ours, we have lost ground and money. And she, too, realistically, will most likely go on to have a baby, and the whole cycle will begin again.

7. We're failing to create beacons for the best women emerging from college and graduate school.

We know that the population is not growing at the pace it was thirty years ago, and that women constitute an increasing proportion of a gradually shrinking work force. Already women constitute half of our vastly reduced pool of entry-level recruits. We also know that women have been absorbed by a growing economy. The end result is that we can no longer consider women fungible. We depend on women to a greater extent than ever. Our company requires all the talent it can get.

Some companies, while admitting their dependency on women at the lower levels, will still dismiss the need for women leaders. They believe they can continue to locate and buy all the male talent they need for the top. You might argue along with them that until we experience the shortages on a widespread basis that are already visible with respect to nurses, secretaries, and engineers, it makes business sense to do only the minimum that is immediately required. To calculate the probability of uninterrupted, ongoing commitment in each woman we interview for a job or make a decision to promote. To continue to make ad hoc changes.

This is shortsighted. Companies that respond to women as a last resort, bringing in a great woman here and there as a supplement, as a patch job, while trying to entice all the best men, will eventually feel the impact of their reactive approach in the one area where they recognize that women are indispensable: they will lose out in the competition for the best and brightest at the entry level.

Here is why. Companies that do not take pains in the present to develop and retain able women will lack women at higher levels in the future, when talent is scarcer. Women graduating from the best colleges and graduate schools in the country will scout out their employment prospects. They will conclude reasonably that those companies with few women at the higher levels offer less prospects for their advancement. They will accept offers from other companies that are able to demonstrate, by the numbers of women at upper levels, that they value women.

These companies that fail to develop women now for leadership positions will be forced to settle later for second-tier women. Given the demographic realities, half of their management will be comprised of women. With half their management second-tier women, they will no longer be able to compete effectively with those in their industry who are able to recruit first-tier women.

8. We could be capitalizing on a tremendous opportunity.

What this all translates to, if we are willing to make some major changes, is a tremendous business opportunity. Given the chance men have to move in their careers without encountering unproductive behaviors and needless barriers, and given flexibility without penalty and real family support systems, women could be leading our company to new profitability. This potential can unfold in numerous ways.

We will vastly expand the pool from which we draw our top leaders. We will see greater talent, creativity, and experience at every level of our enterprise. Enhanced productivity will follow, for all those who are now constrained by artificial barriers. Further, in demonstrating *our* commitment to women's development, we will earn *their* commitment to our organization, at a time when company loyalty is famously scarce. By providing flexibility, we will retain greater numbers of women through their childbearing years—a time of life that often coincides with the onset of professional maturity and the greatest potential contribution a manager can make.

There will be other benefits, too. Once we build a solid cadre of women at the senior levels, they will serve as role models and mentors for the junior women rising through the lower ranks. This relationship will bolster the developing managers' knowledge of our business and will speed their career growth and expand their contribution.

The change in our approach will naturally appeal to the instincts of our stockholders (more than half of whom are women), to whom we are responsible, and our customers, whose support makes or breaks us. Many of them believe women are unfairly inhibited in the workplace now. We will also boost our public image. And that, frankly, is not as secondary as we make it out to be.

When it is communicated that ours is a climate that values women as a central resource rather than one that defeats them, it will surely make us more competitive in terms of recruiting good people (men and women both) at every level, both in our region and in our industry. Then, as other companies follow our lead and remove the obstacles to women's productivity and advancement, it will help to strengthen our nation's global advantage.

PROFESSIONAL FIRMS AS A VANGUARD OF CHANGE

In the real world of today, few chief executives perceive clearly either the costs of responding to women incrementally or the opportunities that would result from a radical change of direction. There is another part of the business community, however, where the need to treat women as a business imperative is much more pressing. That is the professional sector. For a number of reasons, the experience of law and accounting firms can be understood as a sort of early warning system for corporations. The trouble the professions will face if they don't respond to women is much more imminent. At the same time, interestingly, the mechanisms are in place to create a response.

Let me be clear about this. It's not that the professional firms today are uniformly prescient in responding to women as a resource. A few have a nascent awareness; the vast majority have not. But whatever their response thus far, their experience can demonstrate to the corporate community the negative impact of impeding women and the payoff of removing the barriers and providing flexibility for those who need it.

I began in the early 1980s to think of professional firms as a vanguard of change for corporations. Over the years Catalyst had focused for the most part on the corporate sector. But it had become obvious that we would do well to turn our attention to the professions—specifically, at the start, to the field of accounting. Enrollment in accounting programs was rising steadily and dramatically, with projections that women would soon represent at least half of all accounting students.

With that demographic prompt, I scheduled visits with a number of the then "Big 8" accounting firms to discuss their experience with women. One of the things that excited me initially was when Dwayne Kulberg, then CEO at Arthur Andersen, shared his recognition that more than half of the top 10 percent of the graduating classes in accounting were female. He clearly had some inkling that the women emerging from accounting programs could bring quality as well as quantity to his firm.

Catalyst then conducted a study within one Big 8 firm to look at its experience with women. The results suggested some of the obstacles for women in this time-intensive, highly competitive field. When we analyzed their data and the transcripts of our focus groups, we found an almost universal belief that career advancement for women could come only at the expense of family life. The firm had a total absence of flexibility.

Our most important finding was startling: A larger percentage of high-performing women were leaving the firm than of lower or moderate performers. The opposite was true for men. A larger percentage of high-performing men were staying with the firm, relative to men who performed less well. Our conjecture about why the women were leaving was based on our findings about the firm's environment. Our sense was that this firm, perhaps typical of all the major firms, was beaming out to women a sense that they were accepted, that opportunity was there for them—provided that they played by men's rules. The firm required so absolute, so rigorous, a time commitment that women who wanted to start families and a more balanced life were jumping ship in favor of more flexible corporate jobs.

It was a dismaying experience for women and clearly a threatening one for the firm. If they could not retain their ablest women professionals, either their partnership team would be solidly male or it would be comprised of excellent men and mediocre women.

We made our recommendations to the firm in three categories. The first was quick fixes—targeted communication and reinforcement of existing policies. The second included initiatives that would take some planning: programs for child care, further data collection and analysis, and eliminating company memberships in male clubs, for example. The third we termed our "radical" recommendation. It was to establish an alternative career path for anyone who wanted to cut back to a part-time, shared job for whatever period he or she chose and to allow these people, when they returned, to reenter the competition for partner.

Though the firm's response was positive—I was even invited to describe our findings at a conference of its senior human resources people—in the final analysis it was not motivated to move ahead significantly. Nonetheless, that initial immersion in a professional firm reinforced my sense that the corporate community could learn a great deal from, and could be motivated by, the experience of the professional community. Over the intervening years, in order to expand our knowledge base, Catalyst kept in touch with the five accounting firms we had met with initially.

Subsequently I also began to investigate law firms on the supposition that they, too, could be a fulcrum of change for corporations.

Christine Beshar, a partner at Cravath, Swaine & Moore, arranged a luncheon for me to meet with the twenty or twenty-five female partners at some of the large, prestigious law firms in New York City.

I came away from that meeting with the conviction that the first big changes in organizations' response to women would take place in the professions. Why? First of all because virtually half the graduates of law and accounting programs are female, and they are well represented at the top of their classes. So women constitute close to half of all new entrants to professional firms. They have set their course and invested the time and money necessary to become highly trained specialists.

Second, the time line to partnership is much shorter than that required to move from entry level to senior management in a corporation: seven to ten years in law, eight to twelve in accounting, and thirty years in a corporation. As a result, the huge generation of women who entered business and the professions in the late 1970s are waiting in the wings, ready to move to partner. Perhaps most important, the bugaboo about how to evaluate the performance of those on flexible schedules is obviated because the pay structure of professional firms is based on productivity rather than on time in the office. Billable hours and new business can be quantified objectively and without gender bias. In addition, law firms have institutionalized numerous new technologies, from advanced computer systems to facsimile machines, which make it possible to work from home. Finally, teamwork is already a convention in law and accounting. These fields have a tradition of dividing and stratifying assignments.

The professional firms are in great danger when they risk losing women who have worked there for five or so years. By that time many, many women have gone through the rites of passage, proved their worth, and are positioned to move directly to the highest levels of the firm. Additionally, the need to respond to women is made more urgent by virtue of the fact that professional firms on average drive their employees harder than do corporations. This places a woman considering starting a family in a much more difficult position and increases the likelihood that she will leave the firm.

As urgent and as tractable as the response to women is in the professions, even there the action is slow in coming. Still, isolated policies and practices are well worth a closer look.

I visited with several partners at one law firm that would probably rank a 2 on the spectrum of 0 to 5. The firm is proud of its record—

it had instituted a child care resource and referral service, and a parental leave policy that permitted women *or* men to take up to six months away from the job after the birth of a child. The partners told me that they had allowed one senior woman, not yet a partner, to work a four-day week and another woman to cut her schedule back to a two-day week. They expected kudos.

My response? This approach to part-time schedules would probably be counterproductive in the long run. The firm had initiated something that made them feel as if they were being responsive to women. But they had no plan for utilizing women. They had no evaluation points. They had just "permitted" these two individuals, as an accommodation, to cut their hours. It seemed obvious to me that the firm's revisions would come to nothing, because they had been formulated without a direction in mind. Better not to do anything, I thought, than to build expectations and put in place something utterly inadequate that can have no lasting results.

In a different approach, a second law firm launched a policy that allowed women with children to cut back to half-time for up to three years, after which they could return to the partner track with compensatory time to make it to partner. This strategy, it seems to me, is moving in the appropriate direction. Surely it's no "mommy track."

Another positive initiative, I think, is the creation of a new "mezzanine" level, such as "of counsel" or "permanent associate" in law and accounting, where the tradition for so long has been up or out. I see this as an acknowledgment on the part of the firm that it has some professionals who may well have the talent to make partner but are nonetheless willing to trade off the responsibility that position entails for a permanent lower, but respectable, less pressured niche. These individuals (still more women than men) can nonetheless make a substantial contribution to the firm.

If we can get the pejorative aspect out of this, it will be a step forward. Some women today tend to see the mezzanine level as a velvet ghetto. But I see it differently. For many professionals it's just the opportunity they want. To make it work we must change the attitude about it—we have to make it a respectable goal for men and women who are committed both to their careers and their families rather than a second-class option for women. And we should not lose sight of the fact that the women and men who are willing at some point to make the necessary commitment can move without interruption back to the partner track.

This past year Catalyst presented Arthur Andersen, of the (now) Big 5 accounting firms, with an award for a policy it recently formulated. The policy, like that of the law firm I just mentioned, allows any individual who so chooses to cut back to half-time for up to three years and return with compensatory time to reenter the competition for partnership. An important step forward in this policy is the definition of half-time not as half the number of hours, but as half the client load—a measure of productivity rather than simply of time.

Through communicating its policy to entry-level job candidates, this firm will put out two powerful messages. Think about a young woman graduating from an accounting program, starting to consider whether to pursue employment at an accounting firm or a corporation. The accounting firm beckons—despite the fact that the hours are so grueling—because of the training she will get and the opportunities it will provide. She knows she'll have to give her all, but she's young, so it doesn't faze her. In the long run, though, working at the firm will preclude the possibility of family, which she also wants. So she will go to the firm for three years and move on to a more flexible environment, the corporation.

Now imagine she hears about the new policy. Here is the message it gives her: "One, if you are thinking about a public accounting firm, even for a couple of years, ours is the one to choose, because we're thinking about women. Two, you'll want to think of us as a long-term employer because we'll make it possible for you to combine career and family without forfeiting the opportunity to make partner." Although I know that attrition serves the purpose of moving grateful trainees out to corporations that are potential clients, if the woman is an outstanding performer, the firm will want to retain her nonetheless.

The reason I am focusing so much on professional firms, as I have said, is that the writing for them is so clearly on the wall. These firms are small relative to large corporations. To the extent that women still have the primary responsibility for home and children, the time intensity of the demands in professional firms challenge women disproportionately. Additionally, there are only three or four levels, and the single category of partner defines the pinnacle of achievement. But most important, unlike the corporation, where women are still largely at middle levels (because they have not been there for the thirty years required to move up to senior management), the professions already have many women in the wings, poised on the threshold of partnership.

Right now, whether they recognize it or not, professional firms are determining how women will perceive them in the future. Their actions—or inaction—will determine the quality of the women they will attract, their retention rates, and their ability to move significant numbers of qualified women to partnership. So it's worth looking at the different approaches they're taking.

As I see it, law and accounting firms can be categorized in terms of four possible overall approaches.

1. Fast-track firms. These adrenaline-driven firms expect total commitment from all employees and have virtually no policies that are responsive to women or men who have families.
2. Firms that want only driven partners but have formulated policies and promulgated the message that they will respond to the needs of women (removing barriers, providing flexibility) so that they can recruit the most talented female graduates. However, in these firms barriers to women's productivity are left in place, and women who cut back are put on a "mommy track."
3. Firms that have a slower pace and an acceptance, overall, of flexibility. Their policies enable both men and women to partake of other aspects of life: child rearing, caring of ill relatives, public service, and so on.
4. Fast-track firms that are genuinely motivated to capture the talent of women. They identify the barriers that exist for women and take steps to remove them. They also permit women to return after the birth of a child whenever they are ready and, if they choose, on part-time schedules, providing compensatory time to compete for partnership. Essentially these firms accept parenting as part of the lives of the people who work there.

The destiny of the firms I've labeled two and three is fairly obvious. The hypocrisy of number two firms will be exposed by the continued existence of barriers to women's progress. Number three firms will continue to attract and retain women and men who want a slower pace (and are satisfied with lesser rewards) so that they can lead more balanced lives.

I want to analyze here the impact that the culture of the other two categories—let's call them the fast-track firms and the fast-track flexible firms—will have on the recruitment and retention of women, as well as on their movement to the partnership level. Because recruitment, retention, and movement to partner are interconnected, action taken in relation to any one of the three affects all three. (See figure

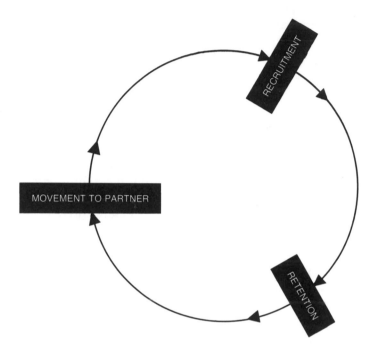

FIGURE 7-8: Interlocking Effects of Recruitment, Retention, and Movement to Partner

7.8.) I'll describe specifically the consequences that these firms will suffer or enjoy.

First, the fast-track firms. In terms of recruitment, the fast-track culture and the resultant paucity of women partners who can serve as beacons to potential recruits will reduce the quantity and quality of applicants. Retention will be a growing problem, certainly for women who have children and want to participate actively in their lives. As we know, women seldom have husbands who take primary responsibility for child care, whereas men more frequently have wives who take primary responsibility for their children, whether or not they hold paying jobs. Increasingly it will prove difficult to retain men as well. In the vanguard of men rejecting the fast-track culture will be those whose first marriages failed and who want their second marriages to succeed. The absence of a mezzanine level will also lower the retention rate of these firms.

What about women's movement to partner? If the rewards of money and prestige are huge, there will probably always be enough driven people who are prepared to make the necessary trade-offs, but considerably fewer women than men will make them. Therefore only a small percentage of women will be partners at the fast-track firms. The ratio of female partners to entering women professionals will be much lower than the ratio of male partners to entering male professionals. The women who do become partners will frequently be unmarried and even more often remain childless.

Long-term consequences for fast-track firms will be harsh. The few women to make partner will be beacons mainly for single-mindedly driven women. As a result, the percentage of female partners will remain small. These firms will fail to attract the talented women graduates who want to be involved in their children's lives. The women who feel compelled to give up family in order to make partner will, additionally, be lonely and isolated at work, because they will have so few women peers and because they will tend to be excluded from the inner circle of their male peers. Finally, the fast-track firms will, on the one hand, come to be known for their callous disregard for family and, on the other hand, be subject to EEO suits and penalties and to class action suits by women who play by men's rules but nonetheless fail to make partner. There is as yet no legal redress for women who are clearly acknowledged to be stars but fail to make partner because they worked part-time (with prorated pay) for a period. But I am confident that women litigators will put their minds and training to this barrier and work their way through it. All of this will be costly both financially and in terms of public image.

Contrast these consequences with those that will attend the actions taken by the firms that want to capture the talent of women—the fast-track flexible firms.

The responsive policies of the fast-track flexible firms will, in themselves, lure women. The significant number of women partners will assure potential recruits that there is a future for them. The retention of women will be radically enhanced.

Combining career and family won't present a problem for women at the fast-track flexible firms. Some women will return from maternity leaves within two or three months, on full-time schedules. Most, I believe, will return on part-time schedules after three months and gradually expand their commitment. A small minority will take longer, full-time leaves.

Finally, the path to partnership will be as clear for women as it is for men, and the number of female partners will greatly increase. And these firms will not be entangled in litigation.

Fast-track flexible firms will see positive results. They will be comfortable places, where the productivity of women will not be impeded. Each partner may take an individually designed route and time line toward the goal of partner. These firms will project a positive image to women clients and to the general public.

The flexible firms will be recognizable for having initiated policies that permit new mothers (and fathers) to cut back to half-time and return with compensatory time to compete for partnership. Those firms that are at the cutting edge of change will do what is now unthinkable: they will employ part-time partners. This policy, which is not yet discussed seriously, let alone practiced, is perhaps the most cost-effective step firms can take. Why? Because the current prevailing cultures require women to work frenetically from the average age of twenty-five to thirty-three to make partner. If a woman waits until then to have children, it is costly to the firm for her to slow down. When the firm has a part-time policy throughout, the woman can work half-time whenever she has a child with prorated compensation—whether before, or after, or before and after she makes partner.

Let me interject here the situation of universities, which parallels that of professional firms. I will take an example from the sciences, both because the need for gifted research scientists is critical and because laboratory work is so time-intensive. And I will describe the situation of a young woman I know well. Call her Elizabeth.

As an undergraduate, Elizabeth majored in literature and minored in music. Her interest in science was ignited by a course requirement in her senior year at college. When she graduated she took a job in a research laboratory and, at the end of a year, knew beyond a doubt that she wanted to obtain a graduate degree and pursue her nascent interest in molecular biology.

Elizabeth was twenty-three when she matriculated again at a prestigious university and twenty-nine when she was awarded her doctorate. She was elected to the Society of Fellows, a singular recognition of her talent and achievement that provided a three-year fellowship. During the third year she became pregnant, and her son was born when she was thirty-three, a few months before she was due to put together her own laboratory as an assistant professor at her university's medical school.

Prior to the birth, Elizabeth was focused intensely on her work, putting in long hours and not infrequently going to her lab in the middle of the night to add a reagent or make a delicately timed adjustment. Her productivity over the next seven years would determine whether or not she would be tenured.

Now, both she and her husband are deeply involved in their son's life. Elizabeth spends time with him in the early morning and returns home by seven P.M. Weekends are family-centered.

As brilliant and productive as this young scientist is, she is—quite consciously—putting her achievement of tenure at risk. The department is in its own right as driven an atmosphere as might be found in a law or financial firm. There are differences: the climate in the typical research lab is not particularly clock-focused; instead productivity is everything. Also, although the competition is fantastic, it's not for the next raise or even enormous wealth in the long run, but instead for recognized achievement. This young scientist does not need or want a part-time position—she could not plan her work, run her lab, and meet her responsibilities to her department and her school on a part-time basis. And her university would not allow that. Instead she wants the legitimization of a "normal" full-time schedule and compensatory time to make tenure. During the "normal" interval, she would be willing to accept a salary that would be prorated accordingly.

Stanford, Dartmouth, the University of Rochester, and a few other institutions have adopted a policy that permits those on the tenure track to cut back to half-time and to have compensatory time to qualify for tenure when they return full-time. The critical question is whether other institutions will remain as unyielding as Elizabeth's or adopt responsive policies that will enable gifted scientists to achieve tenure and to participate actively in their children's lives. Will most institutions continue to open the line to tenure only to those who are childless or are willing to have their children raised by surrogates?

As I've said, the positive steps that professional firms and some universities are taking are not magically going to be translated to corporations. There are too many differences between the two sectors. But professional firms can provide evidence of quantifiable outcomes from alternative responses. What can happen is that as law and accounting proceed, and the business community sees their example, employers can draw strength and confidence from their observation that those firms that take real steps forward are the ones that are most productive, and attract and retain the best women, and that those that do not are not getting the most talented. This will motivate corporations to originate their own approaches to meet this challenge.

THE NEXT STEP . . .

Having spent so much time out in the field talking with corporate leaders, I can't say I hold many illusions about the likelihood of companies suddenly and totally buying into the business motivation to develop women. For some time we are more likely to see greater numbers moving forward gradually, as they are now, out of a desire to do what is fair and right, to respond to women's needs, to bow to advocates' demands, and to avoid litigation. As I've said, I do understand that. Real change takes time.

But this incremental response should not be confused with a vision of women as a business imperative, which is the only motivation that can bring significant and enduring change. Business leaders should not try to convince their managers that women are central from a business standpoint or lead them to believe that they are ready to act decisively to remove the barriers to women's development and productivity, when their motivation is less than urgent. That course can only destroy trust.

You will know when you are beginning to develop a business motivation to bring women into the mainstream. You will start to ask, Can we really afford to continue to think of women as outsiders whom we're admitting to the workplace, to whom we are making expensive concessions, while we feel they really should be back at home?

Then you must return to square one. First, you must look with unobstructed vision at the world as it is now. Take a snapshot of today that isn't clouded by the failures of the past. You'll see that virtually half your work force is female. The supply of labor is shrinking. In terms of innate talent, the Basics, women are just as qualified as men, so they are candidates for the top. There are problems still, but they are not a function of immutable conditions.

You will begin to think how you would deal with women if their entry was an innovation that could bring your company untold profit. Instead of having a few of the best women here and there, you stand to draw from a pool twice the strength in stocking your leadership group—twice the brainpower, twice the creativity, twice the energy. With that as a reward, you would certainly do everything you could to have the best women and men at every level.

To achieve that goal, though, you've got to make a business decision. No matter what it takes—removing the corrosive barriers, providing flexibility and family supports—it will be worth the effort you expend.

Now for the good news. Once the motivation is in place, three things are true. First, the change required won't absorb endless amounts of your personal attention. There is even a functional expertise, human resources, already in place to address issues related to your work force. All the chief executive must do, besides providing the inspiration, is set out goals and objectives, insist on a time line, and evaluate the progress made by qualified staff members.

Making the change won't take endless amounts of money, either. And it won't take much time. You will no longer have the burden of weighing each stage, of asking, "Should we go a little farther down this road or should we not?" You will be ready to pull out all the stops, so the progress you make will be relatively rapid. You won't see the biggest rewards immediately, but you will see a return from the start.

This book as a whole is for those people who are concerned about issues of women and work. The next two chapters are for those who have gone back to square one and made the reassessment I'm talking about. They know that the challenge is not to do three out of five things, but to approach the entire issue as a high priority. And those who are ready to move ahead with no equivocation, no maybes, no measuring and titrating, with no conditions and no holds barred, are ready to reap the harvest of every talented woman as well as every talented man.

CHAPTER EIGHT

Leveling the Playing Field

*T*he compelling need of American business to create profit can be served by assimilating women in every aspect and function.

If only it were that simple.

If you were a CEO and I were sitting across the desk in your office, I think you might be willing to say that a convincing case was made in the last chapter. You would have begun to see that you are underutilizing the talent of women, and you'd probably want to go ahead and do something about it.

At the same time, you'd probably be skeptical. You might well say to yourself, So far, you've defined women's value as a business resource only in terms of the Basics. That's fine as far as it goes, but don't kid yourself for a minute—sheer talent is only one small part of the equation. There's a lot more to making a real contribution to my business than the Basics. There's commitment and moxie and political know-how and aggressiveness. And I'm not at all sure that women have the rest of what it takes.

If women were just like men, you might be thinking, it would make perfect sense to bring them into the mainstream of my company. It would be easy to integrate them fully into management. I'd take immediate action to expand our leadership pool by including every talented woman along with every talented man.

But women are not just like men. I know I'm not supposed to say so, but women in my company keep showing all these negative tendencies and attributes: they're not tough and determined. For most of them, a career doesn't come first; one day they're dedicated and the next they have babies and leave. Most of them are not aggressive enough, and the others are too aggressive. All in all, they disrupt the comfortable ambience I'm accustomed to.

Your doubts would be understandable. Although there are enormous differences among women, perhaps even more than there are between men and women, the fact remains that women as a group *are* different from men as a group. But the problem of how to go about bringing women into the mainstream of your business cannot be solved by forcing women to become more "like men." I don't believe most people would really want that to happen, even if it were possible. On the other hand, I think it's clear that you would miss a tremendous business opportunity if you were to take the "differences" cited above at face value and use them as justification to leave buried the talent of women.

There is a way to avail yourself of the huge potential profit that women can bring your company, but to do it you have to meet a challenge far more subtle than forcing women into a male mode or ignoring them. If you are to pull women into the mainstream of your business, you have to accept, respect, and respond to the differences between women and men in the workplace.

This chapter is about leveling the playing field in order to ensure that you won't continue to bury the talent of women. In this chapter we'll talk about the differences between women and men in a corporate setting. Here we are going to explore how to build on the positive and either eliminate or deal with the negative. We will see that the differences don't have to be a deterrent to utilizing women as a business resource. And it hasn't even occurred to most of us that women are different in ways that could enhance the workplace—that there are things men could learn from women, especially as we move from a manufacturing to an information economy.

To start to address the differences, I'm going to outline four broad areas of action you can take to ensure that the women you employ function as effectively as men. The first is acknowledging the fundamental difference between women and men, the biological fact of maternity. The second is providing flexibility to those women who need or want it. Third is bringing women up to speed by providing them with the Balance—my term for any learned or acquired trait or skill that managers already well endowed with the Basics need to excel. Fourth is improving the corporate environment by removing the barriers that exist for women that do not exist for men.

In the course of the discussion, I'll put forward examples of what other companies have done, taken from studies conducted at Catalyst and by other researchers. These initiatives are useful as illustrations that proactive responses on these issues can be affordable and feasible. But I feel two caveats are necessary.

First, don't assume that any one of these policies or practices is directly replicable in your company. What works in a large manufacturing enterprise may fail in a small high-tech firm. There are countless variables. Second, it's important to avoid the temptation to adopt any initiatives at random, in an ad hoc fashion. What I recommend here is that you use these examples to trigger your awareness of what is possible in the context of a comprehensive, unified strategic plan—a program that can move at once to address all the interrelated issues that might be holding women back within *your* company.

If you were a CEO and we were having this discussion in your office, I would want you to challenge me. I'd want you to raise all the "taboo" questions that are on your mind.

I'd like to try to approximate that experience in this chapter. I'm going to set out every question I can think of that, left unanswered, would inhibit your forward movement. I'll include questions I encounter in meetings with corporate leaders, for which I have had to find answers in order to do my job. Some of them may sound naive or even a bit outrageous, but they are true to those I've frequently heard or that have been implied in discussions I've been privy to.

These are the very questions that are customarily muted by the conspiracy of silence. Here, however, we can lay them all out on the table. As an anonymous reader you need not fear litigation, loss of customers, or the wrath of women.

In these pages I'm going to try my best to prove one point with every logical analysis, example, anecdote, and study finding I can muster: *All the differences that now hold women back in the corporate workplace are remediable*—and at a cost that is infinitesimal compared with the devastating cost of continuing to bury the talent of women.

I won't enter into the mechanics of implementation. This is not a how-to book. Numerous resources are available that can help companies develop policies and programs on a level of detail beyond the present scope of this book. But that doesn't mean my suggestions are "pie in the sky" or something you cannot start in upon today.

If employers can see that what I'm talking about is eminently doable, I will have achieved my goal in this chapter. I want to reach what I think of as a switch in the mind of the policy planner, the one that turns on or off his doubts, because I know that if I can assuage those doubts, he can pull any lever it will take to formulate a plan and put it in practice. By the same token I hope the discussion in this chapter will provide working women and men with the answers they need in order to open a constructive dialogue with their employers.

And I want to give the clearest sense I can of what I believe are the right things to do. Because as it is now, we're getting nowhere, doing the wrong things right.

UNDERSTANDING THE DIFFERENCES

When I say "Women in business are different from men," I'm really talking about a complex interplay of biology, socialization, tradition, and perception.

One stems from simple biology: women have babies, men do not.

Other differences result from women's and men's contrasting traditional roles and upbringing.

Other differences derive from the gap for many women between the Basics and the Balance. One important reason we haven't brought women into the mainstream is that we haven't wanted to admit, understand, or address the behavioral and training needs of women as a result of their recent entry into an environment created and populated by men.

Another set of differences also results from the fact that women are newcomers to the traditionally male world of business but has nothing whatsoever to do with anything that women lack. From the start men *didn't* want or need women in the workplace and *did* want and need them in the home, so they weren't motivated to clear the path for women.

If you want to capture and use the talent of women, it's your job to make sure to coach and help women. You also have to coach and help men, particularly senior managers, to ensure that they don't treat the women in your company the same way they do their wives and daughters. You have to establish certain policies that open alternative doors for women. And you have to deal with the barriers that are there for women and not for men.

Moving in the four directions you'll read about will enable you to make the changes that will allow any woman, at any point in her career, to function as effectively as any man of equal talent.

But first let's think through some basic questions that concern the differences between women and men.

QUESTIONS OF DIFFERENCE

My most basic question is, How in the world can women do it all? I mean, how can they have a couple of kids, and get up at night with them, and worry about their schooling, and get dinner—and still put in a good day's work for me?

The answer is simple: They can't. Men can't, either, but the difference is that they have rarely had to. That's why men wanted their wives to stay home, rear the children, maintain the home, and support their careers. For some time women had the illusion they could "do it all" and "have it all" because they had the illusion that men "had it all." Now that illusion has been cast aside, and women know they have to order priorities and make trade-offs, just as men have always done. If they want high-achieving careers, that probably means they're going to have less time with their children. Conversely, if they want to participate actively, day by day, in their children's lives, they'll probably have to put a ceiling on their career aspirations, at least for a finite period.

Women are not going to go home again, though. So either you're going to force those of them who want to have children to play by men's rules and fail, give up the dream of having children, or turn their children over to surrogate care—or you're going to watch them leave your employ in order to start businesses of their own that will give them career satisfaction and more flexibility, or go to more responsive employers. The alternative is to do everything you can to support the priorities they choose. That includes all the responses you'll read about here.

What drives a woman? What makes her want to enter the jungle of this competitive world when she could be revered and appreciated as the centerpiece of family life?

First of all, you should be aware that the assumption implicit in your question may no longer be valid for vast numbers of women, who either don't have or don't want the option of being "revered and appreciated as the centerpiece of family life." But beyond that, there is no answer to the question as you're asking it, because there's nothing that drives women in general. Women are not a homogeneous group.

Most women, just like most men, want to have one foot in the world of work and one in the world of family. For them, an exclusive career focus would prove too isolating, and an exclusive family focus would deprive them of autonomy, the rewards of mastery, the breadth of life experience they want. Most women, just like most men, need to support themselves and help to support their families. Many women provide the sole support for their children, sometimes for their elderly relatives as well. Some women are just as career-focused, just as driven, as the most driven men in your company. They want power. They want the joy of competing for and winning the top job. They get turned on by the intellectual challenge of tough financial problems or engineering problems.

Why isn't a woman's drive as enduring as a man's?

The drive of some women *is* as enduring as that of many men. The drive of others is not, for several reasons. First, women's drive tends to be undermined by the unsupportive environment of the corporation. Women tend to leave one corporation for another if they see they're not getting anywhere. Perhaps this is interpreted as "lack of drive."

Second, central to a woman's traditional role in our society is the care of her children. It was she who had an intimate physical connection with her child throughout her pregnancy. When the corrosive effects of the workplace converge with her love for her newborn, she's apt to recognize that childhood is finite and decide that her place is there—whether that means dropping out of the work force for a time or finding a position elsewhere, at another company or through self-employment, that will reward her hard work and allow her to spend time with her baby. Her decision is often cemented by the difficulty of finding quality child care at a price she can afford.

How can I find out what she plans to do?

Even *she* doesn't necessarily know, until she has a baby and experiences her response to this event. But you can be privy to her plans and her unfolding awareness—if you have demonstrated your acceptance of whatever she wants to do. Then talking about the possibilities could be natural, rather than adversarial and possibly litigious.

An employer who has put in motion initiatives that respond to women's needs has already begun to demonstrate tangibly his awareness that there are differences among women. If you ask about women's career and family plans when you don't have policies in place or a responsive attitude, it's a form of bad faith, because you can only be asking the question in order to exclude women who don't display total commitment. But if you ask because you know that you want to hold on to women and that you can do that with policies that already exist—that's a different story.

When you talk about the business advantage of responding to the needs of women, you seem to be suggesting that the only reason business would turn to women is if there weren't enough able men—a move, so to speak, born of desperation. You're ignoring—or downplaying—the motivation of corporate leaders to do what is fair and right. Don't you recognize that what you're saying is insulting to the men in senior management position who make these kinds of decisions? That it's demeaning to women to be discussed as a "desperation" alternative rather than as valued individuals?

It is only in the last five years that there has been a business motivation to respond to the needs of women. Prior to that time women were perceived as superfluous to the needs of employers. Nonetheless, women made very significant gains between 1962 and 1987 as a result of several factors: the motivation of women to prepare for and pursue careers, their need and desire to work, the enactment of legislation, corporate social responsibility, and the personal motivation of many business leaders to do what is fair and right.

But a great deal of progress has yet to be made. Additional legislation is required and, I think, will be enacted to ensure the basic needs of women for pregnancy disability insurance, for parental leave (for women and men), and for the removal of discriminatory policies and practices. But I do not think that the other factors, including the personal motivation of executives, will carry us much further than we have come over the past twenty-five years.

I don't see that analysis as insulting to men in senior management positions. After all, the primary purpose of business is to be profitable. However, the fact that business will assimilate women at every level only as a last resort *is* demeaning to women, in that it can suggest that they are viewed as second class. I'm well aware of that.

MANAGING MATERNITY

Women are always going to have babies. The reason it is so huge an issue in business, though, is more in our heads than anyplace else. In other words, just because this is one immutable difference does not mean that maternity must be an insurmountable obstacle. You can learn to manage maternity so that it costs you infinitely less than it does now in terms of productivity and attrition.

A large percent of employers now provide new mothers with a period of disability. But having a baby is more than "disability." It is a continuum that begins even before pregnancy, goes through childbirth and the disability period, and continues into the process of parenting that includes finding quality, affordable child care.

To manage maternity effectively, it's important to separate the continuum into its different stages. One part is a mind-set about fertility. In our era professional women often start families relatively late in life and therefore suffer some anxiety because the period of fertility is biologically limited. Beyond the question of whether to have children is *when* to have them. "How long can I delay in order to establish my career without incurring the risk of infertility?" Of course, fertility is not always controllable; a number of women in Catalyst's studies of maternity in different companies became pregnant without intending to.

Then comes pregnancy itself. There's no denying the emotional and physical impact of pregnancy. On the flip side, most women find pregnancy an experience of happy anticipation and heightened energy. Within the past few decades the average working woman has changed her pattern from one of leaving work at the end of the first trimester to working right up to the month, if not the week or day, of delivery.

What most discourages pregnant women are the attitudes of other people in the workplace. The supervisors and colleagues of mothers-to-be tend to see their condition as a minus rather than the plus it is (for parents the centerpiece of their lives, for the employer his future work force). At best, today, a woman's pregnant condition is ignored.

The majority of your female employees will become pregnant at some point. Practical necessity demands that you allow them to engage freely in this natural process.

Why do so many women leave my company when they have babies?

For many women, the decision not to return to their preleave job stems from the quality of their prior experience at the company as much as from a desire to give their child the best possible experience in infancy. They say to themselves, "It's been unbearable, and my baby is a baby only once." When they leave to have their babies, they may feel certain that they will return, but on a deeper level they may entertain doubts. Most companies don't pay benefits during the leave unless a woman definitely plans to return to work. So unless she has a source of medical benefits apart from those her company provides, she's forced to say she will. Then, if she doesn't return, her employer feels betrayed, and that fans the flames of resentment, distrust, and despair.

Also, women often use their pregnancy experience with the company as an indicator of the company's sensitivity to working parents. If a woman's experience during pregnancy is difficult, she surmises rightly that it will be tough to balance career and family at that company.

A final factor in causing women to leave is that of reintegration after maternity leave. Many women quit their companies six months to a year after returning from their leaves. Why? Their supervisors and colleagues wrote them off during the leave, and no one bothered to reassimilate them upon their return.

If pregnancy and maternity leave were positive experiences in the corporate sector, supported by supervisors and by the general climate for women, more women would surely return.

If I've decided to promote a woman, or to relocate her with a promotion possibly to follow, should I proceed with my plan when I notice that she's pregnant? If I'm interviewing her for a job and she's the best candidate, should I hire her?

Let me separate the two. In the case of relocation and promotion, sound business practice dictates that you proceed as planned. The case of the interviewee is not as clear cut, because you haven't yet invested resources in the job candidate, nor have you had an opportunity to gauge her performance. But the answer is nonetheless that you would be wise to hire her, because she's your best candidate in an era when shortages are imminent. Moreover, you'll win her enduring loyalty and send a resoundingly positive message to the women (and to many men) in your company.

And then what? Sometimes the period that follows is as catastrophic as it was for the woman called K. in chapter 2. But no employer should construe that outcome as a given. The physical reality of childbearing, unlike heart disease or the debilitating effects of alcoholism, can be planned for and managed. But this requires a partnership of the woman with her boss. Also, employers must clearly communicate through their human resources policies all the provisions they will make, as well as what the expectations are for employees' performance during and after the maternity leave period.

I don't know of more than a dozen companies where managers and pregnant women could answer questions like these: When does the period of disability begin and end? What portion of salary is paid during this period, and are benefits covered? Does the company provide maternity or parental leave beyond disability, and if so, for how long, paid or unpaid, and with or without a guarantee of the same or a comparable job? Who plans for coverage of the new mother's work during her absence, and who will actually perform her work? What are her responsibilities, if any, while she is out of the office, and beyond that, at what point do they warrant compensation?

The formulation of policies and practices is complex. It requires careful analysis, which should be conducted in the context of an overall strategic plan. Managers' commitment to these policies plays an equally critical role, as does their clear communication throughout the company. Institutionalized, the process becomes standard operating procedure rather than a continual series of dilemmas, doubts, and crises.

Companies that manage maternity effectively achieve two additional benefits. One is the opportunity to plan for the continuity of work. The new mother is able to plan for the bonding with and separation from her child and to ensure that her pregnancy will cause as little disruption as possible, both for her career progress and for her employer's productivity objectives. The second opportunity concerns recruitment, as high-potential young women emerging from school will be increasingly sophisticated about choosing an employer who will be responsive to their future family needs.

You're suggesting that I hire and promote pregnant women. Why in the world would I do that if I could hire or promote one who's not?

Because most women do have babies. If, in hiring for a job, you skip over one pregnant candidate to choose a woman who's not, hands-down odds suggest—unless she's past childbearing age—that she may well also become pregnant at some point in her career. In the case of the promotion or relocation of a pregnant employee, you've already invested in training her and giving her invaluable experience and company-specific knowledge. Obviously she's one of your best performers—or you wouldn't be considering her for promotion. You may harbor doubts about whether and when she'll return. If your policies are responsive to her needs, she will more than likely return at least on a part-time basis. More important, if you start playing bias games, you'll force the women who work for you into an adversarial role, and you'll foment dishonesty. She's likely to hide her pregnancy as long as she can, and because she is ambitious, she will accept the offer of promotion or the relocation opportunity. Then, if no flexibility is forthcoming after she has had her child, she may well decide it's not worth it to stay on. You'll feel betrayed, and she will have compromised her integrity—not a very good basis for your future relationship.

The only way you could get an edge on competitors by avoiding the cost of maternity would be to hire no women except for those who don't want children, who choose to remain single, who are postmenopausal, or whose children are grown. But even then many women with no children are care givers for elderly family members. If you discount candidates with family responsibilities, you will not reap the talent of the majority of women.

INSTITUTING FLEXIBILITY AND FAMILY SUPPORTS

Now that women are in the work force, children have to have a business impact. Today you must accept parenthood as a cost of doing business. The only way you can reduce that cost is by consciously disregarding the traditional roles of men and women and permitting them, as individuals, regardless of gender, to order their own priorities, to do what they want most to do and can probably do best. The result would be that you, the employer, would get the best and most committed men *and* women, and children would get the best and most committed parents.

Some small percentage of men and women would be what I think of as singularly career primary, while some small number would be exclusively family-focused. But the vast majority of men and women want to combine career and family and want to switch their main focus from time to time throughout their lives. And here is the *major* point: These men and women *require* flexibility in order to be maximally productive at work *and* to be active and responsible players in their children's lives.

As things stand now, the business world must enlarge its infrastructure to support the family needs of employees. It has to be part of the business of business. Then you will benefit from the people who want to work, who are best at work—male or female. Just pause for a minute and think about a woman you know, one who is a real star—and whose husband you know is not as talented as she is. And think of the men you know who are more nurturing than their wives.

What can I do to deal with this reality?

- Accept the fact that you must be flexible and must provide family supports. The alternatives include unacceptable rates of turnover, terrible losses in productivity, and exclusion from the leadership pool of high-potential, high-performing women (and, increasingly, men) who want to be involved in their children's lives.
- Provide the full range of ongoing benefits to women on disability and maternity leave and to those who return part-time.
- Let women who have babies return when they're ready. By "ready"

I mean when they feel well psychologically and physically, when they're getting enough sleep to function effectively during the day, when they feel they've bonded with their babies, and when they have located, tested, and are satisfied with whatever kind of child care they've chosen.

- Let women return from maternity leave on less than full-time or other alternative schedules—part-time, shared, telecommuting arrangements—for as long as they want.
- Permit new fathers to take parental leaves, sequencing them with those of their wives.
- Establish a policy that permits parents to cut back to half-time (at prorated pay) and reenter the competition for senior management levels, partnership, or tenure if they choose. (Translation: Don't put them on a "mommy track.")
- When a woman (or a man) is out on leave or working part-time for a significant period, provide the additional heads and hands that are necessary to get the work done.
- Take responsibility—in partnership with parents, communities, and government—for making high-quality, affordable child care available for every child.
- Find every opportunity you can to enable parents (and other executives who need uninterrupted time to think and work) to work at home.
- Contract out as much work as you can.
- Finally, the sine qua non for all of the above: Learn how to measure productivity instead of time in the office and put systems in place to do so.

I think I understand what you mean by flexibility in a general sense; what does it entail more specifically?

By "flexibility" I mean flexibility in schedule, flexibility in work site (at home or in the office), flexibility to cut back to part-time for open-ended intervals or to take full-time leaves. Companies have already started to recognize that parents will sometimes be late to work or have to leave early or dash out at midday. Some are even making allowances for diminished productivity in periods of stress or illness, or permitting women to return part-time from maternity leave for two or three months. These are natural, humane accommodations to human needs. They are the counterpart of the employer assumption of ready acceptance of periods of high demand, of individuals putting aside personal needs and preferences when it can make a difference to the company.

I think a further and more radical change is necessary in the attitudes of employers, a redefinition of what is meant by flexibility. What I suggest goes beyond stretching the parameters of flexibility to a more direct response to the individual. It is a policy that says, "If you are committed to your career, we will measure your productivity and results and permit you whatever flexibility you need to achieve the results we expect." A career-committed person can cut back to, say, half-time for a self-defined period of time, but half-time would mean half the work, which in a driven environment can come very close to what is 'normally' considered full-time. Additionally, the career-committed person would be expected to take the initiative and responsibility to make provision for the balance of his or her work to be done.

My policy would go on to say that if an employee's primary commitment is to family (at least in this phase of life), the expectation is that he or she will commit to a thirty-five-hour work week with whatever variations in schedule or work site the employee agrees on with his or her supervisor.

But if I institute all these initiatives, won't I be losing out on the prime years of career women's lives?

I suggest that you may not find the two roles—corporate leader and mother (or father)—so incompatible, if you enlarge your vision to realize the ultimate payoff of having women in leadership roles.

I think we must let go of our insistence that the thirty-five high-intensity years be uninterrupted years from twenty-five to sixty. The cost of doing business with a work force comprising half women is to accept and deal with a temporary slowdown in productivity for one or both parents. If you permit men and women to self-select, to decide themselves which of the two—or both—will slow down in exchange for career growth during that period, the situation becomes workable for employer, employee, and child.

This isn't really so strange an idea if you think about it. In fact, there are law firms I know of in which partners' compensation eventually plateaus as they approach retirement, motivated by the partner's desire to slow down. In addition, these partners feel it's only fair and, more important, good business practice for the firm to limit their earnings and invest that money in younger partners, who will then be further motivated to bring in more business and work harder. That decision generally meets with cultural approval, as an acknowledgment that it is unrealistic to expect any individual to function on all cylinders throughout a forty-three-year work life.

There's nothing engraved in stone that specifies the years an individual must work at high intensity. Twenty years ago it was common for men to work well beyond the age of sixty. Today, when couples marry later and are more likely to be the same age, this pattern has changed. A man might work at a high-intensity level as his father did, from twenty-two to sixty. He might begin to think about slowing down for the last five years of his career.

More often than not, a married woman now has a serious career commitment and might work at a high-intensity level from age twenty-two to thirty-one and from thirty-six to sixty-five. She, too, functions for thirty-five high-intensity years. Yet we do not accept her slowdown as natural or inevitable in combination with a business career. We tend to see career and family for women as antithetical, either-or.

Think of it this way. Those to whom career achievement is the highest priority early in life will pursue their careers intensely, without interruptions, from age twenty-five to sixty, retiring at sixty-five. Those who are committed to careers but for whom parenting is also a high priority will pursue their careers intensely from twenty-five to thirty-five, slow down for five years, and work intensely again from forty to sixty-five. If you provide the flexibility these working parents need in that five-year period, chances are a lot greater that they will stay with your company later.

I believe it will increasingly be sound business practice to include those who choose to slow down for five years in the line of succession for the top half of the pyramid and for partnership in law, accounting, and financial services firms.

One minute you're talking about shared parenting. The next you talk about women taking responsibility for children. Where do you really stand?

No matter how career driven the woman, in a two-income couple children are still by and large primarily her responsibility. Even driven men feel driven to have children. They may not want or expect to take the time to raise them, but they still expect to have them. For women it comes down to family *and* career, since they are still expected (and, to varying degrees, want) to shoulder the domestic burden. Therefore it is true that women currently are more apt than men to have periods in which their productivity plateaus. They are more likely to cut back their schedules, change employers, or drop out of the work force entirely for a time.

Nonetheless, the role of fathers is critical. Having a baby incapacitates a woman for a finite time, but being a parent is a lifetime commitment for both mother and father. From the instant of birth—where the new norm is for fathers to attend—fathers are more closely involved with their children than ever before in modern history. Men increasingly desire more family time, and it serves your business interest to enable that participation. Opportunities there start with choosing not to reinforce the socialization of men, include permitting men to participate more in family life, then go even further by recognizing that you are crippling women by not encouraging men to take a greater role at home.

A few employers are already moving in this direction. At a conference last fall, Ted Childs, Director of Affirmative Action and Work Force Diversity Programs at IBM, told a story about a highly promotable executive who decided that he wanted to take a three-month leave after his first child was born. He told his boss of his desire in advance in the context of being offered a promotion opportunity. He said he thought he would have many such opportunities over his career at IBM, but that he would be a first-time parent only once, and he wanted to make the most of it.

The manager of this father-to-be apparently was somewhat confused about how to deal with such an unusual situation. When Childs heard about it, he spoke with the manager and assured him that the high-potential new father would be offered a fantastic opportunity when he returned from his leave, because IBM wanted to use him as a role model to encourage other men to take parental leaves.

IBM is, of course, a forefront employer on these issues, with exceptional work and family policies. My bet is that other companies will soon follow its lead.

But how do I gain by pioneering such policies?

Very few companies want to stay ahead of the pack. They're not sure they want to do anything about women to begin with, so they certainly don't want to take a leadership position. They have enough risk already and don't want to do anything until there is a proven need. But overnight they will be able to see the payoff. As illustration, here are two companies that are taking contrasting approaches on this issue.

I recently spoke with the CEO of a small paper company about his company's response to employees' family needs. "Children are not our job," he told me.

His reasoning? He is in business to make paper and to make money; his is a small, capital-intensive business, and its personnel focus is on the people who make and sell their products. At one point in our conversation he told me that he had been approached about joining a consortium of local employers to create a child care facility. His response had been, "Let our secretaries get their own child care." As I left his office I found myself shaking my head with a mixture of shock, discomfort, and relief. I hadn't had a conversation in years that indicated such a strong conviction regarding women's unimportance to business.

Then there is the Intermedic Company in a little southeast corner of Texas, which is located next door to a huge installation of Dow Chemical. Intermedic was having difficulty competing with Dow for high-caliber people—until they put in a child care center. Overnight they got known as a company that cared about family, and they turned their recruitment around.

What is the the cost to you of treating child care as your employees' problem rather than a shared need? Women are still largely responsible for the care of their children, as we know. Good child care is not yet in place. The result is that women who would stay on the job, possibly as some of your best employees, if they had good child care arrangements are cutting out or cutting back because there is no viable alternative. In addition to perpetuating the distraction of employees whose child care arrangements are tenuous and unsatisfactory, you are interfering with the natural self-selection of those who are truly committed and highly able.

This situation is not exclusive to secretaries, as the paper company CEO I met with suggested. He was implying that his replaceable workers had these problems, that his management women were handling their own child care needs satisfactorily. That attitude might have made more sense when he could say that women were not important to his work force, when they were outside the mainstream of his enterprise. Now that women are a critical part of the mainstream, however, he must do everything possible to retain them.

You cannot afford to look on those who drop out as having the least commitment. Instead they are the ones who are not satisfied with their child care arrangements. They will drop out only if there is no alternative.

Women were superfluous in the past. You must recognize that this is about to change. What yesterday was a risk, is today an avoidance of risk. When you do not address the issues of family supports and child care for the managers you employ, you are absorbing the cost— and it's a substantial investment—of those who do not make it as far as they might because they are constrained by their family responsibilities. This group includes, of course, those who could be the biggest contributors, the real brains and talent and leaders, of your company.

So I have to build an expensive on-site child care center?

Not necessarily. On-site child care is a less-than-appropriate response in many companies, if only because many parents would not want it. For that reason it may even sometimes be underutilized, although most on-site centers have a very small capacity. Nonetheless it's an option that should not be ignored because it's superb in some locations, wonderful for nursing mothers, and valuable for the message it promulgates of the company's concern for children. And I believe it will be one of several alternatives all companies will provide in the future.

There are many other initiatives to explore, whether independently or in partnership with other companies, with parents, with communities, or with government agencies.

Independently, or in a consortium with other companies, an employer can hire a professional to identify, train, and supervise family child care providers, who care for small children in their own homes. This is the first-choice form of surrogate care for a growing number of young parents. First undertaken by a consortium of companies in Hartford, this low-cost way to substantially increase the availability of child care has been replicated by others in Atlanta and many other cities. Dayton Hudson has also undertaken an excellent program to train home child care providers.

Parenting seminars, a generous parental leave policy, and flexibility regarding when and how new parents return to work after having a baby are all additional components of a responsive family policy. So are resource and referral services. These free, community-based information centers have proliferated because they serve an important function. But they have limitations as well, since access to referrals for a relatively static supply of existing child care cannot address a critical need—the creation of new child care resources. IBM's resource and referral service is ground-breaking in that it goes a step further— it encourages and provides training for providers at new facilities.

How can I give some employees something I'm not giving others?

I believe you need to disregard the issue of equity in child-related policies and practices. In the short term children are costly to you to the degree their working mothers and fathers are distracted from work by tenuous and inadequate child care arrangements. The effects of the absence of parents from the home is compounded by the paucity of high-quality, affordable child care and the deterioration of the public school system. The generation emerging now from high school is half the size we anticipated in the middle of the baby boom and further diminished by an accelerating functional illiteracy rate. You are already experiencing shortages of competent men and women in clerical and blue-collar jobs. It is clearly in your interest to make high-quality, affordable child care possible, to ensure a capable next generation. More important, our country's future depends on the health, well-being, and education of today's children.

Why should I make concessions like flexible work arrangements when I can get the real thing—everybody driving full-time?

Because the era when you had a choice is ending. Within the next few years you will no longer be able to fill your human resources needs with men because there won't be enough qualified men to do all the jobs that need doing. The diversification of the work force is the result of the fact that the economy grew at a faster pace than the population. If women walked out today, your company would collapse. Women who used to be home full-time caring for their children are now working for you. They must have flexibility in order to juggle family and work, to be both responsible workers and responsible parents.

In some areas today the shortage of workers is so great that a nurse, for example, can set her own schedule. If she wants to work Tuesday A.M. and Friday P.M., fine. If she has children, the hospital will readily provide her with a space in its child care center. Why? Because the alternative is to shut down a wing of the hospital.

I think part-time opportunities will proliferate in the future, simply because employers will become increasingly aware that flexibility is the key to retaining able individuals who want and need more family time.

One fine example of a flexible system is Steelcase's job-sharing program. The world's largest manufacturer of office furniture and equipment, based in Grand Rapids, Michigan, has offered job sharing on a limited basis since 1982. Last year they set up a formal companywide policy allowing any team with management approval to share a position. In 1989 there were seventy job sharers, or almost twice as many as there were before the policy was companywide. Although reasons for job sharing at Steelcase vary, more than 85 percent of requests focus on child care, usually easing a woman's transition back into the work force after having a baby or enabling a parent to spend more time with children at home. The company still has some concerns about possible problems involving production jobs (though they already have job sharers in production), but management looks forward to reduced turnover and an improved rate of return to work following maternity leave.

Why should I get involved in employees' personal lives, and when does it become intrusive and an invasion of privacy?

That question had more relevance in the past than it does today, because the line between the worlds of work and family has become blurred. In fact, it is emphatically one world, where two jobs have to be done. Say you used to employ five hundred men, who have five hundred wives at home. All told, they have between them four million waking hours per year (that is based on sixteen waking hours per day). In the past the energies of those people would have been divided mostly along gender lines. Men devoted eight of their sixteen waking hours exclusively to work and the preponderance of their eight discretionary hours to work as well. Women devoted eight of their sixteen waking hours exclusively to family and the preponderance of their eight discretionary hours to family as well.

Now we have the same number of hours but a new configuration of time expenditure. Eight of the sixteen hours of *both* men and women are spent at work. However, the fact remains that half of the discretionary hours of your work force are still going to be taken up with work and half with family. One million of those hours are still going to be spent predominantly with children, and one million are still going to be spent predominantly producing goods and services.

Now you are employing five hundred men and five hundred

women, who have a total of four million waking hours. You will have eight male hours and eight female hours devoted exclusively to work, but the focus of the discretionary hours of men and women must be defined by the preference and ability of the individual, not by gender. At its most extreme, you might have a woman who devotes the entire balance of eight hours to work and a man who devotes the entire balance of eight hours to family.

If you don't bring family into the mainstream of your business, the needs of families are going to undermine your company. You're going to have employees who are washing out, distracted, and a business that's centered in a society where children—the next generation of employees—aren't receiving the guidance and nurturance they need.

On the other hand, instead of imposing judgments about which people you think should devote their energies to family and which to work, instead of thinking, All my women employees are going to spend all their discretionary time with their children, and therefore they cannot move up to higher levels in my company, you should allow the redistribution of roles within families so that men and women can self-select for the roles they prefer and do best.

How can I run a tight ship if I allow my management to come and go as they please?

You can run a tighter, more productive ship—if, that is, you measure productivity by what is accomplished rather than by how much time is spent in the office. That's a real challenge because it requires that you set objectives and evaluate performance against those objectives. And I suspect that's very much at the root of the resistance to change. A great deal of time is wasted around the water cooler, tending to personal matters, relieving tension and fatigue in conversation for many of those who spend twelve or fourteen hours at work. (I know some individuals thought of as hard workers who arrive early, leave late, and take care of personal business in the midday hours.) And a lot more can be done by "working smart," by responding to the inner motivation to get the job done and get home to the children, and by avoiding make-work meetings and extended lunches. Just think how much we all accomplish under the deadline of an impending vacation.

I can see from what you say that it would be advantageous for my company to become more flexible, but it's so time-consuming to evaluate where it works, to identify a second person for a shared job, and so on. Is there any way around that?

The undeniable reality is that a new policy or practice is always costly in the initial stages. When TRW and American Can pioneered flexible benefits, their costs were enormous; today experience is widespread and the costs of implementation much lower. Once the practice is institutionalized, the time it requires is minimal.

Those companies that make a total commitment to flexibility will ultimately institutionalize the practice throughout their organization. As they do so in a range of areas, they will make it known that a percentage of the work in each area (a critical mass of full-timers is necessary) can be conducted on part-time, shared, and telecommuting arrangements. I think of it as a cycling process. It will be known, say, that one-quarter of the positions in a given area can be filled by individuals who adopt alternative work arrangements. People will rotate through these jobs—they will leave or cut back for various periods of time, and others will return to fill those places. And when they return, some of them will continue in the family-driven or family-committed mode and others will move to a career-driven or career-committed mode.

How can I get my business done if I can't count on people being there?

You *can* count on them when you structure schedules carefully. What you may have in mind is a desire for your people to be there at your beck and call throughout the day or the week. Instead try jotting down things you need to discuss and call in members of your team once or twice a day rather than buzzing them throughout the day. And, of course, make sure you can reach them at any time for emergencies.

Certainly you're not referring to high-level people, are you?

It's your high-level people whom you can—and usually do—permit a great deal of discretion. That's because they know they're accountable for their turf. They acquired that turf because they consistently delivered on that commitment. You may want to make that clearer to them so they don't feel the need to invent excuses when they want to have an afternoon with a child or go to an after-school activity.

That may be true, but certainly I can't let high-level women take long maternity leaves and return on part-time schedules?

In a Catalyst study we found that after the birth of a child, two groups return at the earliest time possible. One is those women who absolutely depend on their earnings full-time throughout the year. The other is women on the fast track who are afraid of losing their career momentum and of being judged as less than 100 percent committed. The latter is very costly to you. These are the women on whose judgment you depend for decisions that have significant bottom-line impact.

There *are* women who can return with the same degree of intensity and on the same schedules after six or eight weeks—there are even some who can return after only two weeks because they love or need their work or are bored or frustrated at home. Most, however, need much more time to cope with all the factors discussed previously. Unless you permit them to return when they're ready on schedules they choose, you run the risk of losing them from sheer exhaustion, as well as from the yearning to bond with their babies.

Even when these women *do* return at the appointed time, many will just give up down the road. How much better *for your business* to allow them to return refreshed, free of guilt, secure in their child care arrangements, and eager to plunge in to work. They will do this only when you recognize that such an arrangement makes business sense and communicate it clearly to them. Catalyst's research has confirmed that the vast majority of women would return to work much sooner if they could return less than full-time.[1] Smart employers will ensure that when women return on a part-time basis, their specific talents will be put to use and lesser responsibilities delegated to others.

That may be true, but what about those women—most notably single parents— at lower levels, who can't afford to return to work part-time?

If I tell you to pay these women full-time salaries for part-time work, you'll probably laugh and say you're not a charity. But stop a minute and think about this: There's no question that the pressure will mount for more and more paid maternity leave. (Sweden provides eighteen months of leave for the mother or father at 90 percent pay.) You can avoid the whole issue of paid maternity leave if professional women can return on part-time schedules with prorated salaries and benefits. Using some of those savings to subsidize a part-time return for lower-income women makes good business sense, not only for reasons of equity, but to give the children of these women—your future employees—a better start.

I can understand the feasibility of job sharing at lower levels, but certainly it's not possible at higher levels, particularly where clients are involved, is it?

A recent Catalyst study of flexible work arrangements at the managerial and professional levels showed that although prearrangement skepticism still exists, once the client experiences the job-sharing arrangement, resistance disappears.

A condition of success is that the two individuals keep one another informed on a daily basis—and on their own time—of what transpires. In fact, job sharers provide more coverage than full-time workers because one is always there when the other is traveling, sick, or on vacation.

What about the extra costs of office space, benefits, and the time it takes to maintain working relationships?

Cost issues vis-à-vis flexible work arrangements are myth rather than reality, Catalyst researchers have found. At lower levels (and even, sometimes, higher levels) offices can be shared; shared offices facilitate communication because the job sharers have a common filing system, find it easier to reach each other by phone, and are more easily contacted by clients and co-workers.

At all levels benefits can be prorated. Other costs pale compared to the costs of attrition or the lowered productivity of those who are simply overwhelmed. And there is increasing evidence that two job sharers can be significantly more productive than one full-timer.

I accept the reality that women tend to interrupt their careers to have babies and that they can't devote as much time and energy to work because they have to take care of things at home and raise the children. How can you suggest that I legitimize—even that I encourage—men to share that responsibility with women? If I did that, I wouldn't have anyone—save men and women without children—to count on to be committed first and foremost and above all to my company.

Right. But as long as women have the primary responsibility for home and family, their careers (and their contribution to your bottom line) will be stunted. They will tend to arrive later, leave earlier, be less able to travel than men, and they won't be able to attend off-hour meetings without advance warning. If you permitted men to share parenting with their wives, either parent who needed to come in early or work late or travel would be able to call the other and arrange for him or her to cover the home base. Yes, you'd probably lose some time and commitment from men, but your *net* return would be greater, because you'd enable both to have responsible high-level careers.

You talk so much about leaders. What about all the others?
  You tend to think of all those who enter your company or firm as potential leaders, virtually disregarding the vast majority who aren't able enough or don't want to be leaders. So I'm glad you ask that question. With the compression of the pyramid, you're forced to find alternative rewards for those to whom you do not provide constant promotions and salary increases. The one cost-free reward that's enormously valued is flexibility.

What do you think about bringing babies to work when child care arrangements break down?
  I think it's diverting to the mother and disruptive to others in the office. A great alternative is to set up an emergency child care center. The law firm Wilmer, Cutler & Pickering was the first to implement a comprehensive emergency child care program, in 1986. The center, which is open seven days a week, from nine-thirty to five-thirty on weekdays and which serves children ages six months to twelve years, cost $45,000 to open.
  The firm figures it has already made back its investment many times over. The facility paid for itself early on: it gave the firm 1,400 more lawyer hours than it would have had otherwise. Cravath was the first to follow, and the practice, I am sure, will proliferate rapidly.

Why has flextime spread so rapidly in Europe and now in the United States? Isn't it costly to have people coming and going all the time and absent for large chunks of the day?
  People learn to deal with flextime by listing topics that require discussion with colleagues and covering them all at one time in "core hours," typically between ten and three. And the advantages abound. It's an excellent way to provide flexibility without reducing working hours, first of all. Also, employees find that their commuting time is reduced because they can avoid peak hours. Then the availability of staff to clients is extended early and late in the day. Best of all, when flextime is available to two parents, one can get home early by leaving early and the other can stay home during the early hours of the day and work late. The result is that the need for surrogate care or the

time the child spends in day care is minimized, and family time isn't confined to the end of the day when everyone's tired.

Why should I pay benefits to women who have babies while they are on disability leave when I can't be sure they'll return?

Because unless you provide benefits to *all* women you'll force them to say they're returning when they're not sure whether they will or not. When they don't return you're caught short unexpectedly and you don't have time to find and train a replacement. Moreover, the woman who doesn't return feels guilty for taking the benefits. Before you feel betrayed by women who have for this and other reasons dropped out, stop and consider what *you* might have done (or left undone) that forced them to leave. I'm thinking particularly of new mothers who have endured all sorts of indignities and barriers at work and who realize that childhood is finite. It's the confluence of their experience at work with their desire to be with their children that makes them move to a job with a more flexible employer or quit altogether.

PROVIDING THE BALANCE

Despite the fact that they have the innate capabilities, women are not being used as effectively as they might. That's because they're not developed as they could be. They are not being coached and trained as men are, they're not being exposed to the same range of experience, they're not being spotted and tracked and mentored as men have always been. To utilize women effectively, you must do everything within your power to ensure that they get what they need—what I referred to in the last chapter as the Balance—to rise as far as they can.

One example: Historically women have been socialized to be nurturing, a quality that has not served them as well in the corporation as the aggressive, risk-taking behavior that until recently has been imparted more readily to men. We don't have to undertake a huge study to find out whether women are more or less aggressive than men, though. You have only to show women why they need to be and how they can be aggressive if that is what it takes to be successful in your business. And, of course, you must encourage your managers not to penalize those women who are already aggressive or possess other qualities we tend to associate with men. Finally, you can help to overcome the disparate socialization of men and women by resisting the temptation to reinforce traditional behavioral patterns.

Within your company or your industry, if you see something that women seem to lack, recognize it and do something about it. Don't assume it's a fundamental difference between women and men that cannot be bridged.

In addition, we are moving from a manufacturing economy, where command and control works best and authority and aggression is necessary, to an information economy, where orchestration and responsiveness work best and sensitivity and communication skills will be a boon. Indeed, the percentage of women entering the work force is increasing just as the characteristics and skills for which women have traditionally been socialized are important. You may have to begin coaching men to tone down the aggressive military model of the past. So while you are teaching women the rules of the game and how they can play by them, you can coach men also to modify their behaviors.

Sometimes in meetings I find that the women who work for me speak out inappropriately. How can I get them to understand the proper way to behave?

Think about how long it would take you to enter women's traditional world. How long would it take you to make a bed or to cook a meal? All I have to do is watch my husband struggle to get things synchronized for dinner—to come in, as he has recently, to this complicated world of women. The situation is even more complex with the things women do that are generally less well understood and less easily taught—for example, women are the ones in families who orchestrate and support the enormous range of experiences in their children's lives and maintain the links between family members. Is it an accident that families stay together? That people are invited or telephoned? Who writes the birthday cards? These are critical social responsibilities that preserve a very rewarding aspect of life—namely, family and friends—performed by women, which men might find awkward or even difficult to master. Facilitating the experience of men who are beginning to enter women's world is counterpart to the assistance you must provide women who enter men's world.

Men don't come into your business automatically knowing how to behave, either. Everyone needs to be taught—all the way from what to wear to when it is appropriate to speak. But men have an advantage that women don't. On an informal basis, men have always had the benefit of special treatment—the work environment is, in fact, tailored specially to their needs.

Men are comfortable serving as role models to more junior men. They coach them, teach them, expose them to the demands of the culture. They guide them to increasing political sophistication. They evaluate their performance and nourish them with candid, constructive comment on their weaknesses.

Some companies are undertaking formal programs to better prepare women for upper-management positions. One, St. Louis-based Monsanto Agricultural Company, created its eleven-week leadership training program in October 1988. Participants are selected by the company's division vice-presidents, then enrolled in courses ranging from business planning to workplace etiquette. They are also given projects that broaden their knowledge. For example, a manufacturing supervisor who sought a position in plant management gained the marketing knowledge she needed by working on a project overseen by a program "coach" in the marketing division. Although completion of the program doesn't guarantee promotion, almost one-third of the thirty-one women participating have been promoted.

Incidentally, the program has been so successful that it has been expanded to include men.

I can't give a woman candid feedback! She'd just get upset.

That's not the problem. The problem, first of all, is that no one likes to be negative (even when it's appropriately put in constructive terms, as an opportunity to grow). But there's an additional factor with women, and that is that you're afraid to give them feedback. You're intimidated and uncomfortable with coaching women.

You have to recognize that candid evaluation is something women want and need. A performance evaluation, for example, might indicate that a particular woman doesn't perform well at meetings at a certain level. And that's because she doesn't realize that at this level you're talking conceptually and at another level you're meeting on implementation. She won't become upset if the performance evaluation is set up properly, as it needs to be set up for men, too.

In early 1990 Pratt & Whitney announced a revised performance management system as part of its rigorous business plan to improve quality. To measure performance objectively, the assessment is based on a set of "competencies" derived from Pratt & Whitney's mission and culture. Leadership competencies include the ability to create a shared vision, empower others, develop people, and recognize merit. Personal competencies include technical expertise, initiative, and ability to satisfy customers, among others. Employees' performance is measured against behavioral examples of each competency at three levels: exceptional, fully competent, and developing.

In another important part of the process, employees provide their supervisors with written self-assessments in which they express their perception of their performance, accomplishments, needs, and goals. The process promotes open dialogue between supervisor and employee and generates action plans for improvement.

There's another point here, too, that goes back to my earlier discussion of the differences between men and women. While women tend to cry as a response to frustration, men tend to express those same feelings through anger. Within the corporate environment the latter is deemed acceptable—for men, at least. When women get angry, men can't deal with it any better than they deal with tears. I think it would be useful to recognize that if some women cry, it's not the end of the world. Nor would it be a disaster if men learned to shed a tear now and then as well.

I know that a lot of men's advancement comes from their identification with mentors. And I don't have women at those levels to serve in those roles. What can I do?

It's difficult to institutionalize mentoring programs, but it has been done. Corning, among other companies, has found that mentoring is making a difference in its ability to promote and retain women. Indeed, individuals move up faster with the benefit of a sponsor or an advocate higher in the corporate ranks. Corning's program involves formalized coaching of 16 employees a year who are chosen on the basis of their executive potential and interest. The women's mentors help them to hone technical skills, refine their career goals, and to establish a network of contacts within the organization.

From my observation, the process of men serving as women's mentors works best when the men really see the company's advantage, and therefore their own, in choosing a woman with a high degree of raw talent and aiding her professional development. The most important thing you can do, though, is to keep moving women up, because a woman is probably still a better role model for a woman.

Talk about diversity is all the rage today. My human resources people are spending huge amounts of time on it, bringing in consultants, circulating videos, having retreats and discussions, discussions, discussions. And the ground is shifting from managing diversity to valuing diversity. What's it all about?

As you know, diversity *is* a real business issue. It's not that we've suddenly become more sensitive and caring about "others" (though I think diversity *will* enhance sensitivity and concern); it's that we need these diverse groups today because the economy continues to expand and the total fertility rate has been below replacement rate for seventeen years.

Twenty-five years ago equal employment opportunity legislation and affirmative action forced employers to open opportunities to women, mainly in a numerical sense. But these initiatives did not challenge any of the workplace conventions that could inhibit women's progress. In the long run this had some detrimental impact on women's advancement. It was a begrudging, sink-or-swim response, similar to that of "white" colleges in the forties and fifties that admitted "Negro" students who had graduated from separate and *un*equal high schools without providing compensatory education prior to their entrance. As a result, in both instances, many failed outright or managed barely to keep their heads above water by virtue of perseverance and, often, lowered achievement standards, which tended to undermine the credibility of women and minorities as professionals.

Most important, EEO did not recognize differences between men and women. The assumption was that they were alike and that pressure alone could lead to integration. But it couldn't. It was, if not a disaster course, at least one that was doomed to failure. It was the period when the message to women was to be just like men, to emulate the male model—the era of the man-tailored suit and the silk bow tie. As increasing numbers of women, minorities, and immigrants entered the work force, new needs surfaced that could not be addressed by a program that did not acknowledge differences among groups. The result: "Diversity" came into play.

The first impulse was to "manage" these diverse groups—women, blacks, Asians, Hispanics—just as white males had always been managed. But the American tradition of a melting pot just doesn't fly anymore. This is the era of the individual. Businesses now recognize that there is a great deal of talent to be mined among people of varied ethnicity and gender, all of whom can bring new perspectives to the workplace. By virtue of their traditions, life experience, socialization, culture, and values, each group can enrich, expand, and contribute in unique ways to the work at hand. This in turn has led to a realization that not just the employee base, but the customer, client, and stockholder base is becoming increasingly diverse. So it's important to have people with diverse backgrounds in senior management to reflect the needs and values and consumer patterns of all these groups. All this is not only fair and right, it makes good business sense.

You've been talking for the last several pages about bringing women "up to speed," what you call giving them "the Balance." That makes sense to me. As you say, women are newcomers to what has traditionally been a man's world, so there are lots of things women don't know, and it's good business to fill those gaps. My question is, why isn't this part of all the talk about diversity?

Because of 1) employers' fear of litigation, and 2) women's fear of being perceived as different from men. Yet, as I've said, women must be enabled to come up to the starting line with an equal chance to move ahead. The concept of diversity has set the stage for identifying weaknesses (as well as strengths) and needs that tend to be shared by members of each particular group, and there's an economy of scale in addressing them in the group context. The next logical step is remedial, to provide any knowledge or skills that will encourage the needed growth. There have been tentative efforts to provide programs such as assertiveness training, but they've faltered. The necessary first step is yours. With a conviction born of business recognition, you must communicate your belief in women's value to your company and your determination to capitalize on that value by providing the special training that, as a group, women tend to need. Incidentally, it's equally important to provide men with training in areas of women's traditional strengths.

Tenneco's executive incentive program underscores the organization's goals for advancing women and minorities by basing a significant portion of each division's executive bonus pool on whether that division meets all its stated goals and objectives for hiring and promoting women and minorities.

I agree with what you say about the pluses of diversity, but there's something that doesn't sit right with me. I can't put my finger on it, can you?

All the talk about diversity is about "them." It's white males talking about others, it's "we" and "they," the empowered and the vulnerable, and it reinforces the traditional view of the mainstream and the outsiders—of what, for example, men can do *for* women rather than what men and women can do together. It also reinforces stereotypes because it focuses on differences among groups. That introduces another problem in that it fosters the tendency to look to each group for particular strengths (to women, for example, for their communication skills) and to fail to look for other strengths (such as aggressiveness) that do indeed exist in some women.

It's another of these delicate titrations: diversity has to be celebrated, but it can't be overemphasized. It's very much like my sense that we have to talk about *women's* need for flexibility now because corporate leaders recognize that women carry the primary responsibility for rearing children, and they are already beginning to respond to women's needs. But talking about women's needs reinforces the perception that children are a women's issue rather than a parents' issue and a business issue. So as you provide flexibility to working mothers, you must begin to think about expanding the policies, and the practices, to encompass working fathers.

There's an additional danger. In our exuberant discovery of the added value that various groups can bring to the workplace—by virtue of their differing ethnicity, socialization, traditions, and historic experience—we may have, in one sense, set our goals too high. Regrettably, I don't believe we can wipe away in one giant step men's stereotypes and preconceptions about women in the workplace and replace them with a celebration of women's presence. After all, prejudice is simply a judgment that is made with inadequate exposure, experience, and knowledge—and it takes time to change. Just think of the resistance to admitting women to men's clubs, to disturbing the comfortable ambience. I am forced, I'm afraid, to suggest that we start with the more modest goal of becoming comfortable with, of accepting, women in the work force. Celebrating diversity, in that sense, is too ambitious; it strains credibility, and that makes a great many white males scoff at it, disregard it as a short-term objective. I am not for a moment discarding it as a feasible long-term goal. But I think we must move toward it one step at a time. In this decade, I will settle for acceptance of, and possibly a degree of comfort with, women in the workplace.

IMPROVING THE CORPORATE ENVIRONMENT

We've talked about what women as a group need if they are to be brought up to speed in an essentially homogeneous world of men. Men were socialized to enter the workplace. They built it so that it would be comfortable for them. They learned how to function in it. They brought in others like themselves.

Now, an environment that was carefully structured to accommodate men has to undergo further change to accommodate women. It has to become responsive to different kinds of needs.

First of all, men have to accept the reality that women belong in the work force. They have to shed their preconceptions and stereotypes in order to include women in every dimension—formal as well as informal—of their working lives. Men must help women develop, listen to what they say, applaud their progress. In short, men have to recognize that the performance of women has a profound effect on the performance of their companies, and they have to alter their attitudes and behaviors accordingly.

I don't think women are having all that many problems. They don't come to me to complain.

Of course you're not hearing that much is wrong—nobody is talking about it! Why would they come to the boss to complain? They're afraid enough as it is without being perceived as whiners and back stabbers or as disloyal to the company. For your own sake, you have to be sensitive to the conspiracy of silence that prevents women from talking about the difficulties they face. Assume that the environment is more corrosive than you can see on the surface.

The most important thing you can do is get the message out that women are valued as a business resource. Let the people in your company know that if a woman has a problem, you see it as a business cost to you—and you want to know about it so you can solve the problem and eliminate that cost.

If something is forcing a woman to leave, you need to know about it before she leaves so you can take care of the problem. You have to encourage her to talk about the obstacles she's facing, because if you don't know about them, you can't address them. Now, she thinks if she brings up problems, it will identify her as different from men, and different from men means second class. So you have to rectify that impression, by acknowledging that women face more barriers than men and by legitimizing the barriers as subject for business discussion. Go further—show women that their problems are your costs.

I absolutely recognize that I've got to get some women moving up to general management. But I really don't seem to be able to do it.

Catalyst's study of women in corporate management asked corporate leaders what they thought was most necessary to be considered for movement up to general management. The strong consensus was that line experience was a must. Yet in answer to another question, the chief executives responded that it was too great a risk to give women line experience. So women are caught in a catch-22. They need more lateral experience, but corporate leaders are unwilling to place them in areas where they could obtain it.

It's true that women tend to gravitate to staff positions. You can help guide them into the line positions they need to advance to general management. This also obviates the problem of having women concentrated in staff positions and forced into competition with each other (rather than reaching out to assist one another, which is critical). And as we move toward a period of shortages, you can't afford to have all your high-performing women outside the line of advancement to senior management positions.

I think first you have to define what it takes in your company to advance to the highest levels. Catalyst did a study recently at one company that was having a lot of trouble promoting women. We found that senior management could not pinpoint the requirements for promotion to the top. Women can't learn the ropes if they don't know what the ropes look like. And when you don't define the requirements for top jobs, isn't it possible that people are being appointed to them on the basis of qualifications other than innate talent?

Another important factor is the process of identifying talent and competence in women. We have not traditionally looked to women for leadership, and now must make a conscious effort to do so. This means accepting in women the behaviors that traditionally characterize successful men, so that we can make the same effort for talented women that is made to identify talented men early in their careers.

Finally, though, you're just going to have to gamble more on women. You'll have greater attrition among women, but even so you have to bet on everyone with talent. Stop weighing the Balance and go for the Basics, giving women the Balance they need. Everyone evolves. Support women as you do men, instead of perpetuating the corrosive environment that now forces so many women to leave.

Frankly, women aren't moving up in my company to the extent that our efforts warrant. Is there anything to all this talk about a glass ceiling?

Yes, there is, but not in the way it's represented. I don't think there's a barrier that senior management deliberately constructs to hold women down. As a matter of fact, I don't know of a CEO in the country who wouldn't like to have a least one or two really talented women at high levels in his company. But from the day a woman enters management, she faces the barriers I've been discussing—stereotypes and preconceptions, negative male behaviors, and so forth—that men don't face. And as she moves up, she is more and more isolated. It's the cumulative effect of this experience that keeps her from making it, that forces her to plateau or leave. The worst thing about all the glass ceiling talk is that it rivets attention on the problem rather than on what can be done to solve it.

I see women talking about forming groups or task forces, and I think this encourages negativity. Anyway, I don't think women should be talking about women's problems on company time; I think they should be meeting with men to talk about business problems.

Reverse that thinking. "Women's problems" *are* business problems. Encourage your high-level women to come together, to guide each other. You'll have to work hard to encourage them to participate whenever they can, because as it is now they're afraid they will be labeled "narrow" or "disloyal." They know that if a woman gets associated with "women's issues," you tend to cross her off. Instead, turn it around.

One way that men have traditionally advanced is through their mentor relationships and informal professional networks. Catalyst conducted a three-year project that looked at and assisted corporate women's groups. It taught us that many women are afraid of joining such groups because they feel that management views them with suspicion and even penalizes members. Yet membership is constructive for individuals and for the company. As there are still very few senior women, they are unable to provide the widely needed mentoring function, and corporate women's groups can provide a substitute. Members share experiences and learn from and support one another. They help their companies by addressing the needs of women and feeding policymaking. (They also encourage high-level women and provide a feeder system for women at the board level.)

I dread going on business trips with women. It seems to me a no-win situation. My wife worries about what is going on. It's hard for me, too, to travel with or entertain clients who are women without getting confused. These social interactions make me very tense. How is that ever going to change?

When you travel with a woman, your wife is concerned. You're also concerned about yourself. Your colleague may be attractive. However, these are largely mind-set issues. You are there on business together. Acknowledging this is a big step toward dealing with the situation, because then men and women realize they are both concerned. Whether men and women interact socially or in business, the chemical ingredients are there. We're all used to dealing with them socially, but we have to recognize that they exist in business, too.

You know, a lot of what we're talking about comes down to comfort level. I'm just not comfortable working with women.

I know. That's because traditionally we have had a different expectation for women. So many of the behaviors that are appropriate for women in business are alien to people raised in a different generation. If a woman is as aggressive as a man, she's seen as too driven. If she's not aggressive, she's not considered a player. But you need to get comfortable with women departing from the tradition because behavior that is required in the context of business may differ from what you're familiar with in personal life.

No one is asking you to marry the women who act in ways you're unaccustomed to—just to give them every opportunity to succeed in your company and increase your earnings. I know an executive whose daughters are autonomous career women but whose wife resembles June Cleaver. And that's what he wants. I've heard him say, "Why would a man want to marry a woman like my daughters? They're fabulous, but I wouldn't want to be married to a woman like that. I'd be arguing about everything." And that's fine, as long as you don't bring that expectation into the workplace.

I think that though comfort level is a huge factor now, it is ineluctably becoming less of an issue. I'd compare it to the sensation of being taped in an interview. At first you're terribly self-conscious, but soon you get so used to it that you don't even notice it. At entry levels women's presence is no longer disruptive, because women and men have gone to school together, shared dorms, majors, and social experiences, along with career plans and dreams.

What can you do to facilitate the process that is already under way? For one thing, you can take proactive steps to make men aware of negative behaviors, which can change before attitudes, particularly if you emphasize the bottom-line need for the change. This might seem conceptual, but it might help to think in terms of installing a sort of switch in the minds of your male employees. The switch enables them to see women from two separate vantage points. One is personal, emotional, from which they see and interact with women socially, romantically, and sexually. The second is a bottom-line vantage point, which rightfully concerns itself with women's ability to do the job. Some coherence between these two points of view should probably be attempted. Until then men may need to be trained to more consciously accept successful professional behaviors that are not yet acceptable in their personal lives.

To speed this transition, you can find opportunities for women and men to work together in teams. I was struck when I visited the Kellogg School of Management by what seemed to me an unusually large attendance by men at my plenary session. I spoke about it with one of the student organizers of the event. She felt that it was a function of the unusual group approach at Kellogg—all their work is done in teams of women and men together. The outcome is that men start to understand women better as work colleagues, and they develop sensitivity to their own roles with respect to women. At Corning, management retreats achieve much the same effect.

I'm sure there are cases in some companies of real sexual harassment. But I just can't believe that the men in my company would pinch a woman's behind.

You'd better believe it. It happens all the time. It's safe to assume that it is as pervasive in your organization as it is in the work force at large, unless you are taking steps to eradicate these kinds of behaviors.

There's a big spectrum, of course, from really innocent remarks that are misinterpreted to unwanted attention to the most vicious kind, such as sexual favors as a condition of employment or promotion. Nearly as corrosive, however, are demoralizing innuendos, from centerfold pinups to the lightly clad aerobics instructor at a conference in a break between segments, when the next session is led by a woman.

It's a difficult problem—and it's clouded by the fact that women have been conditioned to be sexually attractive and that men expect them to be and punish them if they are not. A female accountant recently won a suit against the accounting firm that refused to make her partner, claiming she was unsuitable after having advised her to consider wearing more makeup and styling her hair in a more feminine manner. On the other hand, another recent suit involved a woman who was fired by her law firm because she insisted on wearing very short skirts to court.

So women are in a tough spot. One of the largest and most prestigious consulting firms had an office in Los Angeles without a single woman partner. They realized that that was going to be terribly costly to them, so they looked into it and found that the managing partner at that location was sexually harassing women. They fired him forthwith.

That's the way it is. And to some degree our confusion regarding this issue is understandable. Men and women have been exposed to each other in social and romantic situations. There has to be a transition now. And employers have to be part of that change.

At Du Pont, for example, a company-wide program called "A Matter of Respect" has been implemented with the goal of creating a responsible and respectful environment free of sexual harassment and discrimination. The program includes a four-hour workshop in which several educational videotapes are screened and discussed. Some of the videos feature vignettes that illustrate offensive behavior in an authentic setting; another shows Du Pont CEO Ed Woolard expressing his disapproval of sexual harassment. "A Matter of Respect" also distributes a handbook that defines company policies regarding harassment, and a confidential phone hotline is available 24 hours a day.

Whether you move women up to places where they can serve your bottom line, or whether you bring women into the mainstream, you must deal with this issue, because their numbers in your management will only increase from now on.

Do I have to accept the fact that women are much less apt to relocate than men?

All of Catalyst's recent studies clearly show that that tendency is changing. In the past, when women's earnings were a fraction of men's, it was unlikely that the family would uproot itself to follow the wife's career. But today 18 percent of women in two-paycheck families earn more than their husbands. There's probably at least another 18 percent who make as much.[2] If women buy into shared responsibility for financial support of their families, their careers will be as important as their husbands' in making relocation decisions.

Furthermore, younger employees of both genders are refusing opportunities to relocate. In focus groups Catalyst conducted, women and men both are emphatic that relocation is a big issue for men, too.

The worst way to handle this question is by second-guessing what any particular individual might want and failing to give her the opportunity to decide. What you find may surprise you. For example, you may think you wouldn't want a commuter marriage, but many people feel that it's a worthwhile trade-off. As a matter of fact, some people find that it works very well in their lives. They work intensely during the week, and then on the weekends they're free to spend time together.

Add to this the high employer costs of relocation, and you have good reason to find new ways of providing needed experience and juggling personnel needs.

I want to do what's right, and we're ready to move on policies. What else has to happen?

Sensitize your managers. First of all, this means communicating the new demographic realities and their implications through training programs for all high-level employees. Only if you do so will they grasp the new realities that affect your company. After all, it is the managers who have to deal now with women and minorities, who have to recognize talent and competence in its many guises, and who have the enormous task of addressing new family needs of women and men while dealing with the everyday pressures of their own positions.

Are you suggesting that if I had an equally talented and qualified man and woman for a high-level line job, I should seriously consider taking the woman?

It would be naive to say "I don't know, they're equally good."

But it would be dead wrong for you just to go ahead and hire the man.

I'd suggest that you consider both and weigh your decision carefully. The explicit bias in your question is due to two factors: babies and barriers. We've already discussed these issues extensively. My point, as you know, is that inevitably your management will be half female, and most of the women will have babies. So the smartest business course you can take is to ignore babies as a factor in hiring and promotion and make sure you're managing every aspect of maternity as effectively as possible. If women are facing barriers to their productivity that men aren't facing in your company, you'd better analyze, address, and remove them as quickly as possible. Every day the toll they take on productivity and retention is huge.

If you're making real progress in leveling the playing field on these two counts, then I would say, Go for the woman. First of all, she's had to overcome barriers men haven't had to overcome in your company. Her stamina and perseverance have been put to the test more than the male candidate's. And she had to be better than he to have reached the point she's at, to be considered as qualified as he is. But the major factor that should tip the balance in favor of the woman is that you have a desperate need for more role models and mentors for younger women and for beacons at senior levels for the best and brightest female recruits.

Let me tell you about a situation that has just emerged at a medium-size public relations firm. This example is somewhat extreme, but I choose it because it points clearly to the potential problems faced by companies employing large numbers of women in their childbearing years and, also, to how companies can address these problems. Jonathan Rinehart is CEO of Adams & Rinehart, a high-quality, widely respected, and successful corporate and financial public relations firm. It employs sixty-plus professionals, half of them female. Fourteen of their female professionals are married. As I write this, in March of 1991, nine of these fourteen have just had babies or are just about to.

Adams & Rinehart's maternity policy provides six to eight weeks of disability at full pay, three months of unpaid parental leave—which no man has yet taken—and, on a case-by-case basis, some quotient of flexibility beyond that time. Rinehart, you might think, is in a terrific bind. If all nine of these professionals choose to take the full three months of leave, as I suspect they will, he's about to lose two hundred weeks (the equivalent of four person years) of billing. Furthermore, one might argue that since these women have been earning enough to put some money away, and since they are all married, they all have enough discretionary income to stay out for a period of years or to drop out entirely.

Has Jonathan Rinehart learned a lesson? Will he radically increase the percentage of male professionals he will hire in the future? I think not. Here's why.

Public relations is a female-friendly field. Ask any senior management male in public relations, and he will tell you that many of the best candidates for entry-level professional positions out of college are women, that these candidates are irresistible, and that it is difficult to find and hire men of comparable talent. So the fact is that Rinehart will probably continue to hire more than half women at the entry level. Given that thirty-one is the average age of first birth for professional women, the firm will employ them for an average of eight years before they start families (in the case of Adams & Rinehart, the women on leave now have been there, on average, for four years). By that time the firm will have invested heavily in the training and experience of the high performers.

That's the first reason. The second is that Rinehart has already taken pains to create a great environment for women at the firm. The women going out on maternity leave know they're valued, and they face no more barriers to their productivity than do men. They identify with the firm and will plan carefully for coverage of their work in their absence.

Third, Adams & Rinehart has instituted policies that permit women to take whatever time they need—in a combination of disability, parental leave, and the option to return on a part-time schedule (the all-important creative wheels in these women's minds will not stop turning when they leave work, say, at midday)—to return to equilibrium after the huge change in their lives, to set up good surrogate care, and to be ready and eager to return to the job.

Fourth, the likelihood of postmaternity attrition is minimal. Women who flourish in this kind of high-paced climate are by nature committed to their careers and need the stimulation, challenge, and autonomy it provides. A career is central to their lives. It would not surprise me if all of them return to the firm, albeit on a variety of schedules.

Finally, word will get out about how maternity is handled at Adams & Rinehart, and as a result the company will attract the best and brightest young female recruits to a greater degree than they do already.

I foresee only two problems for the firm. The first is the four person years of lost billing. That amount is, of course, a substantial expense, but one that will diminish in significance as more companies recognize it as a cost of doing business in a two-gender work force. Consider a similar case: Employee medical benefits were seen by most employers as an untenable expense when the idea was first introduced. Today they are standard in most large companies.

The second problem is that women still shoulder the primary responsibility for home and children. This phenomenon may be more muted here, since many of the new mothers probably earn as much as or more than their husbands, who may in turn tend to play a greater role at home than the average man. You can see that if their employers were to permit these new fathers more flexibility to participate in child care, the women at Adams & Rinehart would be freed up to make a bigger contribution to the firm.

If my company takes a leadership position on family and work issues, if we become truly responsive to the family needs of women and men, what sort of message will we beam out to more driven individuals? Will they all go elsewhere?

I think this is a case where you can have your cake *and* eat it. Your goal is to recruit and retain the very best women (and men) whether or not they have children. Responding to the family needs of women and men is one solution. As your family policies and practices become broadly known, they will serve as a recruitment tool for women and men who have or plan to have children. But you will convey a broader message to the women you employ, as well as to your clients and customers, stockholders and employees. They will understand that you want to be able to recruit and retain the most talented women, so much so that you do everything possible to respond to the family needs of those who have children *and* to remove obstacles to the productivity of all women.

How can I communicate an interest in changing the environment for women without raising all kinds of expectations?

You have to raise expectations. If you don't, your women will despair in the belief that the status quo will go on forever.

It is the employer who has to take the first step toward facilitation and trust. Women cannot; it is still too risky. And in all truth, it would be difficult for employers to do so themselves—if they're not taking significant action at the same time. You must communicate your conviction that able women are wanted and needed in your company, that you value high-performing women, and that you want to do whatever you can to maximize their productivity and retention. Even in the preutopian period, when you cannot have every policy in place, when supports are imperfect and barriers still exist, you can bring up the subject. You may not have the ideal environment, but you can communicate precisely what you are doing and you can draw women into the process—for example, by including them in task forces that are identifying problems and making recommendations about how to address them.

You can say, "This is our parental leave policy. These are our flexible work arrangements. We've identified a number of barriers and are taking steps to eradicate them. Thus far we have a finite number of women at the higher levels. Solving the problems takes time. It won't happen overnight. But we're doing everything we can, because we are driven by a bottom-line motivation. We have stepped back and looked at the situation in our company, and we have made the decision to address the issue very differently from in the past. We want to develop women, so if you are talented, we will do everything we can to help you grow and move up."

Then the women you employ will be free to level with you about their plans. They will know that you will be responsive. You will have begun to break the conspiracy of silence.

And that's terrific. You will be way ahead of the companies I described as going nowhere, doing the wrong things right. You'll be far ahead of those with no plan. You're moving in the right direction.

But you cannot afford only to play catch-up. If you make that mistake, you'll catch up for today only to awaken tomorrow and find you've fallen behind. And you certainly don't want to do that.

You've made all the substantive changes already. You've leveled the playing field for women *as a group*. The final step is to transform your mind-set, specifically as it concerns the deployment of human resources in a successful business. Today you have just as much total talent and drive relative to your needs as you did in the past—it's just distributed differently among the people who work for you. The trick is to learn how to mine it. You must find a way of identifying the most talented *individuals* in your company and clear the way for them. The next chapter will examine how you go about doing that.

CHAPTER NINE

Elevating the Field

*I*n the previous chapter I discussed responding to women as a business imperative. I suggested what can help women as a group and what women can contribute as a group. I enumerated the differences between women and men that employers must recognize in order to clear the way for women.

Leveling the playing field in order to bring women to the starting line with equal opportunity to compete is just step one. The next step requires watching for the strengths of each individual regardless of gender. Once you've ensured that all your people have equal opportunity, a spectrum of capability emerges. Then you can begin to identify the stars: the very best people for each level.

To do that we need to move beyond responding to group needs. We need to design a workplace that can attract, motivate, challenge, and reward every able individual, at any point in his or her life.

I believe we have to think very clearly about something beyond skills: the quality of an individual's motivation. We need to continue to ask how qualified people are for certain jobs, but we must also begin asking what individuals *want* to do.

I've talked about the rings scenario, in which all women were suspect because it was assumed that they harbored commitments to family that might undermine their career commitment. Now the reality is that *everybody* is suspect. Why? Because being male or female no longer dictates an individual's career goals. Today you can no longer depend on a cadre of single-wage-earner males with lifelong, intense career commitment. But that loss is more than counterbalanced by the availability of a whole corpus of women who, like men, have varying degrees of drive and talent.

There is a wonderful analogy for the lesson we must learn in the way a woman named Betty Edwards teaches drawing, which one of my sons experienced when he took her workshop. Her premise is that what prevents most people from drawing realistically is the preconceptions they bring to the people and objects they draw, all learned long ago, in childhood. We can accurately depict an object or person only when we put aside these visual preconceptions—the "knowledge" that stands in our way—and thus really see it as it actually is. Betty Edwards teaches her pupils to do this by making the objects they draw "unrecognizable," turning them upside down or focusing on the spaces that objects create rather than on the objects themselves. Suffice it to say that in five or six days her pupils move from drawing stick figures to creating beautifully modulated self-portraits.

When you drop your preconceptions and look instead at what each individual man or woman may be capable of or enjoy doing, you will begin to appreciate the unique talent of that individual in a way you never could before. You will discover the aggressive, risk-taking woman with business in her bones, as well as the nurturing male who loves to cook and be intimately involved in his children's day-to-day lives. You can embrace and utilize the contribution of the many individuals who today are unacceptable because they do not fit within our gender stereotypes.

The only drawback for employers in dropping their preconceptions is that it will be very confusing at first. Policymakers are accustomed to some framework in which to understand the choices that men and women are likely to make about their career commitment. I think it is valuable to understand the needs of individuals in a structured fashion, even as we recognize that every person is different.

THE BELL CURVE OF INDIVIDUAL CHOICE

Here is the simplest way I can think of to visualize the work choices of individuals. (See figure 9.1.) Some people work to live. Let's call

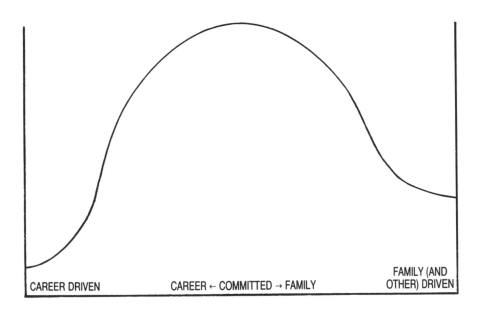

| | | FAMILY (AND |
| CAREER DRIVEN | CAREER ← COMMITTED → FAMILY | OTHER) DRIVEN |

FIGURE 9-1: The Bell Curve of Individual Choice

them "family (and other) driven." Some live to work. They are the "career driven." The bell curve depicts the range of choices individuals make along the horizontal axis. In the middle of the curve are those individuals who are equally committed to both career and family.

Men and women place themselves at various spots along that bell curve. They may change positions in the course of their lives, but at any point in time you could find any individual at some point on the spectrum.

I got into trouble once before for oversimplifying, but I really feel that for the purpose of helping employers understand individuals' work and family choices, it's not necessary to itemize each of the thousands of permutations, each of the endless variations on the proportions of work and family that individuals select. Certainly they are as varied as snowflakes and changing all the time.

Still, if you were to look at the spectrum overall, this is what you'd see. At one end would be the relatively few who are singularly driven regarding their careers. The middle would comprise individuals who want to do a top-flight job both in their work and in raising a family. Within this category the emphasis or priority varies. At the other end of the bell curve, you have those people who work in order to support themselves so they can do other things with their lives. That can mean an intense family involvement or some other activity or role. The reality is that none of these are any longer exclusively male or female goals.

If you were to take a snapshot of the curve at any given time, you'd probably find that most women and most men fall in the middle of the spectrum. They want, to differing degrees, both to pursue careers and to participate in the rearing of their children or to engage in other pursuits. Then there are some men and some women who want to focus almost exclusively on career achievement—more men than women, but even here the numbers are shifting as men seek broader lives and women become more career-oriented. And there are some men and some women who want to focus almost exclusively on rearing their children and maintaining the home. I suspect that this group will be predominantly female in the foreseeable future but will increasingly include men.

It's important to differentiate those in the middle of the spectrum, what I call "committed" individuals, from those who are "career driven," in order to clarify the work expectations we have of each.

For the committed person, career is a central but not exclusive goal. These men and women see work achievement as essential for the challenge and reward it provides but consider other aspects of life vitally important. Even within this group there are variations in the ratio of career-to-family focus and, as important, in the spread of interests outside family. Some people focus equally but exclusively on career and family, sacrificing friends, leisure, public service, or other outside interests. Others focus more on family than on career, exclusive of other concerns.

Although the committed person does not give his all to his career, he can be counted on to fulfill his responsibility to his employer and to be available when he is needed. And he might even reorder his priorities in midlife to increase the level of his commitment to work.

At each step of the ladder the employer must be ready to evaluate the employee and the employee to assess his readiness to alter his degree of career drive.

The driven individual, by contrast, feels impelled by an inner force to move in a specific direction. The force of the drive might range from a high degree of focus to outright obsession. The goal igniting the drive need not be a business goal. It can be on the opposite end of the bell curve I've described—a social mission, say, or a family goal, or a high degree of political, philanthropic, or athletic achievement. Equally various are the motivations that fuel the driven person, including a hunger for power, security, or wealth, a need to excel, or a desire to earn fame, respect, or autonomy. It might come simply from sheer love of the work one does.

It is a combination of many factors that enables people to achieve leadership positions in business and the professions. In the past, at least, most who became leaders positioned themselves toward the career-driven end of the bell curve—although it has always been possible to reach the height of any profession by virtue of sheer talent and only a modicum of application, or through extraordinary intelligence or creativity, or by virtue of competence and political acumen.

Intense drive has one inevitable corollary. The driven individual's life is structured around the focus of his or her drive. The career-driven person, for example, builds his or her life around a career. The family-driven person shapes his or her work around the family. But I believe that for both the career-driven and the more career-focused of the career-and-family-committed people, even in periods of leisure, the focus is always there. It gestates in the recesses of the mind. The synapses are open and receptive. There is what we usually think of as an intuitive awareness, one that nourishes ideas and fosters sensitivity to problems and opportunities relevant to the focus of the drive.

Many individuals are driven from the day they are born. Others find themselves ignited by exposure to a new experience or opportunity. For some it is a single period of finite duration; for others times of intense drive recur at various intervals. I believe that the more intensely driven the individual, the more likely he or she will be to have been "ignited" early in life and remain that way indefinitely.

I know of no evidence that drive is correlated to gender. The focus of the drive, however—whether it is directed in a broad sense toward career or toward family—is greatly influenced by tradition and socialization. It may even be governed in part by responses that are programmed genetically. But the important point here is that the driven person is as apt to be female as male.

It's critical for employers to understand that women equal men in their capacity for professional drive. The degree to which women are career driven gets confused by two factors.

First is corporate executives' tendency to view women as a homogeneous group. All women tend to become blurred into one less driven composite. The danger therein is that the talented woman who is career driven, or toward the career-driven end of the committed spectrum, will not be recognized early enough to get the lateral mobility necessary to advance to senior management. Employers every day distinguish men with leadership potential; obviously it is possible to make distinctions among women as well.

The second factor that seems superficially to negate women's capacity for career drive is the combination of "objective" criteria: lesser work force participation in general, discontinuity of employment over time, and the degree to which women work part-time. But although these trends reflect social mores, they don't add up to less career drive on the part of individual women.

It is most important for future-oriented employers to recognize that they can mine the talents of committed and career-driven individuals much more effectively than they are currently doing. Embracing and utilizing the contribution of diverse individuals requires changing some of the standard precepts with which policy planners approach the questions of who can best lead and manage their organizations.

THE HUGE NARROWING HIGHWAY TO THE TOP

One fundamental change that must take place has to do with the value companies ascribe to career-driven and committed individuals within their organizations.

Traditionally, the gaze of top leadership has been focused only on career-driven individuals, because it is a convenient way of identifying those who are able to rise to the highest levels of the organization. The line of succession to the top quarter (or, perhaps, only the top eighth) is by necessity a front-burner issue to every CEO. He may think of himself as steering the course, finding new products and markets, acquiring and shedding assets. He entrusts to the top three in his company the responsibility for orchestrating, planning, financial management, and sales. But he knows that the high quality of his top nine or thirty or fifty people, depending on the organization's size, is essential—both to the success of his enterprise and to his personal success. He works with these people every day, depends on them, and experiences an acute sense of loss when one leaves. I well remember the anxiety expressed by one CEO I know when he anticipated seeing another CEO whose top HR person he had managed to lure away.

It is natural for every CEO to want to be sure he has excellent alternative people continually available to back up this central leadership group. To ensure that this is the case, every company has a succession plan in one form or another that generally reaches down to entry management levels. At Federal Express, for example, the setup is elaborate and totally computerized. High performers must be identified early so that the pipelines are guaranteed full and so that future leaders are given the lateral opportunities they need to prepare them for general management.

This legitimate emphasis on finding individuals to occupy the pyramid's top quarter goes further, until these become the only individuals the CEO sees or understands in his company. And when this happens, the individuals on the fast track to the top are the only ones the company treats as individuals. It is around them that the company patterns its expectations, its culture—and, most important, its responses.

Out of this emphasis on locating, testing, and training a tiny but essential number of future leaders has developed a perception that the management pyramid is dominated by a huge, central, narrowing avenue of succession to the top. That highway, flanked by what might be thought of as service roads on either side, is occupied by the few individuals who can prove their high potential for advancement. In contrast with what we've been looking at in the last two chapters, this pyramid would probably look something like figure 9.2.

In the past this strategy was cost-effective. Traditional family roles combined with surplus labor in the postwar baby boom to make male managers willing partners with their employers in preserving this arrangement. When the single-wage-earner family predominated, ascending the vertical path to the top was precisely what vast numbers

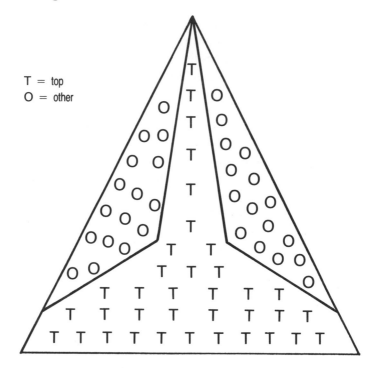

T = top
O = other

FIGURE 9-2: The Huge, Narrowing Highway to the Top

of men both wanted and needed. There was a seemingly unending supply of men who were more than willing to jockey for position on that narrowing avenue. If it meant long hours and weekends, incessant travel, and frequent relocation, fine. Their wives and families depended on them and supported them. Whatever it took to compete for promotion was acceptable. The rewards—family security, personal enrichment, and gratified ego—were well worth it.

Their sheer numbers put employers in a buyer's market. A veritable army was coming into management, raring to compete. It provided a bountiful supply of cannon fodder for top management jobs. The needs of management and the desires of managers were in sync.

In a way, the overvaluing of the leadership group at the expense of all others has had behind it the full force of America's overall economic development. The movement from the small farm to cottage industry to industrialization consolidated and expanded the role of the leadership group, along with its power and compensation. The importance of anyone outside that group diminished in kind.

The emphasis on exclusive focus is widespread in the corporate sector. I spoke with a woman who is in the very top circle at one of the large banks. To be part of the leadership group, she confirmed, requires a total identification with the company, along with a contribution of enormous hours to prove your commitment. This requirement holds true, she said, all the way up the ladder. If you have children, they must come second.

Some universities set a similar standard for exclusive focus. I'll never forget a conversation I had with the president of one university. I asked him how it was that his institution could persist in confining its tenure candidates—60 percent of the faculty was tenured—to those who gave their all to their careers in terms of teaching, conducting research, and serving on committees in the years when they were also often building their families. Didn't he realize that he would likely exclude those stars who had family commitments—especially, at such a point in history, women?

In answer, he described his position as "deliberately uncomfortable." In other words, he knew full well his policy wouldn't capture those stars who were involved in family. He wanted role models for scholarship, he explained, not for balancing career and family. He realized that this screened out many more women than men—and his tenured women were predominantly single—but he was not overly concerned. His explanation: In the pretenure years, aspirants could learn enough to function with less time later. At that later, post-tenure point they could marry and participate in family life. He was suggesting that ambitious scholars build an infrastructure that would free them for greater productivity with less effort post-tenure. And he felt there would always be enough stars ready to give their all during what were, for most, the family years.

The culture that is dominated by career-driven people is epitomized in certain law, public accounting, and financial services firms. Take as an example an adrenaline-driven law firm I know. The whole culture of the firm springs from the quest for partnership, which is the ultimate achievement—the corps of the elite. The magnitude of the financial rewards match the demands on each partner. But though only the partners earn a huge financial return, the driven atmosphere extends to everybody working there. The culture is geared, for partners, toward identifying those with potential and, for associates, toward finding opportunities to prove their commitment and extraordinary talent.

Although somewhat extreme, I don't believe the conditions described to me by some of the partners at this firm will strike many readers as unfamiliar. The firm, one partner told me, must be "the last thing you think about when you go to bed and the first thing on waking." Said another: "You've got to get obsessed and stay obsessed." This firm welcomes "only driven individuals, individuals who are monstrously insecure and need to prove themselves every day of their lives throughout their lives." And the firm's exclusive focus requires time no less than attitude. "The environment feeds on adrenaline, which comes with the 3,500-hour year and just can't come with anything less." Translation: seventy-three billable hours per week.

EXPAND YOUR GAZE BEYOND THE DRIVEN

Today, traditional emphasis on the huge narrowing highway is no longer going to bring employers the best return. Nearly all the societal elements that justified the focus on career-driven people to the exclusion of all others have disappeared. Let's think about the implications for those employers who insist on adhering to the old model.

First, there is the impending labor deficit. Employers who preserve the huge narrowing highway will see, as the smaller baby bust generation moves into the management jobs previously held by members of the baby boom, that there will no longer be an inexhaustible supply of individuals who are both talented and career driven. The labor pool will be neither so large nor so uniform as it once was; a growing percentage of its members who might have been career driven in the past are no longer willing to focus all their energies on their work. Because many of the best will take themselves out of the competition, employers who hold to the model of the narrowing avenue will be forced either to choose for leadership positions career-driven individuals with less talent or to expand their net to include those talented people who have commitments outside of work.

In addition, societal values are changing so that fewer people are willing to make the trade-offs required on the narrowing highway. Increasingly, women and men want broader-spectrum lives, which means the freedom to participate actively in family and to pursue other goals. The more balanced individual, the person with a broader perspective—who participates in family life and other pursuits—is more of a role model, while the career-driven person is less respected or revered. Corporate leaders who insist on valuing only those who are racing toward the one goal of high professional achievement and regarding the progression toward that goal as an unbroken journey are arbitrarily ruling out large segments of their potential leadership group.

One team of organizational psychologists confirms the need for a reexamination of focusing only on the driven:

> Paradoxically, organizations do not necessarily work better when they are full of highly ambitious career-centered individuals striving to get to the top. . . . What organizations need are a few ambitious and talented high achievers (who fit with their jobs) and a majority of balanced, less ambitious, but conscientious people more interested in doing a good job that they enjoy and are adequately rewarded for than in climbing the organizational pyramid.
>
> Organizational practices that overvalue effort and climbing and undervalue pride in one's job and good performance are counterproductive. Economic recessions in years to come will make this even more apparent. As the growth rates of organizations stabilize, the possibilities for advancement and promotion will diminish. People will be productive only if they enjoy the intrinsic value of what they are doing and if they draw their satisfaction simultaneously from two sources—work and private life—instead of one.[1]

Three clear benefits should compel employers to broaden the leadership pool to include committed individuals, at least those at the career-focused end of the spectrum. First, some of the most brilliant stars are those who do not choose to make work the sole focus of their lives. Presently their talent is not tapped for the top. Second is the balanced, broader perspective and life experience a career-committed person can bring to his or her work. Third is the process of self-renewal that can replace the burnout so common and costly among the driven today.

Expand your gaze beyond the driven and you will begin to recognize what you are losing through your treatment of those who have the talent necessary to move up but do not choose to make the commitment required to advance. As it stands now, they are underappreciated and their talent is not cultivated, and their motivation is low because they are not provided with the alternative rewards they want.

Ask the average CEO if a lesser commitment for some employees is acceptable, and he will say no, because he's thinking only of his chief financial officer. And of course a part-time commitment is still essentially unthinkable to him at the highest levels. Now, 88 percent of his people are not at those levels; they occupy the bottom half of his management pyramid. But he doesn't think about the contribution they can make to his bottom line, nor does he see the virtually cost-free rewards that he can painlessly provide to those of his employees who have serious interests outside the workplace.

The problems are similar for those individuals who want to move up but don't have sufficient talent. Needless to say, not everyone makes it onto the narrowing highway to the pinnacle. Those in the management pyramid with less-than-leadership-caliber talent remain essentially atomized, undervalued by top leadership, and with no recourse other than to continue earnestly to try to demonstrate their leadership potential. They put in endless hours, make personal sacrifices, acknowledge no thought of loyalties outside the workplace—as if they were on the fast track to the top. In fact, they are not and will never be.

They are seen by management mainly in the aggregate—necessary to get the work done, but essentially interchangeable. Overall turnover is, of course, always a cause for concern. Still, managers who are unqualified to move up are generally disregarded or discounted. They may even be discarded, or their departure welcomed, to make room for others who can prove their eligibility for advancement. If they quit, management is eager to replace them with others who may have the talent to advance. Yet all you need from these people is a good seven hours. In return you can give them total flexibility through flextime and other initiatives.

Both groups occupy what have always been seen as less important service roads that flank the highway to the top. I suggest that the entire structure is inhabited by employees who should be equally highly valued, albeit for differing levels of contribution. You need them all.

REPOPULATE THE HIGHWAY TO THE TOP

I believe a commensurate change must take place in how employers gauge the eligibility of those who inhabit the narrowing highway. (See

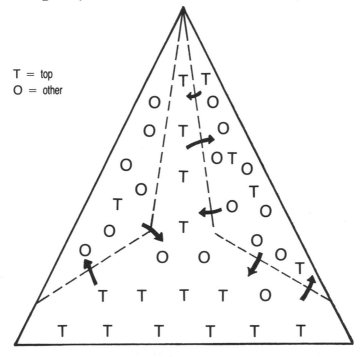

FIGURE 9-3: Repopulate the Highway

figure 9.3.) I think that that track must become more permeable, meaning that it must increasingly welcome individuals who are not driven in the traditional sense. It must also become more porous in order to allow high performers to move on and off the road at intervals throughout their lives.

Why repopulate the highway? First of all, I think we have to seriously question the idea of the exclusively career-driven individual as the paradigm for corporate leadership or for leadership in government, education, or the professions.

Then, is there a point of diminishing returns as working time is increased? Because the business community is threatened globally, it would seem employers' instinct is to press harder on the acceleration pedal. Certainly, up to a point, more can be accomplished. Maybe for some people there is no limit to the correlation of hours to productivity. But are there enough brilliant and committed people to fill the top quarter of the pyramid? There may not be in the future.

Even if we need driven people at the upper levels of the pyramid, how far down do we need them? I know a financial firm in which the assumption is that even the temporary data retrieval staff will conduct themselves as driven. Surely we must ask ourselves if that is necessary.

And what are the implications if all these high achievers opt not to produce children, as is the case with many career-driven women currently, or are unable to spend significant time with their children, as has always been and still is the case with many career-driven men? What we are doing, it seems to me, is punishing the children of very able people (and thereby inflicting some deprivation on society). There's a terrible inequity here for those people, both men and women, who want to be a force in their fields—why should they forgo involvement in a family?

Finally, there is the exclusion from the top levels of working parents—particularly women—who want to be active in their children's lives. Some of these individuals might be the crème de la crème of talent, but as it is now they never get a chance to prove it.

REPLACE THE PYRAMID WITH A JUNGLE GYM

The work force of today is a heterogeneously talented and motivated group. To be profitable, you must capture the best of these people and then place the most talented in every job, at every level, and ensure that they feel rewarded and motivated at whatever level and in whatever job they occupy.

We're moving into a world where it will best serve the employer to structure the work environment so that managers can succeed in a variety of ways. An optimal way to do this is to replace the concept of the pyramid with that of a jungle gym. (See figure 9.4.) In the jungle gym individuals' expectation for limitless upward mobility would be replaced by the option to rise to levels that are self-selected. Managers' choices would be commensurate with their ability, as well as conso-

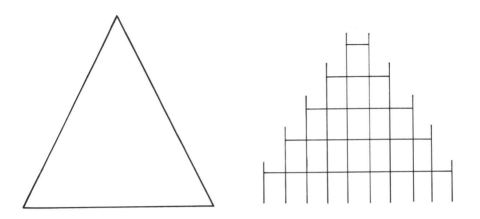

FIGURE 9-4: Movement from a Pyramid to a Jungle Gym

nant with the degree of career focus they choose and the extent of the commitment they are willing to make.

To understand the contrast, consider a simplified picture of career progression within the pyramid. Everyone, as we have seen, aspires to the pinnacle. Those who reach the limits of their capacity to advance hit their heads against the diagonal wall of the pyramid at whatever level they have achieved. They bounce back down. They have to "resign" themselves to remaining at that level, because the assumption is that if they were good enough, they would keep ascending. When the prevalent dichotomy is that you are either succeeding or you're failing, those who crash up against the ceiling feel regret and bitterness. They may stay on as malcontents, or they may leave the company, to join another where their "prospects" are higher.

Related to this idea, I think, is that of the "glass ceiling." People talk about the glass ceiling as a flat, transparent barrier somewhere around the bottom of the top quarter. I don't see it that way. Perhaps it makes more sense to see the glass ceiling inherent in the structure of the pyramid itself, and particularly with women situated as they are now. Women, outside the mainstream, at the edges, are more likely to crash against the sloping roof as they move up at every level.

Now consider the benefits for individuals in an organization structured like a jungle gym rather than a pyramid. The most obvious benefit is that individuals can plot their own careers rather than being forced to compete for the top in an uninterrupted vertical climb.

In the jungle gym, when people move up they do not crash their

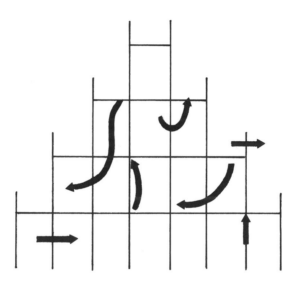

FIGURE 9-5: Movement Within the Jungle Gym

heads and fall back down. (See figure 9.5.) The various levels do not represent ceilings. Instead they are self-determined levels of aspiration. Within the jungle gym there are many avenues to the top; there is freedom to move laterally, vertically, and horizontally. Moving to a jungle gym doesn't have to preclude advancing upward in a steady vertical ascent, but it permits the horizontal entry and exit of people into that core from the bottom to the top. (See figure 9.6.)

Perhaps in the past there has been an assumption that employees aren't capable of plotting their own careers—or that, given the opportunity, their motivation will lag. The assumption has been that only by dangling the carrot of endless advancement—even when it was

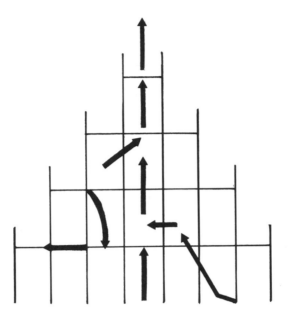

FIGURE 9-6: Advancement Through the Core

not realistically achievable—would managers be driven to do their best in the day-to-day.

I disagree with that assumption. We decide every day of our lives what it is that we want to do and can achieve. We make a decision about our goals, our abilities, and our motivation when we're talking about how far we want to or can walk. When we go on vacations, we ask ourselves, Am I going to climb a hill or do I want to attempt a mountain? Can I hike halfway up in one day or will it take me two? We ask ourselves, What can I accomplish at work today? What am I ready to invest in this aspect of my life—versus that aspect?

There have already been precedents in the corporate sector that attest to the benefits of giving employees autonomy. One study of middle managers asked respondents to rate their top three criteria for a satisfying job. Salary was not the most important value. Instead, the opportunity to take on challenging work ranked foremost, followed by salary, doing what you like, and establishing a balance between career and personal life. When asked to enumerate the best things about their current job, the managers listed autonomy, then challenge, then variety.[2] Studies have shown that CEOs themselves recognize that they must make autonomy a higher priority if they are to continue to motivate their managers.[3] Autonomy in this context means greater responsibility and independence in the course of doing one's job. But I think this can easily be extrapolated to autonomy in determining one's own career trajectory.

When individuals are encouraged to decide where their motivation and talent will carry them, and what it is they want to do, there arises a natural selection—a self-selection—of people who want to pursue careers avidly and are highly motivated to do that and of people who are just as motivated to concentrate mainly on family—and all gradations in between. You'll also have people moving freely from one level to the next and from one region of the jungle gym to the other, as their needs and values change throughout their lives.

Of course, individuals cannot make up their own minds about their career goals and paths unless their alternatives are clear. The jungle gym structure makes this possible. As in the traditional pyramid, rewards and responsibilities increase as managers advance in the hierarchy. (See figure 9.7.) But masking the legitimate equation of rewards and responsibilities in the pyramid has always been the overarching demand for exclusive focus. The requirement that everyone be driven has permeated the environment and confused everyone's understanding of the expectations at various levels and in different job categories.

The confusion about what it takes to get where you want to go has been detrimental particularly to women managers. Catalyst research within numerous individual companies has established the lack of clarity about career progression as a particular obstacle for women. Wellesley College researchers Anne Harlan and Carol Weiss found similar difficulties in their landmark study of the barriers corporate women face.

> Many managers, regardless of sex, experience lack of clarity about how the promotion process functions. It often appears to the managers that decisions are made haphazardly in the absence of objective criteria. . . . When criteria for promotion to higher level positions are unclear, sex bias may freely affect the selection decision.[4]

The jungle gym model makes it possible for individuals to understand both the rewards and the requirements as they reach each level.

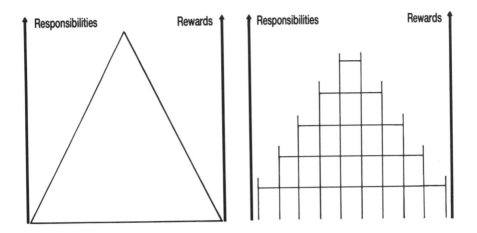

FIGURE 9-7: Responsibilities and Rewards in the Pyramid and in the Jungle Gym

Individuals equipped with such knowledge can determine for themselves how far they want to progress and in what direction.

Let me be absolutely clear about one point. I am not proposing a once-in-a-lifetime choice, but a lifelong process. In the jungle gym employees can reevaluate and move anyplace at any interval. All they have to do is move on the horizontal bar that is already there, waiting for them to step on it, or on the vertical bar, which is there for them to grasp. There's a place for everybody to go. You can find out about the opportunities, too, because communication is better in the jungle gym. You can stand on the top of one level and talk directly to the very top.

And there's a safety net—a structure that never existed in the pyramid. There, you were not only hitting your head against the ceiling, you were falling into nowhere. You were even falling from grace. In the jungle gym you see clearly where you can move next. The structure is all visible. Exposed are all the formerly mysterious channels through which people could move up. You know you can move up to open spaces and see the sky. Not only that: as low down in the structure as you may be—even if you're sitting on the ground—above you, it's *all* sky. It's just a perception of how ready you are to climb.

A third benefit for individuals is that the jungle gym legitimizes the preference of those who choose, even though they have the ability, to limit their career aspirations in order to spend more time with their families and friends or in leisure activities, politics, or public service. The jungle gym also allows such individuals to reenter the competition for further upward mobility if they so choose, with no penalty.

Finally, the jungle gym minimizes the incidence of career "failure." It replaces insistence on the universal pursuit of upward mobility with respect for the individual's right to determine his own career aspirations at any time in his life.

There will always be individuals who have both the talent and the commitment to move up but who lose out in the competition. They will still feel thwarted, undoubtedly. Still, I could almost guarantee that you will find more people happy where they are than you have now.

In some people, for example, the intensity of family drive will override career drive. Then—and perhaps this is most important of all—you have to make that choice respectable. At some point you must allow them to make a lesser commitment and to accept more limited rewards because they choose a lesser commitment. Don't discount them—in the present or for the future—because they have "failed" in their commitment when in truth they are committed to your enterprise and at the same time to some other aspect of their lives.

These benefits for individuals all have a flip side in benefits for the employer who replaces the pyramid with the jungle gym.

The first positive result for employers is the loyalty of employees who appreciate the flexibility in time and location and other alternative rewards of this new arrangement. Providing for different and changing levels of commitment is beautifully consonant with your need to find rewards that are meaningful, that will motivate diverse people.

Catalyst's study of flexible work arrangements at the managerial and professional levels asked participants who were currently on flexible work schedules how long they would prefer to remain in that mode. "Permanently or as long as possible," was the response given by a third of respondents, while another 20 percent said more than five years. In the words of one study participant: "This [job sharing] is not a way to zoom forward on the fast track . . . but staying in a holding pattern is preferable to stepping off the ladder completely . . . or, for that matter, staying on full-time and burning out."[5] Clearly, a valued reward for many, many people will be the flexibility you can provide without long-term career penalty.

In order to make this happen, however, employers must learn how to evaluate productivity rather than hours in the office, so that people can work at home and on flexible schedules. I am reminded again of the law as a good example of where this shift is already starting to occur. Billable hours make it possible to measure productivity rather than time in the office, so women are able to prove their abilities. This also holds true for financial services organizations. Because some women are highly visible as deal makers, I am convinced that women in general will be more readily accepted into the mainstream of the enterprise. It is crystal clear that they are profit centers.

Companies will also benefit when they see a reduction in turnover of able people who have become embittered.

A third benefit: The quality of people at each level is higher, because many who have the ability and talent to move ahead have chosen to step out of the competition for an interval of time or even permanently. I believe increasing numbers of people are uncomfortable with the degree of commitment required to move up to levels commensurate with their ability and would welcome the opportunity to trade off varying degrees of upward mobility and compensation for the greater freedom to participate more fully in family life or pursue alternative interests. They would be satisfied with lesser career achievement because they will be achieving other goals—rather than remaining disgruntled, resentful, and less than productive, as many are now.

This situation could be the converse of the one you have now, in which the majority of women are more competent than others at the levels they're at. They're not satisfied there because their positioning is not self-selected. In the meantime, the cliché of the Peter principle dominates for many male managers who rise to the level of their incompetence. When you allow people to select their own goals, you will find that many—though perhaps not the ones you expected—are ready to stay at levels below their level of competence. Their performance can prove a bonanza in an era when the corporate pyramid is compressed, upward mobility is severely curtailed, and competition is increasing, so the best are needed at every level.

The fourth benefit for employers is an expanded leadership group. The individual who is not career driven in the traditional sense can now move up to a leadership position. You can include both those men who are newly unwilling to give their all and women whom you have until now not considered adequately committed to their careers. These individuals may be committed to other aspects of their lives, but they can nonetheless function effectively and produce critical bottom-line results.

Then the structure of the jungle gym allows employers to do what is to some unthinkable at present: welcome back the woman (or man) who wants to leave the company altogether for an extended family hiatus—as long as five or even seven years—and return to a comparable position (joining a smaller generation where the employer's need for able people is greater) and rejoin the fast track if that's what she (or he) chooses, with no career penalty.

Want to quiet a room of senior executives real fast? Make that suggestion, as I have on occasion. As uncomfortable as the proposal makes people, as anathematic as it may be to the present corporate culture, I believe we must move in this direction. If we do not, we are sure to incur the comparatively greater cost of forcing the best and brightest to make either-or choices and, ultimately, to lose many of them.

Here's an illustration of what this responsiveness might make possible. A woman entered your company in, say, 1980, straight out of college. She was born in 1958, at the peak of the baby boom, so there were many, many entry-level candidates to fill her job. She proves herself able, promising. She takes a leave of absence in 1990 to raise a family and returns in 1995—reentering *at the same level she left.* This is a crucial point.

Now, remember that the generation she rejoins will, like her, be at the ten-year point in their careers. However, they have worked at an uninterrupted pace for that period, are closer to their academic training (having started work five years later than she), and are well known to the boss, who is most likely a different boss from when she stepped out. Those are the pluses for her colleagues.

Yet the woman who stepped out brings competitive advantages of her own. Her colleagues are younger than she is and less mature. Further, she has had her children and is ready to resume her career. She knows she wants to be there and is refreshed and raring to go. The process could even be treated as an institutionalized cycling—a second-stage entry from various levels, with some people leaving as others return.

ONE WORLD OUT OF TWO

What locks all this into position is that you're not dealing with two conflicting agendas. You're creating one approach that works for everybody.

You have a workplace, and it has two functions: it has the function of rearing children and the function of producing goods. And you have people who are to varying degrees committed to one or the other goal. By enabling them to self-select, you're allowing both things to take place in your enterprise. You're making room for those people who want to do the things that are not traditionally a part of business. You're giving them a place on the jungle gym—perhaps not always a place in the center, but a respectable position. You're creating a workplace that accepts and values every kind of person. And if you want to be a leader in the corporate community, if you want to stay ahead of the game, you can't just be thinking about producing goods and services. You've got to think about how these two worlds are going to come together.

PART IV

The Irrelevance of Gender

CHAPTER TEN

Breaking with the Past

*O*ver the years the conversations I've had with career women have given focus and impetus to my work with companies. I've spoken with women in different fields, at widely varying levels of achievement, and from environments ranging from highly supportive to grossly undermining. Their stories have provided a continual affirmation that women today are dedicated to excelling in their jobs. They have underscored my sense that companies that remove the barriers to women's advancement will earn a significant dividend: women's increased loyalty, energy, and productivity, along with their obvious talent.

Yet it has also become clear to me that the obstacles women encounter in business and professions aren't the only deterrents to their success. The conventions of family life and the social mores and traditional roles women and men have inherited also contain barriers for women. I've come to believe that women themselves can play a significant role in changing the status quo. To do that they must make a mental change that is perhaps comparable to the turnaround I've already suggested is necessary for employers. In this chapter I want to suggest the benefits for women of making this mental change. First, though, I want to share two stories that illustrate especially well the multiple challenges women face as they become more self-determinate.

The first story concerns a woman I'll call Alice, who telephoned me seven or eight years ago after I'd addressed a group of marketing professionals on the West Coast about the barriers women face and the responses they can make. She asked if I would meet with her when she next visited New York, and we scheduled a date to talk.

Alice was thirty-eight, married, and childless.

She told me she had met her husband, Keith, at the company where she worked between college and business school. They were both gung ho for their careers, and both wanted children eventually. They didn't talk specifically about how they'd manage it all, but Keith was already launched in his career and entirely supportive of her plans to get her graduate degree in business. They married. Alice took her MBA in New York, where Keith worked. While still in school she accepted an unusually good summer internship in Chicago, and the couple learned something about the pros and the cons of commuter marriages. When Alice got her degree they decided to move to Los Angeles, where both Alice and Keith had excellent offers from good companies. They also felt that southern California would be a relatively easy place to raise children.

Alice had faced obstacles throughout her career—bosses who had low expectations for women; a senior manager who essentially stunted her growth for two years because the good opportunities required travel and he was uncomfortable traveling with a woman; one ugly exposure to sexual harassment. She also spent another stint, this time for two years, in Chicago, and again she and Keith commuted to be with one other. This, to be truthful, she told me, was not all that bad: they worked intensely during the week and enjoyed weekends together. Over time she developed a protective coat at work, loved her job, and was finally, just recently, accepted by almost all of her all male peers as an "exception"—a woman who was also a member of the team.

Alice told me then that she had, year by year, postponed having children. Until recently Keith had gone along with the delay, albeit reluctantly. She had just been promoted to the first rung of senior management and identified in her company's succession plan as a contender for the very top level. This was the time when Alice truly had to give her all. But her biological clock was ticking, and she and her husband desperately wanted to have a child.

To understand Alice's frame of mind, you have to know she was surrounded at work by men who had children. Some had wives full-time at home, the balance had career-committed wives who nonetheless took primary responsibility for the upkeep of their homes and the care of their children. These men, with all their support systems intact, were Alice's competitors as well as her colleagues on the job. When she thought about what she might do, she reflected that her husband had made it clear that he was willing to help out, but not to share equally on a day-to-day basis in rearing their child. In fact, Keith thought it might be best for her to have a child and then drop out of the work force for a few years altogether or at least cut back to part-time. Alice's very significant salary—higher than Keith's—had enabled an expensive life-style they both enjoyed. They'd have to live much more modestly if she quit or cut back, and Keith insisted he was willing to do that. This didn't surprise Alice, as she had always suspected that it was somewhat difficult for her husband to be the secondary earner.

When she came to see me, Alice had reason to fear that her marriage might suffer irreparable strain if she decided to forgo having a child. But she was equally frightened about the prospect of having a baby now, in which case she felt she'd jeopardize her chance to move up. The only way to avoid any career slowdown would be to hire a full-time care giver for her child, and Alice felt she couldn't handle that, because she'd want to be a major player in her child's life. She was also afraid that Keith's minimal participation would be difficult for her, insofar as she believed strongly that a child should have two involved parents. And, of course, Alice knew that even with a good deal of surrogate care, it would be virtually essential for Keith to share in rearing their child if she were to continue to advance in her career.

Compounding Alice's worries and fears were a number of personal regrets. In college she had been something of an environmental activist, but in the years since, she'd been so pressed for time that she'd felt forced to give up that involvement. Then, too, although Alice used to meet frequently with other women to talk about their common problems, since her career accelerated she hadn't. It gnawed at her that she wasn't lending other women a helping hand, either by providing whatever guidance she could or by using her senior position in the company to speak up for women.

As Alice and I talked, we drew up a balance sheet.

What were her possible courses of action if she followed her heart and had a baby? She could take a six-week disability leave and the three-month parental leave her company had recently adopted as policy, but she'd be viewed with suspicion: career-committed individuals weren't out for over four months at her company. And until her child went off to nursery school, Alice knew she would no longer put in ten- or twelve-hour days routinely or be available for any sudden crisis. I advised her to talk to her boss, to discuss her plans and assure him that she was comfortable with limited growth for a few years, but that she definitely wanted to reenter competition for the pinnacle in a couple of years.

Alice was almost willing to try that. She felt confident that she could work around her child's needs when she returned to the job, work smart, and achieve the results that would ensure her continued growth—but not if her employer continued to be as inflexible as he had in the past, and not if she alone had to handle most of the child-rearing responsibility. She felt sure of this, even though any form of child care she desired and any other services that could make juggling work and family simpler were well within her means. So alternative one didn't seem unfeasible to Alice.

Alternative two was to have the baby, stay on for a few years at a slower pace, and then move to another company. That course seemed viable, but she'd put in many years with her current employer and had gained a great deal of credibility, so it had an element of risk.

Another idea was for Alice to find employment elsewhere, with the understanding that she could cut back to half-time for a couple years after having her baby and then return to the fast track. This was her top choice, but, she and I agreed, quite unlikely given the dearth of part-time opportunities currently available for professionals at her level.

The alternative of staying home full-time for a few years to take care of the baby and reviving her career later was inconceivable to Alice.

One last possibility was that of forgoing a child entirely. That was a painful prospect indeed. Nonetheless, it was somewhat easier to accept because Alice recognized that motherhood would almost certainly lead to a high degree of career risk, constant fatigue, conflict with her husband, and some tension over how involved she could be day to day in the life of her child.

When Alice and I said good-bye, she had no definite sense of what she would do, but the options were at least a bit clearer.

Flash forward to a few months ago, when I visited her company to meet with the senior management group of eight. Alice was among them. After the meeting we went out for a drink to catch up. Alice is now forty-five, divorced, and still childless. When she finally decided not to have a child, it ended the marriage.

She talks of a "hole in her heart" that will never be filled, and there's an edge of bitterness when she refers to her seven peers at the meeting, five with intact marriages, all with children. Alice feels isolated at work, both because she's usually the only woman present at internal and external meetings and because she tends to be excluded from the golf, after-work drinks, and social circles of her colleagues.

On the positive side, Alice still loves her work and enjoys her sense of achievement. She can be somewhat more flexible now about her schedule and gives considerable time to an environmental group that draws on her marketing skills and her business contacts. She hasn't been truly assimilated into the company's women's professional group—she thinks because she doesn't represent a desirable role model for them, since she's not balancing career and family, and they resent the fact that she didn't reach out to them on her way up the ladder—but she *is* a voice for women in the top management circle. She is proud that she's learned how to enhance sensitivity to the barriers women face by presenting them in business terms. The conditions for women entering her company now, she told me, will improve, though she's not sure how rapidly or ultimately to what degree. She's not entirely sure that the basic perceptions that have to change will do so in the near future.

The second story I want to relate also speaks directly to the dilemmas women confront in combining work and family. It was told to me by the highest-ranking woman at a large insurance company. Currently Katharine is president and CEO of one of its major subsidiaries. What she confided has much to do with her beginnings at the company.

Her career with her present employer began ten years ago, with an excellent interview. Katharine's interviewer told her she shouldn't expect to hear from them for a week, but there was a high level of good feeling on both sides.

Directly after that meeting Katharine happened to have an appointment with her doctor. She was astounded to discover that she was three months pregnant. Immediately she called the search firm that had arranged the interview. Her contact assured her that her condition shouldn't be an issue and that he would convey the information to her prospective employer.

The executive recruiter never got a chance to make that call. So impressed with Katharine were the people in charge of hiring at the insurance firm that they decided to call her at home to make their offer the very night of the interview.

When the man who had interviewed Katharine reached her by phone that evening and offered her the job, she immediately informed him she'd just learned she was pregnant. There was a pause. He said he'd call her back. Katharine later learned that he didn't know what to say or whether he could rescind the offer without risking litigation. When he got off the phone with Katharine and checked with his sources, he learned that he couldn't. She also found later that everyone assumed she was taking the job as an interim move, in order to add this higher-level job to her résumé, and that she would not return from maternity leave. The company had never before had a pregnant woman at so high a level.

Katharine went through her pregnancy in what turned out to be a supportive environment and returned three months after delivering twins. For two years both she and senior management leaned over backward to make it work. (When she was first introduced to the board, the CEO said they had gotten three for the price of one—a remark that might offend some women. Katharine, however, interpreted it as a cordial remark by a man who had grown up in another era.) After four or five years Katharine's status as a mother of two young children became so accepted as to be almost a nonissue. When some important activity was taking place at school or otherwise in the lives of her children, she made it a point to attend; even if it presented a conflict with work, she found the conflict could usually be resolved. Katharine travels a good deal, works evenings, produces. She's senior enough now to have a fair amount of flexibility, and her bosses (she's had ten in as many years) have been understanding. She finds it gratifying not to have to hide the fact that she has children—many pictures of them adorn her office.

Katharine instituted parties once or twice a year for the children of all employees. The reception by men was great, she told me—they like to bring in their children, and although it's inevitably somewhat disruptive, they've found the work gets done because people are glad to compensate for the time spent with the kids. There needs to be a recognition, she said, that work is not all of one's life, a greater understanding that at some times employees can give 150 percent and at others they have to cut back. If an employer wants the long-term loyalty of an employee, he has to recognize the ebbs and flows in people's lives.

The important thing here is that Katharine would have been forthright at the interview had she known she was pregnant. She called the search firm as soon as she knew, which was well before her interviewer was supposed to call her. But had those in charge of hiring Katharine known she was pregnant when she came to the interview, they probably would not have hired her—though she was such a good candidate that they made their decision to hire her virtually on the spot. Indeed, she has worked out extremely well for the company, as her level of responsibility indicates. They chose Katharine, probably not for the sake of numbers, but because she was the best candidate— and they would have lost her by their own hand had they known she was pregnant.

That was the gain. Here's the private pain: Katharine's husband has never been an especially participative father. He works longer and less predictable hours than Katharine, which is in part why she has been the parent principally involved in the children's school-related activities, despite the fact that she travels a good deal more than he does.

Now they're in the midst of a nasty and trying divorce. Tension had been mounting about his psychological detachment from the children and about the extent to which she was out of town. He wants custody, she believes mainly out of vengeance. The children, who are now 9½, want to be with their mother. Katharine feels the system is working against her, insofar as judges are trying to redress a historical imbalance by giving custodial preference to fathers in the courts. There is a presumption that since women have entered the work force they aren't putting in their due as mothers, along with a continuing but unarticulated presumption that the mother ought to be central. Katharine may be able to gain custody by bringing in a reputable psychologist, but she's aware of her rare good fortune in earning enough so that she can afford to. Still, she may lose primary custody.

I can't put forward a clear moral to either of these stories, only communicate my sense of their complexity. Each of the two women in these stories faced an array of obstacles as she tried to combine high career achievement with a satisfying personal life. Each chose a different approach to surmount the obstacles. Though both women felt some pride and gratification in the turns their lives had taken, there was just as surely a sense that somehow they had lost out.

This sense of loss, and the consequent tone of bitterness, is fairly prevalent among the many women who have confided in me over the years. They often ask for advice or wonder what I would do in their circumstances. Answers to these questions are difficult to provide, mostly because each individual is so different in her history, her aspirations, and her levels of satisfaction. Notwithstanding, I feel it is important at this juncture to offer some new ways of thinking about the decisions we make as individuals and the way we put those decisions into practice.

These new ways of thinking and acting have their roots in what I see as women's capacity to become much more self-determinate about their lives.

BECOMING SELF-DETERMINATE

"Be self-determinate." But of course. Isn't that just a substitute phrase for the shopworn bromides of the self-help movement? Be all you can be. Go for it. Just do it.

Well, no, it's not.

I think we have to stop for a moment and assess what we're really talking about here. After all, many of the people I speak with these days, including the women in the stories just preceding, believe that they're making deliberate personal choices, to the extent that it is possible to do so. They believe that they *are* "all they can be."

There's no question that we've made a transition. Even thirty years ago the notion of a person not adhering to gender-defined choices regarding career and family set off danger signals. Women were home. Men were at work. That was the rule, in cultural mythology if not always in fact. Anyone can spot the shift that has taken place in that mythology. You need look no farther than the popular culture of self-help books, service magazines, talk shows, and advertisements that both feed and feed off of the new cultural ideals: women who juggle, men who nurture.

Yet the lives of ordinary individuals are not quite so far beyond the role strictures of the past. True, most women have set aside the ultimatum of full-time, lifelong homemaking. But they still carry the concerns of the home; they've brought those concerns with them into the workplace, and they feel overburdened, sometimes overwhelmed. Men have indeed grown more involved in the life of the home, but with rare exceptions they haven't been able to abandon the charge that they build their lives around a career. So their participation in family life is by necessity circumscribed.

I think that we have the potential to go much, much farther. We seem to be trapped, still, in the framework of *what is*. I'm convinced that we're missing the larger picture, that there is a whole dimension of choices women and men aren't even conceiving of—decisions that can be made in the boundless context of *what can be*.

NEW OPTIONS

We've inherited a set of assumptions that limits our awareness of what options we have. Indeed, a brief survey of history reveals that our social roles have grown increasingly polarized over time, even as the need for them to be sex-linked has steadily receded.

Go back to earliest human history and you will see the beginnings of a role division between the sexes. In those early years women's ability to gestate and nurture children made their protection critical to the survival of the tribe. At the same time, owing to their superior physical strength, men were assigned the role of hunter, to literally bring home the bacon when it was still on the hoof. Men's relatively limited role in procreation made their frequent exposure to danger culturally acceptable—they were, to put it baldly, more "dispensable" in terms of the overall survival of the species than were women. Two aspects of that early division of labor hold true. First, it made sense from the perspective of survival. Second, although men's and women's roles differed, the sexes lived and worked in close proximity, and their roles were rather loosely defined.

Later, in the agricultural era, the division of labor between the sexes might have been less critical to outright survival, but it still made economic sense. At the same time there was a real sense of sharing between men and women. The family was the central economic unit. People relied on their children as a source of labor, and with a devastating mortality rate for children, it was a lifelong job just to raise a healthy family that could help work the farm.

After the Industrial Revolution, the traditional allocation of sex roles was still comfortable and expedient. It made sense for men to go to one central workplace, where the machines were located, and for women to center their child rearing in the home. As that occurred, the married couple agreed in essence with the goals and objectives they sought to achieve, though they might negotiate to some degree or another the specifics of their complementary roles. This was usually some variation on one theme: the man was to provide an adequate standard of living and the woman to maintain the home and rear the children, the former at a level and the latter in a manner that was acceptable to both. Each member of the couple had the primary responsibility and was respected in his or her separate domain.

Then, toward the middle of this century, the expedience of gender-defined roles began to fade. New conditions had come about that freed women to enter the world of men. The pulley, the lever, and the wheel and, later, more advanced technological achievements removed the need for superior strength to participate in the world outside the home. With the substitution of brains for brawn, "men's work" could easily be done by women.

I think that maybe, if the converse had been true—if all of "women's work" could have been done by men—we might have moved directly into a new, wholly androgynous world. But that didn't happen. Why? Because there is one part of women's work that cannot be done by men—the bearing of children. Now there is no reason to believe that men cannot be as nurturing as women. But the processes of gestation and childbirth and breast-feeding, in which women play the central biological role, are so powerful, so vital to our future as a civilization, that I think we became needlessly conservative about divergence from roles that had grown familiar. The fact is that except for those functions related to childbearing, the roles of men and women as parents could be virtually interchangeable. That, of course, is still not the common perception.

Both psychological and social trends in the middle of this century strengthened the division between men's sphere and women's sphere. Freudian precepts in particular had a rigidifying effect on the division of roles in the postwar generation of the 1950s. Yet the vehemently polarized ideological message that went out in the postwar era—Men, make goods! Women, make babies!—came at a time when children were an expense rather than an economic asset to the family, when child mortality had fallen dramatically and contraception was readily available. There was no cultural reason for women to spend their whole lives at home rearing children.

Traditional assumptions were certainly challenged when women surged into the work force in the mid-sixties and seventies. Many people had to rethink and redefine their values and attitudes. Still, there wasn't a realization that women were taking on a second job. And sharing roles at home barely came up as a possibility. Nor would men have been receptive to the idea had it been raised at that time.

Today we're beginning to move in a less gender-defined direction. And yet . . . I speak to group after group of people who seem mired in past assumptions. When a two-career couple has a baby, it's still almost without exception the woman who cuts back in her career, regardless of whether she wants to or not. Men who resented their absentee fathers are still largely absent from their own families. Women are understandably wary about breaking new ground in traditionally male fields. Working mothers assume that after maternity leaves that are too brief, they must return to their jobs full-time. They believe that the only options open to them in terms of child care are those posted on the bulletin board at work or those the local referral service tells them exist. They continue with draining commutes rather than finding an employer closer to home or a home nearer their employer.

We're in a new era, one in which the justifications for the role divisions of the past no longer prevail and all the options are within our grasp—but we're running on old tapes. Today it is both possible and desirable for women and men to make their own choices. Men and women can pursue careers with a singular focus. They can work just enough to support their families. They can change the pace of their lives, switch careers in midlife, move to new places, explore different life-styles. They can choose fields where the projections of shortages are great or new industries that do not have a history of male management—that came into being when women already represented close to half the entry-level managers. They can combine work and family in a manner and in a sequence that is both personally satisfying and workable.

Yet both women and men have been lulled—and lull themselves—into performing roles that are still essentially defined by gender. Just as employers have to recognize that the incremental change they have initiated so far is fundamentally inadequate, so too must men and women begin to see that the steps they've taken toward new options are often faltering and incomplete. There is a whole new way of responding to the circumstances of work and family that goes far beyond what is now being done.

This generation is the first that must ask, What does parenting mean to me, and what does work mean to me? And this double question is perhaps the most profound that we have ever had to ask of ourselves. There are no rights and wrongs, no easy givens. Whatever we do should be a conscious choice, one that is reassessed at intervals throughout our lives.

When I refer to becoming self-determinate, I'm talking about a fairly challenging, rigorous process—not a rhetorical flight or a knee-jerk yuppie mantra, but a realistic approach to living one's life. Not an ideal to which only a privileged few can aspire, but an act in which any person can engage, regardless of age or sex, field of work, income bracket, or family status.

I recently looked up the dictionary definition of "proactive." It means to insert oneself as a link between the real and the wished for, between what *is* and what the individual wants to *make happen*. The action taken need not be a radical departure from past norms, from the mainstream. However, it must result from a conscious choice to either adopt, modify, or reject the norms on one's own terms.

Becoming self-determinate means not allowing oneself simply to drift with the current, but to be proactive in creating the conditions of work and family that will be personally fulfilling. That can mean deciding to attend a unisex college or choosing a career that is nontraditional. It could mean making the decision to live in a part of the country where the tempo is slow, the climate is great, or culture abounds, where housing is cheap or adrenaline flows. It could mean dealing with an ambitious spouse by choosing a "portable" career or rejecting a spouse who won't support your career or share in rearing your children. It could mean documenting for your employer the case for working a part-time schedule or tracking down a partner to share a job. It could mean helping to institutionalize an alternative work practice in an organization so that the wheel need not be reinvented with each new arrangement.

I'll give one example of what I mean. Several years back I met with a director of marketing at a company in St. Louis. The day we met, she had just hired a woman for her department and subsequently learned that the new employee was pregnant. When I asked, she said that had she known, she would have hired her in any case.

Why was the director of marketing so confident? She informed me that at least thirty women in her department had gone on maternity leave in the last few years. Only one failed to return; one came back on a part-time schedule. The rest came back full-time, just as before. No wonder she viewed maternity not as a problem, but as an issue to manage.

We came to the conclusion that this wonderful but unusual experience was a function of several factors. First of all, everyone in St. Louis is home by six, because all the offices close at a reasonable hour and because the average commute is less than thirty minutes. The result for full-time working parents is minimal separation from children. Second, there's an abundance of child care of all kinds in St. Louis. Third, this woman's company is very flexible with regard to the needs of working parents.

I recently asked the marketing director for an update on the story. She said that although a couple of people had been bothered by the circumstances under which the new manager began with the company, she had done so well in the interim that their concerns had faded. The moral of the story is that combining family and career can certainly work, and that the choices people make have a lot to do with making it work. The conditions at this company are certainly better than average, but women and men can work toward replicating their policies and practices in their own companies. Also, however, living in this particular city—and others like it—offers clear advantages regarding child care and conventional working hours, advantages that are in individuals' power to choose.

There is an essay by Roger Rosenblatt that describes the 1989 uprising in Czechoslovakia, specifically the relationship of the individual citizen to the ground swell of mass activity. "People are born yearning to be independent," he writes. "But however they are born, people can be made quite comfortable in their dependencies. It takes very little energy to accede to one's imprisonment, but an enormous exertion of will to decide to want to be singled out, to be noticed, to make public the singular creature you know yourself to be." Later in the essay he continues, "To avoid a collective tyranny, one must learn self-rule, the idea that a democracy is made up of each separate individual, recognizing that he or she is a system on its own, frighteningly alone, magnificently alone in a crowd."[1]

THROUGH THE TRANSITION

I think this would be perceived by many women as a very risky proposition. It's easier to accept the legacy of the past, even if those roles do not serve us as well as they once did.

It sometimes amazes me to see the degree to which people invest in the assumption that they cannot make choices. They are too frightened to move more dramatically beyond the gender-defined roles that have been handed down to us.

Their fear is evident in a pattern I have often observed in talking with women of different ages and experiences. For the most part women do not often raise with men some of the questions that are pivotal to the success of their relationships with the men in their lives. What does parenting mean to each of us? What level of involvement does it require from each of us? What does career mean to each of us? What is the priority of career achievement for each of us? Whose career, if either, will take priority in our marriage? When I ask women why these questions are seldom raised, the answer has in one way or another to do with a fear of jeopardizing the relationship.

Last year I flew to Atlanta to address members of the Foundation for Student Communication, which is a group of two hundred high-achieving business students from the best colleges and universities across the country. A young man and woman came to meet me at the airport. He drove and waited in the car while she came to the gate to greet me. I was planning to talk that evening about shared roles in marriage, so I used that time to probe this student's attitudes. Yes, she told me, she and her friends talk about family and work issues among themselves—but not with the young men they know. She wanted to have children and, when pressed, said she'd probably take a year off for each. Would her future spouse share in the responsibilities for housework and child care? She said she hoped he would help out.

On the ride in to the hotel, I put the same stream of questions to my driver. Yes, he certainly wanted to have children. Surprised at my question, he was quick to respond that he *couldn't* take time from his career. Did he expect his wife-to-be to raise them? Well, yes, maybe, but of course she would be free to make her own decisions.

At the center of the silence about who will play what role in the family, and at the heart of women's resistance to facing the risks they need to take to exercise their new options, is women's subliminal feeling that they are dependent economically on men. Certainly there is some truth in this conviction. Yet I believe that even in this arena women are in fact much more capable of autonomy than many believe. Knowing the danger areas can lead women to make informed choices that will help ensure their financial security—if, that is, they understand their options and exercise their opportunity to choose among them.

This has its genesis in two misconceptions. One is the little voice in the recesses of women's consciousness that says, "Someone will take care of me." Hearing that voice, women tend still to think that their earnings are not important or at least not primary. I know many women who earn more than their husbands (18 percent of married women in two-paycheck couples do) and yet see their earnings as secondary, if not dispensable. Complicating this is that men come to depend upon the woman's income but also want her to be the all-giving nurturer in the family. This forces women into the superwoman role, which we have come to realize is a sham.

Traditionally, women left the shelter of their fathers' homes to enter the homes of their husbands. It is important that they consciously shed the dream that a Prince Charming will always protect them. Women can become self-determinate only when they recognize that they must assume financial responsibility for themselves and be prepared, if necessary, to support their children as well. After all, the vast majority of women today launch their careers before they marry and have children. During that period they have ample evidence that they can be financially independent. Nonetheless, an attitude of passivity lingers.

THE TRUTH ABOUT THE WAGE GAP

The second genesis of women's sense of economic dependency on men is the dialogue that surrounds the pay differential between men and women. I think the wage gap is often used (consciously or unconsciously) by women to rationalize why they can make no further progress. And out of the feminist usage of the wage gap as a banner with which to rally the troops has come a distortion of the concept, probably inadvertent, that has added to a climate in which many individuals are unwilling to take risks that could enable them to have more control over their lives.

The differential between the earnings of women and men is somewhere around sixty-four cents earned by women to every dollar made by a man. I often hear commentators cite the size of the gap, then emphasize the snail's pace at which it has changed over the century, or over the past thirty years, or over the past decade. In truth, in 1890 women earned forty-six cents for every dollar earned by men. By 1939 the ratio had risen to fifty-eight. In the years that followed, despite EEO legislation, it rose by only one cent, to fifty-nine cents, by 1981. The fact that the wage gap is such an effective symbol of the exploitation of women, such a powerful weapon in the battle against men for the equality of women, probably accounts for the fact that little fanfare is made concerning the tremendous rise that has taken place recently, to 68 percent, between 1981 and 1989.[2]

Discrimination certainly plays a part in women's overall work experience, and we should fight it in every way we can. But discrimination is only a partial cause of the wage gap. I am afraid that promoting it as so impenetrable has the effect of reinforcing women's sense of inadequacy—and how can an inadequate person make the case for removing discriminatory practices? To a degree it has become a self-fulfilling prophecy.

If, instead, we understand its additional causes, we see that the gap is based to a significant degree on factors over which an individual can exert considerable control. The first and most important of these is choice of field. The second and almost as significant is continuity of employment. Third is the investment in careers by women, which has traditionally been low but is increasing steadily. An individual can make choices in all these areas that will ensure she is at the leading edge of equality between men's and women's earnings.

First, let's look at the major reason for the difference in earnings between men and women: the difference in where men and women tend to work. Women are clustered in fields that pay less than those in which men are clustered. For example, they make up 99 percent of the secretarial field, 95 percent of all registered nurses, 96 percent of licensed practical nurses, 85 percent of librarians, and 85 percent of elementary school teachers.[3]

This is beginning to change. Women today are setting their career sights at much higher levels than their mothers, who were more ambivalent, less confident, and faced a male phalanx in the corporate and profession sectors. According to Gordon W. Green, Jr., assistant chief of the population division at the Bureau of Labor Statistics, "Women are entering the kinds of occupations traditionally dominated by men—professional, managerial, and technical positions—and the male-female wage gap within those occupations is narrowing."[4]

Comparable worth advocates make the important point that women's jobs have traditionally been devalued, and that sexism makes it difficult for women to enter or remain comfortably within male-dominated, higher-paying professions. But there may be reasons aside from discrimination why women continue to enter low-paying fields.

> The psychological stress attached to the position of "token" is clearly a component in the refusal of many women to try to break out of the area labeled women's work, a refusal that ensures the continuation of unequal wages. Paradoxically, the economic motivation that brings so many women into the work force may also decide them to stay in stress-free areas rather than take the risk of moving up. They need the jobs they have too much to take any chances with them.[5]

Even when women go into traditionally male fields, they have tended to self-select into jobs that fit more with their traditional socialization, such as management positions in the field of engineering. A good example of this in corporations is the preponderance of women in "softer"—and less high-paying—staff positions rather than the line jobs that lead more frequently to the pinnacle. Part of the reason is that the climate within traditionally male occupations is still harsh.

Recently I heard about a situation that reflects this harsh environment. Although somewhat extreme, I'm sure it's not without parallel in other male-dominated organizations. A woman engineer was one of only a dozen in similar technical positions at a large British fuel corporation. She was responsible for monitoring production on the night shift at a fairly remote company facility. There were no women's rest rooms on the site. The men who worked there made it clear to her that she could not comfortably use their facilities. When she needed to use the rest room, she got on a bicycle and pedaled a mile and a half into the neighboring village. In order to do this, she had to leave her station unattended and risk an industrial accident in her absence.

The wage gap is also a function of how continuously men and women are employed. There is still a sizable difference in the work patterns of men and women overall. It has been estimated that the average man will enter the labor force 3.9 times and exit voluntarily 3.6 times, while the average woman will enter 5.5 times and exit voluntarily 5.4 times.[6] It is for reasons of childbearing and family responsibilities that women tend to have discontinuous work experiences, which can slow salary increases over a lifetime and thus lower the average female wage.

Averaging across generations creates one picture of women's earnings. When you examine the pay differential between women and men of differing age groups, you see a different picture. The wage gap is a much more respectable (but still far from ideal) 86.2 cents to the dollar for the twenty- to twenty-four-year-old age bracket, according to economists James Smith and Michael Ward.[7] This is in part because younger women are on average better educated than ever before. Look at the starting salaries of MBA students. At Wharton, for example, the average starting salary of women graduates in 1987 was $44,074, a figure that *exceeded* that of their male peers.[8] (Isn't it fascinating that it was these very Wharton women who had received so strong a message from the corporate community that they even bought into the idea that they must remove their rings at job interviews!) Besides educational credentials there is another reason the gap is narrower for younger women: at a younger age women haven't yet had babies and begun to work intermittently. It doesn't show that the wage gap is disappearing overall, only that it would if women weren't penalized for cutting back when their babies are born.

This aspect of the wage gap contains a lesson for women who want to increase their financial autonomy: the woman who plans to "take a few years off" from her career to raise a family is making a decision that will ultimately affect her earnings. In the short term, obviously, she forgoes a salary and treads water in her career. She may be willing to make that trade-off in growth, because she feels she would otherwise have too little participation in her baby's development. Her work hiatus may well also affect her future earnings after she has returned full-time if she suffers a loss in credibility and is not given the opportunity to pursue her goals. Clearly, however, she can limit both these losses—in the short term if her husband also takes parental leave, and in the long term if she makes both her goals and her commitment clear to her employer.

Underlying all these explanations for the wage gap, I see the tendency for women and men both to buy into the pattern of women taking primary responsibility for the family. That can mean accepting a job that's closer to home but offers less advancement prospects, or opting out of the work force for a significant period to raise the children. Meanwhile, men for the most part perform the role of major breadwinner and therefore pursue both a higher wage and an uninterrupted career trajectory. In addition to the "someone will take care of you" voice, women hear a voice that says, "You must be the nurturer of your family." For their part, men receive the silent assurance, "Your wife will take care of the emotional needs of you and your children." It is this inner dictum that leads many women to shelve their career aspirations for a time.

When women see that the decisions they make about the fields they enter and the career paths they pursue, and the consistency of their work pattern can lead to the same degree of financial autonomy as their husbands, I think the wage gap will gradually close.

Pay equity advocates propose comparable worth legislation as an alternative solution to close the wage gap. I think that pay equity misses the point, because discrimination is not the primary cause of the wage gap. The state of Washington was the first to implement a comparable worth program to close the gap between the average wages of men and women. By upgrading the wage scale of jobs traditionally held by women to those of men in comparable jobs, the pay gap has been narrowed from 20 percent to 5 percent, and women have achieved a new level of pay and respect. Nonetheless, men and women continue to work in the areas they occupied traditionally. Indeed, the above market wages for these jobs causes women to continue to work in traditionally female fields, thereby consolidating occupational stereotyping and undermining their motivation to enter traditionally male fields. These jobs are now more attractive in the short term, but Washington's solution tends to divert women from the single most effective route to higher pay—namely, entering traditionally male fields (for example, doctors rather than nurses, lawyers rather than legal secretaries, line rather than staff jobs, and construction rather than production control workers). Additionally, to cover the $400 million cost of equalizing pay, the state had to reduce cost-of-living increases, causing a drop in traditionally male fields of as much as 30 percent. As a result, government has lost out in the competition for the best male workers: private industry has been able to lure them with higher pay, resulting in a 3 percent drop in the males employed by the state of Washington.[9] My sense is confirmed that the only practical means of closing the wage gap is to encourage and enable women to enter traditionally male fields.

THE DANGER OF INERTIA

Practical fears of economic dependency may account in part for women's reluctance to become more self-determinate, but surely another explanation lies in a widespread tendency toward inertia that is motivated partly by anger and partly by a fear that we cannot succeed in doing anything differently from the way it has been before. Symptomatic of working women's inertia is their eagerness to endlessly rehash the problems confronting them instead of working toward solutions. It may sound contradictory, but in my experience all the breast-beating seems to deafen people to any talk of change.

I saw a good example of this in a discussion I had with a group of executive men and women from different companies. The purpose of the discussion was to explore a question I posed: Could a woman take five years off and rejoin the fast track?

These are people who are committed to finding solutions to the problems women face in the workplace. Yet for the duration of the discussion they offered no solutions, only explanations for the status quo. Most were stuck on their observation that they did not know successful women who had taken a long-term career hiatus. Once they'd left their jobs, observed several of the executives, women seemed satisfied with their lives at home. Transitions from family to work or work to family were difficult. The thought of making two transitions just didn't fly with them. The possibility that a woman might return to work gradually was not raised, nor was there any suggestion that after a substantial hiatus a woman might come back to her career refreshed, free of guilt, enriched by the profound rewards of having immersed herself in the lives of her children for a solid period. When I mentioned it, they seemed to find the idea unimaginable. I am not saying that their observations were wrong; what I am saying is that their conjectures derive from observations of current behaviors. They were commenting on what is, not on what might be or what is possible.

Yet examples abound of accomplished, highly visible professional women who have taken off years in midcareer to raise a family. Marilyn Laurie, who as senior vice-president of public relations at AT&T is in their circle of top thirteen, worked part-time from home as a freelance writer for four years when her children were small. And Barbara Preiskel, who has served on ten corporate boards (including the boards of such giants as General Electric and American Stores) and more than a dozen not-for-profits, stayed at home with her children full-time for more than four years. Later, she worked from 9:30 to 2:30 as General Counsel for the Motion Picture Association, gradually expanding her schedule there to full-time. It might be argued that these women are exceptional. Certainly it is true that these extremely able women are fighters. They are proactive when it comes to making their way.

But if they have done it, isn't that proof that it can be done? Again, I believe we have to start conceiving the unlikely—that which our inertia, our fear of the unknown, tells us is unimaginable—in order to move toward a different way of finding satisfaction in our lives. We have to goad ourselves to be wary of accepting a homogeneous societal pattern that is "comfortable" for everyone and challenge ourselves to create patterns of work and family that make sense for us as individuals.

DEFINING GOALS AND MAKING TRADE-OFFS

Comedian Steven Wright says, "You can't have everything, where would you put it?" Becoming self-determinate has to start with a recognition that no one can "have it all." It's a vague and meaningless goal that can only drive one relentlessly, frenetically, in an insatiable quest for more without even the time to take pleasure in the process or to savor the rewards. I think the notion that having it all is possible or desirable stems in part from the mistaken assumption that helped launch women into the work force thirty years ago, the premise that men had it all.

You can't have it all, but you can *feel* you have it all—if you have what you value most.

We are entering an era when companies will be forced to accommodate to the needs of working mothers and of women (including those who have children) who aspire to the highest levels, because there will be a shortage of able, educated people. In this period the obstacles that women face will be identified and addressed, and more women will be able to define the conditions of their employment, including the hours they work and the location of their jobs. But there will always be a delicate balance of what accommodations employers will make in order to retain good people—and what individuals must sacrifice to achieve their goals. The central question we will always have to ask of ourselves will not go away: "What do I want most, and what am I willing to trade off to get it?" It is only to the extent that we search out the answers within ourselves that we can hope to pursue our goals with minimal energy and psychic drain and with a maximum sense of fulfillment.

The question must be repeated throughout life, because of shifts in one's attitudes and goals and in the way in which one's existence is bound to that of others over the years. I visualize the process of evolving dependencies as an atom with the individual at the center, in the nucleus, with or without a partner at various phases of life, enclosed by surrounding circles of relationships. For most the atom comes to include children who, as they grow and achieve independence, move out of the nucleus to the nearest ring and then to more distant rings. They no longer inhabit the nucleus but nonetheless stay in the inner circle with the relatives and friends who moved to more proximal rings over the years.

Some of the dominant thrusts of our lives can be recognized early on—an unusual talent, say, or a love of children, or a drive for money or for power. Our evolving personalities shape the pace of our lives, inform our search for goals, and help to establish our priorities. They will change as the demands on us from the various quarters of our lives increase or diminish.

A crucial element in the process I've described concerns the need for the individual to develop self-confidence. We must accept as right and good whatever we determine is right and good for us alone.

We must free ourselves from traditional values, define our individual needs, and recognize that today, for the first time, we are free to choose. There is no longer a rigid structure into which we must fit, no longer rigid rules to which we must adhere. We can truly say, If I as an individual am comfortable with my choice, then it is the correct choice.

CHAPTER ELEVEN

Essential Trade-offs,
Unexpected Rewards

*U*nderstanding what it means to be self-determinate is one thing. Putting it into practice is a more specific challenge. To uncover new options, I think it's useful to focus on the major arenas of decision making and activity for most people: work and home life. I cannot write a prescription that will guarantee fulfillment in either. I do know that fulfillment is next to impossible without knowing how to evaluate the realities of one's job and profession or how to interpret the long-standing patterns of behavior on the home front. What I'd like to do here is offer some observations and some questions that might help in finding the approaches that best suit women (and men) as individuals.

SOME BASIC CAREER REALITIES

There are two questions individuals must explore in order to define their priorities and make trade-offs in the work arena: What do I want to achieve in my career? and how do I go about achieving it?

Let's think about the dimensions of the first question. Included, certainly, are choice of field, where in that field the individual aspires, and the nature of the rewards he or she seeks.

I continually hear references to wanting to "make it to the top" in one's career. That's a vague and ultimately useless expression. I don't believe most individuals define the level they want to achieve in the corporation, although there are some who enter with fire in the belly and the drive to make it to the pinnacle.

What is natural is to move from one step to the next, with one's goals changing as more is learned about the field and the organization. Still, an individual can early on get a sense of what he or she wants to achieve in terms of the nature of the work, the degree of autonomy and responsibility desired, an optimal objective for standard of living and therefore for salary, and a sense of priority about money status, family life, service, power, autonomy, recognition, fame, and leisure.

In defining career priorities, you may find it useful to recall the dimensions of the pyramid I referred to earlier. The top quarter of the pyramid contains less than 2 percent of its inhabitants. Do you mean the top quarter when you refer to "making it to the top"? The second quarter contains 11 percent of the pyramid's inhabitants. Are you willing to commit to the requirements at that level—to give up a substantial degree of time, peace of mind, and freedom for other pursuits? What does it take to make it to the top half of the pyramid? To reach the middle level means that you are in the thirteenth percentile, that you are achieving a higher level than 87 percent of the individuals in your company. In any given professional firm, the ratio of partners to other professionals is, on the average, one to five. In public accounting firms the ratio is one to twenty. The commitment that is necessary to achieve a particular level varies with such factors as the industry or profession and the culture and location of the enterprise.

Understand that no matter what the organization's overall structure—whether we're talking about a pyramid, a jungle gym, or, in the case of professional firms, a rectangle topped by a cupola—as an individual advances upward, both the demands and the rewards increase. Every level requires trade-offs. Even at the lowest levels one might be trading off some of one's desire to be at home with one's family or engage in a favorite recreational activity for one's need to earn a living by working or, conversely, to qualify for the fast track. And at the highest levels the desire for greater rewards (money, status, power, perks, the expression of one's talent, or the pursuit of one's self-described "mission") motivates one to trade off other things to get them (time with family or friends, leisure, or service). It makes sense to work toward moving up the narrowing hierarchy until you reach your comfort level—that is, until from a personal standpoint the rewards are in equilibrium with the responsibilities.

The second question people must ask themselves is, How do I go about achieving my career goals? To answer that, one must be reasonably conversant with some of the realities of what it takes to reach the next level and to reach the level one ultimately wants to achieve.

Those realities differ, of course, from industry to industry and from job to job. Nonetheless, some broad indicators hold true concerning the relationship of time to performance, the rituals of corporate or professional life, and the levels of drive and focus necessary to move to various levels at various places. To explore some of these issues, I talked with a group of high-level corporate managers.[1]

TIME, PRODUCTIVITY, AND ADVANCEMENT

Since one set of realities pertains to time, I asked the group to probe the question of the correlation of time put in to upward mobility. Could they generalize about the employer expectation regarding employee time commitment at various levels? What did they see as the relationship of time to productivity? At what point does one have to perform in a certain way to get into the pool of people with leadership potential? And does that performance ever *not* have a time component?

Their consensus unquestionably linked time to productivity to advancement, with a caveat. Certainly, for aspiring managers, the expectation is of hours beyond the normal nine to five day. The amount of time expected doesn't necessarily increase, however, as the individual advances. Still, it would be wrong to imagine that time is not a component of advancement—it's unacceptable to say, "I'll just get my work done."

The time requirement for corporate advancement poses special questions for women, of course. Because most have dual responsibilities at home and on the job, women are forced to make choices men have not, to date, had to make. Women have more time limitations than men during the early family years, so it is critical to know whether ambitious individuals need to get on the fast track and give their all right from the start or whether they can do so with an interval of lesser intensity and whether there is a pattern of time required at each level within a particular company or firm or institution.

What about the eighteen-hour day? Must women buy into this total commitment in order to move up? Can women change it? This is another of those delicate titrations, like that of working to achieve flexibility for women without perpetuating their primary role at home. Women can't refuse to make the time commitment because it's the current reality, and they won't achieve success in certain fields unless they do. Of course they can choose fields where inordinate time is not a requirement. Certainly a woman with modest goals can work at a slower pace and take a few years off, if she's ready to return to the level she left. But the common perception is that an individual cannot do this if she is shooting for the highest levels.

I put these questions to Richard Heckert, former CEO of Du Pont. His response was that as long as a person was working full-time at the level at which the company spots people for top leadership, she'd be counted in the running, even if she had taken time off or slowed her pace earlier in her career.

The problem, of course, is that if a woman hasn't joined the race with the starting gun, or if she has slowed her pace for an interval before the period of selection, she is almost invariably discounted as a candidate for senior management. One alternative course she can take is to start her career with one company, work with intensity so that she can move up as rapidly as possible, and then have her children. If her image suffers as a result, she can seek employment at another company that will be impressed by the level she achieved during the first high-paced decade. The new company is likely to be unaware of the interval in lower gear, recognize her track record and her high potential, and hire her. Bravo for her and condolences to the company that invested heavily in her training and experience, had time to put her through a narrow screen of ongoing evaluation, and suffered with the relatively short period of lessened productivity.

A second alternative might be to meet with her boss, to evaluate her performance to date, at some point after she knows she's pregnant and before she goes out on maternity leave. Assuming that the evaluation was positive, they would begin to discuss her plans for the future. She could use this as an opportunity to articulate her long- and short-range career goals. Her boss would then be clear as to her commitment. He'd be more inclined to leave her on his high-potential list and be ready to respond in kind when she goes back into high gear.

Of course, what I am proposing is a bit like putting together a jigsaw puzzle without having first seen the whole picture. Yet I think we can get closer to thinking about and articulating what we want to shoot for more in advance than many people do now. Consider the case of a strategic programs manager I met at a company in the Bay Area of San Francisco. She was divorced when her second child was six months old. Then, after a five-year stint as a single mother, she remarried. At that point she decided to cut back her time, and her pay, so that she could spend more time with her children.

I find it instructive to examine the process she went through to determine her new status. The hours worked at her company are quite long, so, feeling she would not be comfortable if she cut back too far, she decided to work 80 percent of her former schedule, to come in four days of undetermined length rather than work a specific number of hours per day or week. She stressed to me her belief in reciprocal flexibility, which is necessary on the part of employee as well as employer. Thus, when she was essentially on a four-day work week but was needed for a fifth day, she unbegrudgingly put in that day. And she subsequently made another change, which demonstrated that she hadn't locked herself in to a different status when she put this schedule together. This time she decided to switch from a line to a staff position and to up her hours and pay to 90 percent of full-time. I'm sure that if she wants to make future changes, her willingness to explore options and articulate her needs will make it possible.

BUSINESS RITUALS

Time is only one issue that must be understood by managers who want to advance. Sensitivity to the culture plays a critical part in understanding what it takes to reach one's goals. "You have to understand the company rituals and honor them," one executive told me. The rituals do not necessarily require endless amounts of time, but they may require the "correct" amount of time.

For example, at one company ritual might dictate that lower-level managers be at work fifteen minutes early and stay fifteen minutes late. You're marked out of the competition if you are in the elevator at 5:10. The consensus will be, "They're going nowhere—they're going home." It's not, therefore, a question of the number of additional hours a person is willing to put in, but that those hours—or minutes—are visible and are put in at the appropriate time. If you work all the time, are there all the time, you can be perceived not as a go-getter, but as inefficient. These rituals vary from company to company, industry to industry, department to department within companies. If you want to make it to the highest levels at a Goldman Sachs or an American Express, you have to put in the time. Right or wrong, not knowing the differences between cultures is what kills careers. In these cases being self-determinate isn't bucking the culture but knowing the variables in order to respond appropriately or to select a company with a culture you can live with or where you can comfortably make the requisite trade-offs. Being self-determinate is keeping informed.

Also, if a person can deliver the business, make the sale, that person is given a lot more latitude in conforming to the company's rituals than someone who doesn't produce as visibly. In other words, flexibility can depend to a high degree on measurable output. And, of course, in line jobs productivity is usually more measurable than in staff jobs. Therefore the observance of ritual, such as time in the office, tends to have a bigger impact on the career advancement of staff managers. This presents an interesting dilemma for those who want to limit their hours. Women often perceive staff jobs as having less urgent and immediate demands, but they may require more hours because they provide less specific measures of productivity.

DRIVE, FOCUS, AND RISK TAKING

Individuals must create opportunities for their growth and movement, rather than wait for opportunities to present themselves. That is probably the most important reality of career advancement, and one I think many women find it convenient to minimize. Ray Smith, CEO of Bell Atlantic, makes the point that the ambitious executive needs to take the initiative to know "whether she is on the short list" of high-potential employees—she should not wait to be told. I have observed almost without exception that individuals who seek experiences beyond their defined responsibilities and who volunteer for additional responsibilities are upward bound.

I believe advancement comes with intense drive. There is a self-selection of people who have real talent and for whom putting in the time is no sacrifice, because they love the work or because they love the rewards. This is the individual for whom there is what Cam Starrett, senior vice-president of Human Resources at Nestlé USA, Inc., described as "an integration of personal and professional goals." Scholars, for example, never retire, because they love to spend their time doing their work; many computer programmers, teachers, marketers, and writers truly love their work to the extent that they find it more satisfying than leisure. These individuals are truly fortunate.

Some people thrive on pressure, need the constant flow of adrenaline to survive. Others tolerate it with equanimity: if it "comes with the job," it's not painful because it's getting you where you want to go.

One executive described a period in her career when she was worn out from the demands of her job, which included incessant travel. Even then, she said, "I paid that cost without thinking. I was tired, and felt isolated, but the choice wasn't painful. I was accomplishing a career objective that I really wanted to accomplish."

Another said, "You are constantly making trade-offs. Executives are always, *too*. It's never status quo. And that causes time pressure and other kinds of pressure, and you either thrive on it, love it, or you don't. Those who do it, do it because they like it."

I think that women can extend this positive approach to barriers they're facing so that the problems will get addressed. Whenever I address professional women, sooner or later one of them asks, with a tone that reflects both resignation and anger, what I have come to think of as the "What can I do if" question. What can I do if I'm repeatedly passed up for a promotion that's given to a less able man? What can I do if I'm not being given the kind of critical, constructive evaluation that will help me to grow? What can I do if my ideas are consistently ignored? What can I do if I never get the challenging assignments? What can I do if my boss is condescending, if he humiliates me publicly?

Women face obstacles that they perceive as insurmountable, because they feel that to bring them up is to be adversarial. They're afraid to be adversarial because they think they can't afford to be, that they'll be taken off the short list or maybe even squeezed out altogether. I welcome the opportunity to talk about this fear, because I believe a more useful approach is feasible. Women might try expressing their problems to their employers with the following analysis: If there's a barrier there that impedes my productivity, it's costly to my employer. He's in business to make a profit for his shareholders and to grow, so he wants me to be maximally productive. Eliminating the barrier, therefore, is to our mutual benefit. He'll welcome the discussion *if I state my case clearly and provide him with solid documentation and viable alternatives.*

For example, if a woman believes that she is definitively more qualified for a promotion than any of her peers, yet she has been passed over three times, I suggest she bring her performance evaluations to her supervisor—it will either speak eloquently to her case or demonstrate the need for change in the process of evaluation in her company.

I always remind women that what they're seeking is not retribution but resolution; what they're engaging in is not confrontation but facilitation. I would only add another observation made by Ray Smith: "All those actions we see as risky in bureaucracies—taking responsibility, correcting error, speaking one's mind, going outside the chain of command—these are precisely the actions that are *rewarded* in a well-functioning system."[2]

THINKING ABOUT FAMILY PRIORITIES

What about defining family priorities? In this critical arena, too, individuals can take more control of their lives when they recognize some basic truths.

Some years ago I saw a Planned Parenthood subway poster that depicted a wooden cradle filled with bills. The legend read: "An expected child can really rock the cradle." A Manufacturer's Hanover Trust ad message more recently read: "If you want a bundle of joy, you'll need a bundle of money."

I was delighted when I saw these ads. First of all they implied that having a child was not such a sacred act that it could not be questioned.

And it stated clearly that a couple should make a deliberate decision about whether or not to have a child, that either choice was acceptable, and that responsibility was entailed in the choice.

Today, for the first time, when children are no longer an economic necessity, and when society is no longer exerting pressure on young people to have large families, the decision about whether and when to have children is discretionary.

The question of timing is, in part, affected by the impact parenthood is perceived to have on the individual's career progression. My own sense is that later is better, not only for the maturity it permits, but for the opportunity it provides to establish credibility and confidence with one's employer, based on high-level performance over at least a five- or six-year period. But I don't think it's necessary to press the limits of the biological clock.

In any case, whenever couples decide to start a family, the point is that they make a conscious choice, and the outcome is wonderfully positive: a far larger percentage of babies are born because they are wanted and when their parents are mature and established enough to make them the centerpiece of their lives.

THE PRESSURES ON PARENTS AND CHILDREN

This doesn't mean all the problems of children are solved. One troubling aspect of child rearing today is that parents who want and need to pursue careers are forced to work full-time with only minimum time for childbirth and parenting. As a result children are often separated from their parents for nine or more hours each day.

I think any child care arrangement can work—a full-time, at-home parent along with a parent at work full-time, two parents who both work three-quarter-time schedules, two parents who work full-time with one who structures work around family, or even parents who are both intensely focused on career achievements. All, of course, are best served by solid, ongoing surrogate care arrangements. Even single parenthood with a strong support network can work. Any of these alternatives is feasible, provided it is carefully considered and freely chosen and that the parents are willing to live with the implications of their choice for their children.

The prerequisite, however, is that people evaluate for themselves what parenting means to them—and I believe this isn't done frequently enough or probed deeply enough. Part of the problem is that new parents are being pressured from every side.

One source of pressure, of course, is parental. After I addressed a women's professional group in Denver recently, a woman asked if she could walk with me to my car. She told me she'd been married for three years before her two-year-old son was born and that she and her husband had an ideally egalitarian and sharing relationship until the previous year. At that time her mother-in-law started to comment on her son's "excessive" involvement with the care of the child. Although the woman in question had a high-level job, her mother-in-law felt that the child was really her responsibility and that she was exploiting her husband. At first the son shrugged off his mother's comment. Gradually, however, as the daily demands of parenting increased, he began to grow convinced of her position and his participation lessened significantly.

This young woman—obviously sensitive, intelligent, and caring—was distraught. She felt overwhelmed by the idea of having sole responsibility for their child. She felt outnumbered by what she had come to think of as "the opposition."

A further pressure that parents experience is financial. For the vast majority, wages have not risen commensurately with either the cost of housing or private higher education.[3] This increase in the cost of living is compounded by the ubiquitous marketing message that has elevated to the level of necessity the need for a second car, a larger home or apartment, or a second telephone and television. It's important for young parents in two-income households to recognize that they may be working to satisfy their consumer needs in part at the cost of being forced to delegate the care and rearing of their children to surrogates. In addition, conscientious parents feel they must start squirreling away money in the children's infancy for their future college tuition. The multiple pressures are so great that the tendency is to succumb to the perceived necessity for both parents not only to work full-time, but to compete endlessly for higher pay and promotions. I wonder, though, whether it might not benefit young children more to have more time with their parents, rather than their parents spending time away from them in order to enhance their lifestyle.

The government sets up pressures of its own to farm out the care of children. Social critic Charles Siegel points out that "the law discriminates against families that take care of their own preschool children. A dual-career couple earning $60,000 a year with two preschool children get a child care subsidy of $960 taken off their federal tax liability. If the employer provides a child care plan, they can get as much as $10,000 a year. If this couple both worked part-time and sacrificed $30,000 in income, they would get no subsidy."[4] Parents who want to be much more involved in the rearing of their children can lobby for subsidies or tax benefits for at-home parents.

Parents today, increasingly alarmed and guilt ridden, are for the most part faced with an untenable choice *between* family and career. Men and women have been denied the flexibility that would permit them to reduce their schedules while their children are small and to return to full-time, satisfying, high-achieving careers if and when they choose. Those who choose to cut back, with a few isolated exceptions, do so at great financial risk and career penalty.

The results border on the disastrous. I have already discussed the price that employers pay in turnover, loss of productivity, and impairment of children who are their future workers and leaders. The price for parents is anxiety and guilt, fatigue and deprivation. Men, I think, suffer anxiety almost as much as women. When most men worked and most wives stayed at home, men felt secure that their children were loved and cared for. They could give their full attention to their work. Now parents tend to be equally concerned about their children. Women, however, feel a greater guilt, because responsibility for rearing the children was traditionally theirs.

Children suffer most. For the most part, in two-income families, one parent can get home, at best, at five-thirty and the other—usually the father—at a later hour, both tired and wound up. It's the end of a day that probably started before dawn with a rush that included getting dressed; getting the children up, dressed, fed, and to the child care arrangement; and traveling from twenty minutes to two hours. Evenings are not apt to be a good, relaxed family time.

This raises the question of quality time as it has typically been portrayed. Is there such a thing as "efficient" time with children? Can we be more energetic, competent, and motivated in the time we spend with our children and thereby make it more productive?

I am afraid the answer is no. I don't believe that parents can make up for minimal time spent with their children by trying to make the time maximally enjoyable and enriching. The interaction tends to be contrived, unnatural, and frenetic.

Parenting cannot be time out from life; it has to be a central part. Of course it is important to be there for significant occasions in the life of the child. It's even more critical, I think, to be around when nothing is happening, when life just goes on and play or learning or conversation takes place spontaneously.

On the other hand, parenting is a combination of the focus of attention, involvement, the depth of love, patience, support, the degree of relaxation and pleasure, the willingness to discipline that makes for strong family ties, strong values, and a strong sense of self in children. Time spent with children is a sine qua non, but it is not the only factor. I believe that the parent who has limited time but cherishes it is better for the child than the full-time parent who is always there but resents it.

CHOOSING HOW WE RAISE OUR KIDS

The terribly frustrating thing about all this is that there *is* an answer. Individual choices that are not only tenable but rewarding *can* be made. And these choices can work for everyone—parents, children, employers.

In previous chapters I have described what is required of employers. In short, men and women must be enabled to share the responsibilities of parenting. Men's role in the family must be legitimized and facilitated. Flexibility for working parents and high-quality, affordable child care alternatives must be made available.

Individuals, too, must take action. The first step is to evaluate to what degree they want to be involved in the day-to-day lives of their children. What constitutes a comfort level for them? It can't be a reactive process, as it is now, in which a parent suddenly finds him or herself in a situation with unacceptable child care or watches a fragile arrangement crumble, only to drop out of the work force temporarily or switch to a job that's less demanding. Then everyone loses out—the woman, her husband, the employer, and especially the child.

When parents recognize the need for trade-offs, they can work toward structuring a mixture of work and family time that meets their needs as they've defined them. This might start right at the beginning, at the birth of the child. I believe that the vast majority of women, given the option, would choose to return from maternity leave on part-time schedules. To be honest, I think that given the choice, most would continue on part-time schedules for at least three years with one child, five if they had two. The interval would probably be shorter in those cases where fathers also cut back for some time in the early childhood years. In a Catalyst study of flexible work arrangements at the managerial and professional levels, we found that many companies are beginning to provide part-time, shared, and telecommuting arrangements, but these practices are by no means broad-scale or extensive. Women themselves can accelerate the proliferation of these policies and practices.

One promising approach involves first identifying a series of desirable jobs and a person with whom the jobs could be shared. I suggest going into the interview independently and, when the job is offered or the offer imminent, returning with the suggested partner and presenting a cost-effective case. I think it's important that job sharers commit themselves to keeping in touch on a daily basis, on their own time. The benefits to the employer, as I detailed in an earlier chapter, include two good minds focused on the job at no additional salary. In addition, there is growing evidence that because the energy level is high, because the part-timer is motivated to plan her work carefully, more is apt to be accomplished. Some job sharers also find that many of their best ideas surface in the nonworking hours of the day or week. And, of course, there is more than full-time coverage because the alternate partner is available when one is on vacation, sick, or traveling.

The woman who works full-time and wants to cut back the job she currently has is well advised to analyze her job very carefully and identify how it could be divided. The most desirable division is one I think of as split-level, in which a large component of the work could be done by a well-supervised person with less skill and experience and lower pay. This enables the higher-level part-timer to continue with the most important aspect of her job and to train someone from within or from outside to do the balance.

In either of these cases it is important to define elements of the job, along with management's expectations and the parameters for evaluation. Equally important, in the long run, is to carefully document what has transpired. If the arrangement hasn't worked well, it should be fully described on the record so that mistakes will not be repeated; if it has worked, those who have demonstrated the case can be instrumental in promulgating it to other areas of the company and working to institutionalize it so that the practice will be available in the future to others.

Beyond helping to create alternative working arrangements, there is much that individual parents can do to expand their child care options. First, of course, is to choose a community where many alternatives are available—St. Louis, for example, or Cincinnati—or a company that has an on-site center without a waiting list or a community-based center run by a consortium of companies. Another approach is to choose a company that has hired a professional to identify, train, and supervise home child care providers or to persuade one's company to form or join the growing number of companies that have adopted this inexpensive but immensely useful service. Resource and referral services abound in the corporate and professional community, and it is useful to tap that source of information, but that should not preclude thinking of alternatives—for example, organizing a cooperative nursery school or two families with children the same age hiring a teacher or otherwise trained professional.

Again, this is only a sampling of the questions to be raised and ideas to be explored by women and men if they are to regain a measure of control over how they can build a life for their families. But no matter how proactive they are in effecting a balance between home and work, I don't believe enduring change will happen before women and men reexamine and redefine the roles they play within the family.

NEW ROLES: TWO STORIES

If you look around, there are families who have already broken with traditional patterns and created new ones, albeit not without a degree of uncertainty and difficulty. Here are two families whose stories show that it is possible to move beyond traditional roles.

I have a friend who is forty and facing a totally new set of life circumstances as she and her husband decide whether to have a child.

Helen has an M.A. in education and psychology, and she taught in the New York City public schools for five years during her first marriage. When she was divorced, she drove to Los Angeles, where she waited tables, then worked in a book store. In Los Angeles Helen met Bob. He held an M.A. in English literature and had a passion to paint. While Helen worked as an administrator in the mental health department of a free clinic and thought about pursuing a social work degree or a Ph.D. in psychology, Bob supported himself with odd jobs and immersed himself in his art. She was anxious and uncertain, searching for a sense of involvement that the not-for-profit world did not seem to provide. The couple decided to move to New York City, where Helen could explore the business community and Bob the art world. At a Columbia University program for women who wanted to change careers, a workshop in public relations excited Helen. Afterwards she secured an entry-level job with a large public relations firm, where she prospered.

Helen and Bob married in 1981, when she was thirty. Their working assumption was that she would pursue her career in public relations and become the couple's primary earner; Bob would paint, primarily, but would take whatever part-time odd jobs he had to in order to contribute to the upkeep of the household.

Today, Helen is advancing steadily, although not yet to the very top of her field, and Bob is immersed in his painting, though his work is not yet widely recognized. He spends three evenings each week as a freelance word processor in a law firm, which he enjoys both for the change of pace and the supplementary income it provides. Most of the time their roles are clear and comfortable: they are both doing what they love.

Nonetheless, some already existing tensions have been heightened as they anticipate having a child. For one, Bob occasionally feels guilty about not supporting the family as his father did. Sometimes Helen feels resentful about carrying the primary responsibility for their support. Neither can predict how they will feel when Helen's earnings rise to a level that make Bob's earnings superfluous. On the other hand, the couple's lifestyle is still short of grand—which is of less importance to Bob than to Helen—and although they feel they can afford to enlarge their family at this point, and it would seem natural for Bob to continue in his primary role as manager of the household, Helen cannot help but wonder what would happen if she ever wanted to cut back in her career for a period. She knows she doesn't relish open-ended time with her nieces and nephews, but she can't predict how she will feel about a child of her own. The paradox here is that there would be no problem if Helen had the passion to paint and Bob for public relations. I believe the two will succeed by force of their courage in breaking new ground, but I'm sure it won't always be easy.

The second story concerns Marcy, a young associate at Catalyst who accompanied me on a day-long visit to the university from which she'd graduated the year before. I had observed her unusual sensitivity and her uncluttered motivation to public service and looked forward to learning about her life experience as we drove.

When her parents were married in 1954, Marcy told me, her mother worked as a pharmacist and her father as a manager in a small company. The couple wanted children, but, unable to conceive a baby, adopted a son in 1962. At that time Marcy's mother cut back to a part-time schedule. A year later their son was diagnosed as retarded. Marcy's sister was born in 1964, Marcy in 1968, and in 1969, their brother went away to a school for the mentally disabled. For the first ten years of her life Marcy grew up in a traditional family, where her mother was the primary care giver and her brother lived away from home.

In 1978, Marcy's father suffered a back injury and was permanently disabled. Unable to perform his job, he was still able to function at home, where he could have intermittent periods of rest. Thus, when Marcy was ten and her sister fourteen, their mother returned to work full-time and their father assumed responsibility for the care of the girls and for home maintenance, shopping, and cooking. Five years later, Marcy's brother returned home. He had the mental capacity of a five year old, and required full-time care.

The lifestyle of Marcy's family was twice dramatically altered— first by her father's injury and the reversal of her parents' roles; then, when Marcy was fifteen, by her brother's return.

Marcy's father, she told me, was by nature a more nurturing person than her mother. As she saw it, the circumstances of their lives forced the members of her family to overcome the prescriptions of gender by thrusting them into roles for which they happened to be better suited. Moreover, Marcy's brother's abnormality, which at first engendered confusion, embarrassment, and resentment, ultimately added a new dimension to her life, as he came to represent "everything that's pure, innocent, helpful." The subject of Marcy's senior thesis in college was "Confronting the Dubious Status of Normalcy: The Idiot Figure in Literature and Film," and was dedicated to her brother "for his unconditional love." For Marcy, the norm is not the traditional. She is free of preconceptions and her life is the richer for it.

SHARED ROLES FOR MEN AND WOMEN

It is people like these who strengthen my conviction that men and women sharing roles on the basis of preference rather than arbitrarily by gender benefits everyone: women, men, children, and employers.

Most couples today, regardless of the career arrangement, still structure their relationships along traditional, gender-linked lines, although many do so inadvertently. The only thing this has in its favor, it seems to me, is a degree of simplicity. In so many other ways I've already described, it is less than advantageous for everyone involved. One of the biggest drawbacks is that both partners end up adopting responsibilities they would prefer not to assume and may not be very good at. Moreover, it puts pressure on the primary earner to support the family, forces him to give his all to his work and so reduce his involvement in the life of the family. The at-home mother has to sacrifice her career ambitions. Additionally, in view of the fact that half of all marriages end in divorce, and given the decline in alimony awards and lack of dependable child support, she is put at enormous risk by not having job experience to fall back on in a crisis. The child also suffers—instead of having two involved, nurturing parents, there is only one.

I'd like to pause a moment to focus on the impact on a child of having two parents who are both intimately involved in its day-to-day life. Think of the enrichment that comes with the spectrum of talents and capabilities brought by two persons who may enjoy different ages in the life of the child and may respond to different developmental needs. It offers so many more possibilities for exposure to humor, to art and music, to intensity, serenity, drive, pleasure. Two parents bring varied interests: sports, music, science, literature. Think of the breadth and complexity of emotions and responses—the timbre of the environment in which the child is raised. Think of having two parents with whom one feels totally secure, a security that can minimize the trauma of separation when one parent is ill or must travel. Think of the positive identification with a father and mother both who are nurturing and autonomous, effective, fulfilled in their careers, and of the profound effect this identification will probably have on the child's relationships with other men and women as he or she matures. Compare all this enrichment with the paradigm I just described of the full-time mother, who often feels constricted and resentful, and the absentee father.

A movement toward freedom from gender-linked roles within relationships has already begun. More couples choose to divide responsibilities so that both individuals are to a greater degree involved in both career and in family. Of course, what we're striving for, here as elsewhere, is not an exact balance of home and work responsibilities, but simply the freedom to choose on an individual basis and within the relationship an optimal balance. It's probably inevitable that career will be more important to one member of a couple and family to the other. That difference, when freely chosen, can certainly facilitate managing a household. But even when both members of a couple are deeply involved in their careers, there are still ways to make it work. For instance, the general pattern of one can be to leave early in the morning and get home early and the other to pursue a complementary schedule. This arrangement is particularly practical when the career-committed partner's work week is confined to thirty-five flexible hours. In such cases one parent can be home with the child for two or three hours in the morning and the other in the afternoon, leaving a great deal of shared family time and requiring minimal child care. When parenting is interchangeable, one parent can usually cover the home base at the beginning or end of the day when the other has to work.

On one of my visits to business schools, my hosts were a tenure-bent academic couple, both of whom the dean described as "stars." They had a two-year-old child and a meticulously planned schedule. In the morning they breakfasted together. The father dropped the child at the home of a child care provider, and they both proceeded to work. At six they both left work, and the mother picked up the child. Each stayed on to work late one evening each week, and on weekends each worked without interruption for a half-day. Of course, both were free to work in the late evenings, after their child was asleep.

It was fascinating to me to find such a rigid—and far from optimal—schedule in the university environment that, by its nature, is capable of providing flexibility. I could not contain myself from suggesting that if the couple alternated staggering their hours throughout the week—one leaving early in the morning, the other going to the university later, and each returning home accordingly—each parent in turn could have relaxed, high-energy time with their child every morning, unencumbered by the problems of the day. Furthermore, the child's time with the child care provider could be reduced from nine to four or five hours.

These are just a few of the options that will become more evident as increasing numbers of married women and men begin to share parental and work roles. What will help us move in these directions has, in my estimation, a lot to do with further change in the behavior of men. Until men grow more involved in family life, women will be greatly limited in the degree to which they can fulfill their career goals.

WHAT ABOUT MEN?

It's women who set in motion the revolution that has taken place in the home and in the work force, so it's understandable that all the discussion, all the press coverage, all the legislative efforts regarding changing roles, have focused on women. Here and there, and only very recently, articles have appeared that laud men's changing role in the family. A few commercial films in the past decade have explored and celebrated the sensitivity of men. But one has to listen intently to hear the still-muted voices of men who yearn for greater freedom and broader lives, who want to be active players in the lives of their children.

This is not to say that the women's movement hasn't had a huge impact on men. Women's exodus from the home has affected not only how men feel about themselves, but what they want as individuals. It's important to understand the continuum along which men have moved since the start of the feminist movement in the mid-sixties, so we can see not only why more dramatic change hasn't yet taken place but also what it will take to continue to move forward.

In the beginning, few husbands were totally supportive of their wives or partners when they pursued paid employment. (Some were. That's important. Their husbands' support is the first thing most successful women mention when asked how they achieved their success.) When husbands watched their wives join the paid work force, they accurately sensed the loss it would mean for them.

Now, more than two decades later, men have begun to discover that the advantages of having working wives can more than offset the losses they experienced when women left the home. Probably the greatest boon is the freedom a second income provides from the inexorable pressure to climb the career ladder. Husbands have a vested interest in their wives' increasing career success, as their income can make possible a career change in midlife and give the family a security net in case he loses his job. This was notable for the first time in the 1974 recession, when the hardship of layoffs was mitigated in two-income families.

Other advantages have also emerged for men whose wives hold paying jobs. One is the purchasing power of a second income. Another is the opportunity it provides for the man to forge his own personal identity. His wife, who was always Mrs. John Doe, has now become an autonomous person. Consciously or not, he has begun to recognize that he too can become something more than Mr. John Doe, in his white shirt and briefcase—or with his work boots and lunch box. He can overcome the early socialization that made him equate his masculinity with his earnings, that inculcated him with the belief that it was his role to prepare for a career and to pursue it full-time, without interruption, because it was his responsibility to support the family—like the little plastic man street vendors sell that can be wound up and pointed in a direction it pursues until its spring is spent. Just as his wife is freeing herself from her socialization, going beyond it, so can he. Men are beginning to enjoy the freedom to enlarge the scope of their world by participating in what was previously thought of as women's world. Witness men discovering the fun of cooking, becoming much less rigid in their mode of dress, sharing decisions that range from choosing furniture to interviewing child care providers.

Partly as a result of these changes, men have grown more invested in family life. To date, though, their involvement shows more in the level of their concern than in their behavior. Psychologist Joseph Pleck, who has been in the forefront of research on the changing roles of men, writes that today "the majority of men are more psychologically involved in their families than in their jobs."[5]

Unlike in the past, when most mothers were home with their young children, fathers today cannot leave behind their worries about their children when they go off to work. A study of employees at one large Minneapolis company found that almost three-quarters of employee fathers under the age of thirty-five had serious concerns about problems they were having managing work and family conflict with their spouses. Some 60 percent of the men said family concerns were affecting their work goals and plans, noting that they were often not seeking promotions and transfers because they needed to spend more time with their families.[6]

Although men seem to be changing more in the emotional arena than in behavior, I think we should not overlook the remarkable degree to which they have begun to share in child rearing. Sociologist Arlie Hochschild found that in 70 percent of the families in her study of how two-career couples share domestic responsibilities, men were substantially—though not equally—involved at home.[7] Today, fathers of small children, even in single-wage-earner families, rarely come home after work to don slippers and read the newspaper.

There is one complaint I often hear from women and that I'm ambivalent about. It usually starts with a pretty positive statement about the husband's role—that he's very helpful, does a lot, maybe even takes close to half of the responsibility for home and children. The lament is about his having always to be asked, of his failure to take the initiative, and the need therefore for the woman to be the orchestrator. She feels acutely the burden of keeping track of everything that has to be done, of remaining on perpetual alert. My strongest feeling, always, is delight at the husband's participation, because a change in behavior represents a healthy first step toward the change in more stubborn values and attitudes.

That said, I want to explore what it will take specifically for men to move toward greater sharing. There are four things, two of which are fairly inevitable—we need only clear the way and let them happen. The other two depend on women.

The most immediate motivation will derive from young men's rejection of the absentee father model they experienced in their own childhood. Men will increasingly discover the deep satisfaction and immediate pleasures of being part of their children's lives. They've already begun to see the beauty of being an integral participant in their children's birth, a partner with their wives in the experience, and to savor the bonding that comes of it. As men increasingly feel the rewards of intimacy with their children, they will want to take more of a day-to-day role at home.

The second factor that will push men toward greater sharing is more general but also terribly important. It is simply that the overall cultural climate is moving in that direction. Today we are seeing a cultural shift that is a positive movement, rather than a painful renunciation of power. Men have discovered the rewards of being a part of their children's lives. And the message in the air is that that's not only acceptable, it's good.

In this regard I find it compelling that social scientists have found men are participating more at home, in terms of housework and child care, *whether or not they have wives who work*. Add to that the curious fact that women don't seem to be expressing dissatisfaction so much with their own work overload at home as with the low level of their husbands' contribution. It seems that husbands are influenced to contribute more at home as much by a general cultural climate as by specific circumstances within a particular marriage.

The third factor that will push men forward is a recognition that men's sharing at home is only half the equation of the change that is necessary. Women, I think, have to be aware that men are carrying a second shift of their own: their feeling of responsibility to support the family, which I've already described. A man may increase his home participation in order to lessen his wife's overload, at her insistence or because he cares about her or in keeping with the spirit of the times, but the distribution of roles remains as stressful for him as before because he continues to carry his extra burden of financial responsibility. (The extent of the financial burden varies, but the effect is the same.) In fact, he probably has a tougher time psychologically, because by taking a bigger role at home, he opens himself to the possibility of diminishing the career achievement on which he knows his family relies.

When women recognize men's deeply felt responsibility to support the family, they'll see that their husbands are driven, quite independent of tradition or the need for power, to work harder, to persevere more, and to be more ambitious in their careers than women. If this is the case, then there's ample room for negotiation about roles within the family unit. There are solid, equitable grounds for both to support the family financially and to rear children.

In other words, rather than simply asking men to share more in domestic responsibilities, women should look toward a redistribution of total responsibilities within each individual couple—not so that each member is equally concerned with family and with career, but so that a wife and husband will divide responsibilities (and take ownership for them) as much as possible. The aim, then, is for each to do what he or she wants most to do and does best.

Many women today are successfully on the fast track and enjoy it. Nonetheless they choose to be family-centered for a period because they feel it is an important role, because they desire it, and because in the corporate culture it is still perceived as more acceptable for a woman to cut back than a man. There are other women, still, who want and expect to be taken care of financially by their husbands throughout their lives. They can remain in that role comfortably in part because they are married to men who prefer a more traditional relationship. When roles are chosen freely, a woman can be career driven and a man family-centered. If the arrangement was accepted by individuals themselves and by society at large, the resulting relationship would not be tense or combative, but comfortable. All these options fall well within the realm of possibility—if women and men both face up to the fact that each is now carrying an extra burden, if they consider what part of that burden they want to shoulder and what part they can purchase in the form of services, and if they work with their partner to arrange an equitable division of the rest.

Now for the final element that will bring men toward greater sharing. This one, I predict, will prove most difficult for women to accept and act on, yet it is absolutely critical: women must begin to let go of their domestic turf.

Now I can hear people say, "Well, of course. They're anxious to— any time men are ready!" But the reality is not so straightforward.

Women in the past had all their eggs in one basket: the home. They grew dissatisfied with the limitations of that basket. But they don't want to shift many of those eggs until they have the other basket, their position in the workplace, firmly in hand. That's understandable. Everyone needs to derive a sense of ownership from some area of life. It's natural in this time of transition that women would be reluctant to let go of their turf in the home before they acquire a solid sense of worth and confidence at work. Men, likewise, hold on to the power they derive from their paycheck, because they have not yet fully experienced the rewards of intimacy and involvement in family life.

There's a problem here, though. When women hold on to their traditional turf, men cannot lay any claim to it. They cannot learn to perform the essential tasks of home and family without the patient instruction that women resent having to give them even as they refuse to let go of the primary responsibility. Equally important, women are going to have to let men into the home and allow them to participate so that they will be able to make the work commitment they desire.

To start the process in motion, women need to give men the space, guidance, and understanding they need to enter the world of the home, just as men need to coach women to be comfortable and to perform effectively in the workplace. One way to get this ball rolling might be as simple as a woman suggesting to her husband that he begin to engage in simple things: planning events for a birthday party or taking the children to visit a place that is being studied in school or instituting a new ritual of bicycling out for Sunday breakfast.

RAISING THE QUESTIONS

It seems to me there is one initiative supporting all the others that individuals can take in order to make shared family roles a reality. Not surprisingly, it concerns challenging one tenacious aspect of the conspiracy of silence in which women and men both engage.

Earlier this year, in the course of researching this book, I had dinner at the home of Arlie and Adam Hochschild in San Francisco. I had been intrigued by Arlie's book, *The Second Shift*, in which she reported on her study finding that over the course of a year, women in two-paycheck marriages work a full month of twenty-four-hour days more than men. I was immediately aware that Adam, an accomplished writer and editor, was serving the meal and responding to the needs and questions of his son. At first his gestures seemed understandable on one level—after all, I was Arlie's guest, and it was appropriate that he "help out." But I gradually recognized that this was no exceptional occasion, and that Adam was entirely comfortable in the traditionally female domestic realm—he knew not only exactly where the kitchen utensils were, but exactly how to use them, and his relationship with his child was obviously deeply grounded and intimate.

As I left I asked, "What makes you act as you do? How did you buy into this?"

His answer: "It was Arlie's condition of marriage; of course she does the same for me."

That response thrilled me. It suggested that it was indeed possible to be proactive in this terribly important arena of men's and women's work and family roles. I'm aware that it doesn't sound romantic. How can you fall in love with somebody and then make something a condition of marriage? Isn't love quintessentially unconditional, after all?

Still, I think it's essential that women and men raise the questions and state their own expectations right up front, openly, with their partners. Because there's nothing in a relationship that can be more destructive than the anger generated by feeling exploited and not being able to talk about it for fear of the loss that would ensue if the partnership failed.

The purpose of business is to create wealth, and women will be assimilated at every level because they serve the bottom line of business's need for talent. The purpose of marriage is to provide emotional rewards. Don't we owe it to ourselves to achieve them? The one way to do so is to become as self-determinate in love as we must at work, by clarifying our desires and our expectations and by summoning the strength and creativity and perseverance that will bring them into being.

CONCLUSION

Looking to the Future

*T*hroughout this book, I've talked about today's hard realities. Now I'd like to look forward to what is likely to happen in the future as a result of the action we choose to engage in now. I foresee two very different possible alternate scenarios unfolding.

As I envision it, the hallmark of the ideal scenario is integration: work and family no longer represent conflicting demands but forces that fit smoothly together. In this version of the future, the halves are reassembled to make an energetic, vibrant whole. Work supplies energy to the home, and home revitalizes life on the job. A crucial element in this consummate vision is fulfillment, both personal and professional—again, the two are no longer opposed. Men and women are able to define and pursue their goals freely, regardless of gender.

Is this ideal way of life achievable? Certainly we can begin to approach it. It's what would come into being if the revolution that began thirty years ago, when women poured into the work force, were now accelerated. I believe further movement toward the ideal is not only logical but eminently practical.

But it is not inevitable. If we are to continue in the present mode, I foresee the emergence of a set of conditions that would be diametrically opposed to the ideal. If the status quo were to remain unrecognized and unchallenged I believe there would be a gradual increase in the quiet sense of failure felt by both women and employers. Working women's bitterness and frustration would persist, or it would be supplanted by resignation. The obstacles would finally seem too great, the work load too heavy, advancement too difficult—and the rewards would no longer appear to be worth it.

Many more women would then move out of corporations and professional firms to become entrepreneurs. There, female executives' talent and drive could run free. The conditions of a workplace they create themselves would not put a lid on their spirit or their achievement.

Yet women would continue to enter business in flood tides. Most would continue to hang in because they must—for the income, the autonomy, and the self-expression their careers provide. At the same time, corporate employers would become increasingly entrenched in the status quo. Yes, they'd continue to implement ad hoc, well-meaning programs, but as the incremental efforts result in minimal real change, their discouragement too would deepen.

As we face increasing pressure to compete in a global economy, I worry that employers would drive men to work harder, to travel more, to put in longer hours. This would lead to a point of diminishing returns, the result of fatigue and the frustration born of men's desire for broader life participation. Men would become further estranged from their families, which would in turn put greater pressure on women to take responsibility for managing the home and rearing the children. As a result, the careers of women with children would be stunted. They would be forced to take less demanding jobs and to exclude themselves from the leadership pool—a huge loss of bottom-line potential for employers and a prospect that would make women not only bitter and resentful but more vulnerable in the case of divorce.

Most likely, the pace of change would be just fast enough to perpetuate the conspiracy of silence. Women would refrain from demanding more—of the workplace, of themselves. In that case we would probably remain at the point where we are now, where it's not working, and everybody knows it, but nobody is talking about it.

If we were to continue in this way, it would appear to be progress. It might even seem as if a sort of natural selection were taking place between those women who were "innately" career-oriented and those who were family-centered. But this would be a deceptive distinction. We would be separating women according to their level of drive, perhaps, but also to some extent by virtue of which individuals are able to develop a tough enough hide to withstand so corrosive an environment. The division would not take into account genuine desire or real talent. We would essentially eliminate from the running the vast numbers of women who would pursue their careers with pleasure and satisfaction if they had the conditions that men have.

That is the frightening picture that would emerge if we continued to experience the everyday pressures and refused to confront the issues that create them. We could instead draw impetus from all these negative outcomes. We could stop short now, face the issues, and take action in order to move toward a future that is more satisfying for both women and men.

We might start by asking ourselves some tough questions. How many of us can truthfully say we are doing what we want to do? How many are supported and encouraged and assisted in our pursuits? How many take satisfaction in our work, or find intimacy and emotional rewards in our personal lives? Who can say with certainty that they are giving all they want to give to their children, to their loved ones, to their community—or even to themselves?

In a business setting, how many executives feel they are adequately responding to the needs and desires of the people who work for them? Have any corporate managers not sensed discontent among their most promising people?

Negative answers to any of these questions will provide some personal motivation to take a different approach than we have until now. But there are other factors that will drive us perhaps more forcefully toward the idea that our most rewarding course at present is to complete the revolution already begun—to bring into being the change that will serve all of us.

I believe the process must begin with corporate leaders, after which there will be a ripple effect throughout society. The primary reason executives don't want to assimilate women at every level is because they cling to an image of the past. That image tells them that women should be home rearing children, that women are dropping out or plateauing in their careers because work achievement is not really as important to them as to male employees. Women, to them, represent problems that are impossible, or at least, too costly to resolve. Further, they believe there will always be enough male high performers to replenish their leadership ranks.

I think those beliefs will change because business is quintessentially realistic, and the realities of the workplace have changed. Senior executives will recognize that the pool of labor is expanding much less rapidly than it did in the recent past, and that its composition is growing much more diverse. They will see that the traditional primary source of competence and talent—white males—is no longer adequate to meet their personnel needs. Business must utilize new sources of talent in order to survive.

Corporate leaders are gradually waking up to the fact that the vast majority of women no longer want to be full-time mothers, but to engage in work that is fulfilling and challenging and, for most, to maintain a real commitment to their families. Already, men have begun to yearn for a life beyond their paid jobs. As a result, the separate worlds of home and work have for the first time merged—into one world, where we must both produce goods and rear children. That unified world is inhabited by virtually equal numbers of men and women, some of whom are more interested in and more qualified to nurture and some to work. Their preferences increasingly have less to do with gender than they do with personal preference, so it serves the self-interest of their employers to permit men and women to define their own priorities.

It is a recognition of these realities that will cause corporate leaders to turn their thinking totally around. They will take the first step toward the future, which is to cast aside the stereotypes and preconceptions they hold about women. They will recognize the sweeping demographic changes already underway, and analyze the enormous competitive advantage women can provide for their business. Then they will act decisively, systematically, to remove even the more subtle barriers to women's achievement, to enable women to be productive, to function at levels commensurate with their ability, and to have the same opportunities to advance as men.

These first steps will unlock the process for everybody else. Women's forward movement will start with an acknowledgment that the status quo is unacceptable and that not talking about the obstacles they face on the job, and in combining family and work, only make them more difficult to remove. They will begin to recognize that they must share their experiences and talk candidly about their needs—both among themselves, with their colleagues and family members, and with their employers.

As the movement ahead accelerates, I think we will see more women and men break with traditional sex roles. We'll see greater numbers of the kind of woman I think of as self-determinate. These women will take more responsibility for generating whatever is their share of family support, and will insist on their right to combine career and family to the extent they desire as individuals.

At the same time, more men will expand their identities beyond that of principal breadwinner, and will come to feel ever more comfortable and competent inside the home. Their involvement in the lives of their children will grow. Husbands will begin to understand some little-imagined benefits of women's empowerment—the freedom their wives' earnings give them to take risks at work, to question endless relocations, even to change careers in midlife.

As the life choices men and women make begin to be dictated less by tradition than by personal preference and ability, I foresee a new ease in communication between women and men about what is meaningful to them, about what they want out of life. Men and women will feel more secure in broaching their career and family expectations and priorities throughout the "courtship" years and when they decide to marry. As they grow and evolve together, couples will be able to build partnerships that preclude feelings of exploitation and anger.

Other motivating factors will continue this chain reaction of change, pushing us toward the ideal life of the future. On a global level, I believe it will become clear that America cannot regain its competitive position in the world economy unless we mobilize our best human resources in every sphere and at every level. To do that we must develop and enlist the greatest talent we have. Women are the largest underutilized resource in this country, one that no other country can match.

Another motivation: we cannot survive unless the next generation—today's children—are committed to leading productive lives. Sometime in the near future employers are going to recognize the loss they suffer when they denigrate parenthood as they do currently, both by failing to make possible the part-time return to work that so many new mothers would prefer and by limiting so severely the leave time working parents can take at the birth of a child. I find it interesting to compare the current situation with the one during World War II, when there was no question that the call to battle was more urgent (and important) than the call to work. Men went to war, and when it was over they returned to their careers without penalty. Today, insofar as employers keep parents from fulfilling their responsibility to their children during the first years of life, by imposing the penalty of career derailment (putting them, so to speak, on the mommy track), they are saying, in effect, that the needs of children are less urgent (and less important) than the call to work. That too will change, as business leaders understand that how our children are raised will determine the stability and confidence, and the competence, of tomorrow's work force. The logical next step: their commitment to a unified effort by business, government, communities and individuals to create quality affordable child care.

These are the forces that will inspire us to move ahead, to take the risks, to absorb the costs of assimilating women into the work force, and to encourage men to take a bigger role at home. It will be enlightened self interest on the part of all involved that sets the process in motion.

That is why the role of the facilitator is paramount at this juncture. Feminism will continue to have a central place because we must have a sound, workable, coherent ideology, a clear vision of our goals and how we can go about achieving them. Advocacy will also continue to be pivotal; we must make the case for what we believe is fair and right. We must keep the issues affecting women in the forefront of attention—help men to recognize their preconceptions and biases, and to become comfortable with the changing roles of women and of men. However, we cannot afford to undermine our credibility by overstating the facts, nor should we resort to the bully tactics of the ideologue. The feminist strategy of confrontation was, I believe, an important one in the 1970s, but it tends to be counterproductive today. Why? Simply because more than in the past, the goals of men and women are shared, and the opportunity is at hand to work toward them together.

As women and men and their employers unite to deal with these new realities of work and family, companies will find that attrition of working mothers will be greatly reduced and that the productivity of those who are currently overburdened and exhausted will increase dramatically. Then their business motivation will carry employers' responses to women far beyond the necessary infrastructure that legislation provides—specifically, for example, as employers recognize the enormity of the benefit to them, the rigidity of the workplace will be replaced by flexibility. In fact, I think it will come as a surprise to corporate leaders and to family leave advocates alike that as companies satisfy working parents' needs for flexibility, the push for a legislated, extended paid maternity leave, which is imminent, will be averted, because the vast majority of women, given the opportunity, will return to work on part-time schedules. It will be superfluous to lay down the law—good business sense will provide its own mandate. Employers will even embrace some alternatives that at present seem unimaginable—the subsidization, for example, of part-time return from maternity leave of those women who could not otherwise afford to cut back. And business will learn how to reabsorb those able women (and men) who want and can afford to take extended unpaid full-time leave.

I've named some of the factors that will inspire further change. But how will we be certain that we have gone in the right direction? What will ensure that the change will continue to spread from one company to the next and from one person to the next? The answer is fundamental: what works for one party in this process of change works for all the others as well.

I predict that tremendous benefits will accrue to companies that clear away the obstacles women face and give working parents the time they need for family. Those employers will gain a clear competitive advantage in terms of recruitment. They will attract both the vast majority of men and women who want to achieve a balance between career and family, and those whose exclusive focus is their work, whether for some part or all of their lives, but who nonetheless see the benefits of joining flexible companies. They will find that the pool of high achievers will be significantly enlarged.

As more companies experiment with innovative flexible policies and programs geared toward working parents, it will become evident that pregnancy and childbirth in the workplace can be effectively managed and the costs minimized. And employers will learn the value of making a clear distinction between these finite and relatively predictable processes and the long-term responsibility—for men and for women—of being a parent.

Giving women flexibility in the workplace will not entrap women in the traditional domestic role. As men take an expanded role in child rearing, it will become ever clearer that only tradition decrees men cannot be as nurturing as women. Then corporate leaders will recognize that when they encourage men and women to select roles for themselves, they wind up not with a loss but with a greater net gain. Employers will begin encouraging men to be more involved as parents, and as a result women will be as free as men to make a resolute commitment to their careers.

Even the new technology of the computer age will contribute to bringing the new life into being. The industrial age brought us into cities, where the clock synchronized the convergence of men in one central place of work. Since women joined men on the job, the clock has more than ever come to tyrannize the family.

Now the computer, the fax, the multipurpose telephone system, and overnight mail, can make it possible for more families to move back to the home-based work site, where parents and children can share experiences in a way that is more attuned to natural, biological rhythms. All that's required of employers is a change of perception, as they learn to measure productivity rather than time in the office. Furthermore, as the service sector of the economy expands, the proliferation of small companies in the areas they serve will permit employees to live closer to home.

The result: those who want it will have more time for intimacy within families and among friends. And I think, too, that among those who choose to live life at a slower pace or to cut back for intervals in their lives, some will bring a different, important perspective to a world caught up in an ever-accelerating pace.

All this lies in the future. It's the reality of the possible, rather than the present. But it will not just happen, and it won't be brought about by somebody else. Each of us must reach this recognition, face the truths that we now tend to dismiss, and take action to change the current reality. Only then will the future ideal become the present reality.

As I write this, my thoughts return to those women in the Wharton MBA class of 1991 who felt compelled to remove their rings when they interviewed for jobs. As we emerge from the current recession and job opportunities open up, I don't think it's unrealistic to imagine that the graduates of 1993 will have less temptation to remove their rings. Nor do I think it a mere flight of fancy to imagine a graduate of Wharton 1995 walking into an interview with a ring on her finger, confidence in her manner and a pregnancy well underway. What seems impossible today will, I believe, become tomorrow's facts of life.

END NOTES

CHAPTER ONE: *The Riddle of the Rings*

1. Unpublished transcript, focus group at Wharton Business School, February 12, 1990.

2. Ibid.

3. Ibid.

4. Ibid.

5. "Labor Letter," *The Wall Street Journal* (February 13, 1990).

6. "Facts About Today's Women's Colleges," Women's College Coalition, August 1990.

7. Capitol Forum quote from unpublished notes, April 6, 1990.

8. Smith Management Program, July 27, 1990.

9. Unpublished taped discussion with faculty, Tuck School of Business Administration, April 18, 1990.

10. Private conversation, April 18, 1990.

11. Private conversation, April 11, 1990.

CHAPTER TWO: *The Conspiracy of Silence*

1. This and all subsequent quotes in the "K" story from unpublished transcript, working mothers focus group at Catalyst, August 7, 1990.

CHAPTER THREE: *What Aren't We Talking About?*

1. Reuben Mark, CEO of Colgate Palmolive; Edith Boen, vice-president at Boeing; and Marian Spragings, a managing partner at Smith Barney: "CBS This Morning," July 23, 1990.

2. Unpublished transcript, working mothers focus group, Catalyst, August 1, 1990.

3. Carol Hymowitz, "Women on Fast Track Try to Keep Their Careers and Children Separate," *The Wall Street Journal* (September 19, 1984).

4. Anecdote courtesy of Marilyn Machlowitz. From June 1990 Financial Women's Association Downtown Working Mothers Group meeting.

5. Unpublished transcript, working mothers focus group, Catalyst, August 7, 1990.

6. *Work and Family Benefits Provided by Major U.S. Employers in 1990* (Linconshire, Illinois: Hewitt Associates, 1990).

7. Catalyst, confidential study of maternity within one company.

8. "Bars to Equality of Sexes Seen as Eroding, Slowly," *The New York Times* (August 20, 1989).

9. All quotes from unpublished studies, Catalyst.

10. Alison Leigh Cowan, "Trend in Pregnancies Challenges Employers," *The New York Times* (April 17, 1989). Study cited was conducted in 1987.

11. Martha O'Connell, "Maternity Leave Arrangements: 1961–85," *Work and Family Patterns of American Women*, Current Population Reports, series P-23, no. 165 (Washington, D.C.: U.S. Government Printing Office, March 1990).

12. Catalyst, *Report on a National Study of Parental Leaves*, 1986.

13. Study by Decisions Center, Inc., a N.Y.-based marketing research firm. Cited in CAM report, January 15, 1990.

CHAPTER FOUR: *Public Progress, Private Pain*

1. Suzanne M. Bianchi and Daphne Spain, *American Women in Transition* (New York: Russell Sage Foundation, 1986).

2. U.S. Bureau of the Census, Current Population Reports, series P-23, no. 163, *Changes in American Family Life* (Washington, D.C.: U.S. Government Printing Office, 1989).

3. Bianchi and Spain, op. cit.

4. Bianchi and Spain, op. cit., and *Employment and Earnings* (Washington, D.C.: U.S. Department of Labor, Bureau of Labor Statistics, May 1991).

5. U.S. Bureau of the Census, Current Population Reports, series P-23, no. 163, *Changes in American Family Life* (Washington, D.C.: U.S. Government Printing Office, 1989).

6. Bureau of Labor Statistics, unpublished statistics, 1990.

7. This is 52.5 percent as of 1989. *1991 Edition, Educational Statistics* (Washington, D.C.: U.S. Department of Education).

8. Ibid.

9. Ibid.

10. Ibid.

11. Ibid.

12. Ibid.

13. Ibid.

14. U.S. Bureau of the Census, *Changes in American Family Life*, op. cit.

15. Ibid.

16. Sheila M. Rothman, *Women's Proper Place* (New York: Basic Books, 1978).

17. James R. Wetzel, "American Families: 75 Years of Change," *Monthly Labor Review* (March 1990).

18. Elizabeth Douvan, "Differing Views on Marriage—1957 to 1976," *Newsletter, Center for Continuing Education of Women*, vol. XII, no. 1 (spring 1979. Ann Arbor, Mich: The University of Michigan).

19. Rita J. Simon and Jean M. Landis, "Women's and Men's Attitudes About a Woman's Place and Role," *Public Opinion Quarterly* (summer 1989).

20. Private correspondence, May 13, 1968.

21. Private correspondence, April 18, 1969.

22. Merle A. Gulick, vice-president, public relations-personnel, Equitable Life Assurance Company, "The Role of the Educated Woman in Today's World," a speech given on Founder's Day, William Smith College, December 11, 1960.

23. Mary P. Rowe, Ph.D., "Prospects and Patterns for Men and Women at Work: To Be Able Both to Love and to Work," a speech by the special assistant for women and work, Massachusetts Institute of Technology, at the Centennial Convocation, MIT, June 2, 1973.

24. Bianchi and Spain, op. cit.

25. Schwartz, E.G., *The Sex Barrier in Business* (Atlanta: Georgia State University Press, 1971). Cited in Anne Harlan and Carol Weiss, *Moving Up: Women in Managerial Careers* (Wellesley, MA: Wellesley College Center for Research on Women, 1981).

26. Gary N. Powell, *Women and Men in Management* (Newbury Park, Calif.: Russell Sage Publications, 1988).

27. Virginia Slims poll cited in Maureen Dowd, "Many Women in Poll Value Jobs as Much as Family Life," *The New York Times* (December 4, 1983).

28. Jessie Bernard, *The Future of Marriage* (New York: Bantam, 1973).

29. Catalyst, *Corporations and Two-Career Families: Directions for the Future*, 1981.

30. Felice N. Schwartz, president, Catalyst, "The Two-Career Family," remarks at Fourth Annual Awards Dinner, March 6, 1979.

31. Heidrick and Struggles, *The Corporate Woman Officer*, 1986.

32. *Korn/Ferry International's Profile of Women Senior Executives*, Korn/Ferry International, 1986.

33. *The Wall Street Journal Study of Women Executives*, conducted by the Gallup Organization, 1984.

34. *Korn/Ferry*, op. cit.

35. "Probing Opinions: Executive Women—20 Years Later," *Harvard Business Review* (October 1985).

36. The 1985 Virginia Slims American Women's Opinion Poll, conducted by the Roper Organization.

37. "Taking Stock: Wharton Women Face Tough Decisions Ten Years Out," *Wharton Alumni Magazine* (fall 1989).

38. Bar graph printed in Horst H. Stipp, "What Is a Working Woman?" *American Demographics* (July 1988).

39. Simon and Landis, op. cit.

40. Tamar Lewin, "Women Say They Face Obstacles as Lawyers," *The New York Times* (December 4, 1989).

CHAPTER FIVE: *The "Mommy Track": Anatomy of a Reaction*

1. This and subsequent quotes in this section are from private correspondence, 1989.

2. Ellen Goodman, "Why Do Women Execs Cost More Than Men?" *Newsday* (January 24, 1989).

3. Ibid.

4. Ibid.

5. Dana Friedman, "Why the Glass Ceiling?" *Across the Board* (July/August 1988).

6. Maureen Orth, "Home and Glory," *New York Woman* (October 1988).

7. Felice N. Schwartz, "Management Women and the New Facts of Life," *Harvard Business Review* (January/February 1989).

8. Ibid.

9. Jennifer Kingston, "Women in the Law Say Path Is Limited by 'Mommy Track,'" *The New York Times* (August 7, 1988).

10. Unpublished letter, August 15, 1988.

11. Tamar Lewin, " 'Mommy Career Track' Sets Off a Furor," *The New York Times* (March 8, 1989).

12. Felice N. Schwartz, "Management Women and the New Facts of Life," op. cit.

13. The 1985 Korn/Ferry survey of corporate leaders contrasted with 1982 Korn/Ferry survey of three hundred executive women.

14. Janice Castro, "Rolling Along the Mommy Track," *Time* (March 27, 1989).

15. Nora Frenkel, "The Mommy Track," *The Baltimore Sun* (March 14, 1989).

16. "Advocating a 'Mommy Track,' " *Newsweek* (March 13, 1989).

17. Karen Croke, "Making Tracks," *New York Daily News* (March 19, 1989).

18. Mary Sit, "Misunderstood?," *Boston Globe* (March 15, 1989).

19. Beverly Beyette, "A New Career Flap," *Los Angeles Times* (March 17, 1989).

20. Barbara Ehrenreich and Deirdre English, "Blowing the Whistle on the 'Mommy Track,' " *Ms.* (July/August, 1989).

21. "Why Not Many Mommy Tracks?" *The New York Times* (March 13, 1989).

22. Joseph Pleck, "Fathers and Infant Care Leave," *The Parental Leave Crisis: Toward a National Policy* (New Haven and London: Yale University Press, 1988). Eds.: Edward P. Zigler and Meryl Frank.

23. Gail Collins, "The Mommy Track to Nowhere," *New York Woman* (September 1989).

24. "Notes and Comment," *The New Yorker* (October 2, 1989).

25. The apology in the September-October 1989 issue of the *Harvard Business Review* read as follows:

> It is the practice of the *Harvard Business Review* to stimulate discussion and encourage debate about its articles in order to expand awareness, enrich understanding, and generate creative ideas and solutions. This is done in various ways, including letters to the editor.
>
> To debate the ideas raised by Felice N. Schwartz's article, "Management Women and the New Facts of Life" (January-February 1989), people were invited to submit letters. Many who responded were highly visible individuals with a history of advocacy or at least a predictably adversarial point of view. Three days

before the press deadline, to expand the range of opinions, the editors solicited additional comments from a list provided by Ms. Schwartz. However, this time constraint limited the representation of corporate leaders—men and women—who are in a position to effect the changes that Felice Schwartz predicts will take place. *HBR* apologizes to Felice Schwartz and readers who feel that the process produced an imbalance in the printed letters.

26. Women in the media were my biggest adversaries, and women in the media are having the toughest time of any industry. The two are probably not unrelated.

27. Rick Gladstone, "Catalyst Owner Spends Her Time Repudiating 'Mommy Track,' " *Sunday Democrat and Chronicle* (March 18, 1990 Rochester, New York).

28. Ellen Hopkins, "Who Is Felice Schwartz and Why Is She Saying Those Terrible Things About Us?" *Working Woman* (October 1990).

CHAPTER SIX: *The Demographic Imperative*

1. Frederick W. Hollman, U.S. Bureau of the Census, "United States Population Estimates, by Age, Sex, Race, and Hispanic Origin: 1980 to 1988," *Current Population Reports*, series P-25, no. 1045 (Washington, D.C.: U.S. Government Printing Office, 1990). Table M.

  Gregory Spencer, U.S. Bureau of the Census, "Projections of the Population of the United States, by Age, Sex, and Race: 1988 to 2080," *Current Population Reports*, series P-25, no. 1018 (Washington, D.C.: U.S. Government Printing Office, 1989). Table A-3.

  Both sources cited in: Cynthia Taeuber, *Statistical Handbook on Women in America* (Phoenix, Arizona: The Oryx Press, 1991).

2. "Projections of the Population of the United States, by Age, Sex and Race: 1988 to 2080," U.S. Bureau of the Census, Current Population Reports, series P-25, no. 1018 (January 1989).

3. GNP trends provided by Stern, Roe & Farnham, prepared from the following data:

  Business Statistics, Washington, D.C.: U.S. Dept. of Commerce, Bureau of Economic Analysis. Biennial volumes 1951–1971, issued by the Office of Business Economics; 1973– by the Bureau of Economic Analysis.

  Survey of Current Business and Supplement, U.S. Department of Commerce, Bureau of Economic Analysis (December 1990).

4. This inexorable downward trend will not necessarily translate to full employment. As we move toward a service and information economy, the primary demands of the service sector will be for relatively unskilled workers and the primary demands of the information sector will be for highly educated workers. As a result, a large group of those people who are overeducated for the former and undereducated for the latter might go unemployed.

5. U.S. Department of Education, Division of Adult Education and Literacy, Office of Vocational and Adult Education (January 1990).

6. Lorraine Dusky, "Are You Ready for the '90s?" *Working Woman* (January 1990).

7. David Kearns, speech to the Industrial Management Council, November 13, 1989.

8. "Demographics of the '90s: The Issues and Implications for Public Policy," R. Scott Fosler, vice-president and director of government studies, Committee for Economic Development, speech delivered to the Public Affairs Council, Washington, D.C., April 12, 1989. *Vital Speeches of the Day*, July 1, 1989.

9. Harry Bracas, "Desperately Seeking Workers," *Nation's Business* (February 1988).

10. Pamela Kruger, "A Game Plan for the Future," *Working Woman* (January 1990).

11. Cindy Richards, "Agency Cooks Up Job Lure to Keep Students in School," *Chicago Sun-Times* (May 10, 1990).

12. Quoted in Lynne F. McGee, "Innovative Labor Shortage Solutions," *Personnel Administrator* (December 1989).

13. Ibid.

14. *Workforce 2000, Competing in a Seller's Market: Is Corporate America Prepared?* survey report on corporate responses to demographic and labor force trends, Towers Perrin and the Hudson Institute (August 1990).

15. Howard N. Fullerton, Jr., "New Labor Force Projections, Spanning 1988 to 2000," *Monthly Labor Review* (November 1989).

16. U.S. Department of Labor, Bureau of Labor Statistics, "Employment and Earnings," table A4, (May 1991), 10.
Future projections from Howard N. Fullerton, Jr., op. cit.

17. U.S. Department of Education, *1991 Digest of Educational Statistics*, forthcoming.

18. Ibid.

19. Bickley Townsend and Kathleen O'Neil, "American Women Get Mad," *American Demographics* (August 1990).

20. Bureau of Labor Statistics, *Current Population Survey*, annual averages for 1990.

21. Private conversation, April 11, 1990.

22. Thomas J. Espenshade and Tracy Ann Goodis, "Demographic Trends Shaping the American Family and Work Force," *America in Transition: Benefits for the Future.* An EBRI-ERF Policy Forum, Employee Benefit Research Institute (1987).

23. John Naisbitt and Patricia Aburdene, *Megatrends 2000—Ten New Directions for the 1990s* (New York: William Morrow and Company, 1990).

24. Marvin J. Cetron, "Class of 2000: The Good News and the Bad News," *The Futurist Magazine* (November-December 1988).

25. Jeffrey J. Hallet, *Worklife Visions: Redefining Work for the Information Economy* (Alexandria, Va.: American Society for Personnel Administration, September 1987).

26. American Management Association, *Survey on Downsizing and Outplacement 1989*, summary of key findings.

27. General Electric, annual report, 1989.

28. Here are a few estimates.
Elizabeth Fowler, "Careers," *The New York Times* (March 20, 1990): "The average employee today will stay in a job about four years, according to government figures, which means a large number of job changes in a lifetime."
"Labor Secretary Seeks to Require Workers to Save," *The New York Times* (May 17, 1990): "Each year, one in five working Americans changes jobs and one in ten changes careers, "Mrs. Dole said. Some experts predict the average worker will soon hold up to ten jobs before retirement."
Naisbitt and Aburdene, *Megatrends 2000*: According to the U.S. Labor Department, they write, the average American changes careers (note: careers, not jobs) three times.

29. Veronica F. Nieva, "Work and Family Linkages," *Women and Work: An Annual Review*, vol. 1 (Beverly Hills, Calif.: Sage Publications, 1985). Eds.: Laurie Larwood, Ann H. Stromberg, and Barbara Gutek.

30. Joseph F. Coates, Jennifer Jarratt, and John Mahaffie, "Workplace Management 2000," *Personnel Administrator* (December 1989).

31. Florence Skelly, president, Telematics, Inc.; vice-chairman and director, Yankelovitch Group; vice-chairman and director, WSY Consulting. Presentation for the New York chapter, American Association of Public Opinion Researchers, January 10, 1990.

32. *Beyond the Transition: The Two-Gender Work Force and Corporate Policy.* A roundtable discussion, New York City, June 20, 1984. Copyright 1984, Catalyst and Touche Ross & Co.

33. Ibid.

34. R. Scott Fosler, op. cit.
   Also, U.S. Department of Labor, Bureau of Labor Statistics, annual averages from Current Population Reports, published monthly since 1948.

35. Steven R. Weisman, "In Crowded Japan, a Bonus for Babies Angers Women," *The New York Times* (February 17, 1991).

CHAPTER SEVEN: *The Cost of Burying Women's Talent*

1. An alternative way to conceptualize the management structure would be as a tree. I chose the pyramid because it is a familiar symbol in the corporate community. Were this information to be presented in tree form, its overall shape would be similar, save for a broader base. That difference would only accentuate the presence of women at lower levels.

2. Here is my reasoning:
   a. Men and women are equally endowed with the Basics.
   b. In fact, there is a random distribution of the Basics throughout the population and therefore within the population of men and within the population of women.
   c. My premise is that the Basics can be evaluated accurately by the employer.
   d. As a result, numbers can be assigned to women—and likewise to men—in descending order, and the number 1 woman has the same Basics as the number 1 man; the number 37 woman has the same Basics as the number 37 man.

3. Bureau of Labor Statistics, unpublished data, from *The Numbers News*, published by American Demographics (April 1989).

CHAPTER EIGHT: *Leveling the Playing Field*

1. Catalyst, *Report on a National Study of Parental Leaves*, 1986.

2. U.S. Bureau of the Census, Current Population Reports, Series P-60, no. 165, *Earnings of Married Couple Families: 1987*.

CHAPTER NINE: *Elevating the Field*

1. Fernando Bartolomé and Paul A. Lee Evans, "Must Success Cost So Much?," *Designing and Managing Your Career*, Edited by Harry Levinson (Boston, Mass.: Harvard Business School Press, 1989).

2. "Middle Managers Have High Hopes," A Survey Conducted by Dunhill Personnel System Inc. in Conjunction with the Columbia Business School, 1989.

3. Sally Solo, "Stop Whining and Get Back to Work," *Fortune* (March 12, 1990).

4. Harlan and Weiss, *Moving Up*, op. cit.

5. Catalyst, *Flexible Work Arrangements: Establishing Options for Managers and Professionals*, 1989.

CHAPTER TEN: *Breaking with the Past*

1. Roger Rosenblatt, "Season of Crowds," "MacNeil-Lehrer News Hour," November 28, 1989.

2. June O'Neill, "Women and Wages," *The American Enterprise* (November/December 1990).

3. *Occupational Projections and Training Data*, BLS Bulletin 2351, Table 6, "Occupational Employment, 1988 and Projected 2000, and Selected Employment Characteristics," April 1990.

4. "Earnings Gap Closes for Women," *The Collegiate Career Woman* (spring 1988).

5. Elizabeth Janeway, *Cross Sections from a Decade of Change* (New York: William Morrow, 1982).

6. Suzanne M. Bianchi and Daphne Spain, *American Women in Transition* (New York: Russell Sage Foundation, 1986).

7. Arlie Hochschild with Anne Maching, *The Second Shift: Working Parents and the Revolution at Home* (New York: Viking, 1989).

8. Anne L. Alscott, " 'Comparable Worth' Is Unfair to Women," *The New York Times* (May 24, 1986).

9. "Comparable Worth has Its Price," *HR Focus* (September 1990).

CHAPTER ELEVEN: *Essential Trade-offs, Unexpected Rewards*

1. Catalyst board of advisers discussion, October 13, 1989.

2. Raymond E. Smith, Remarks, Executive Women International Conference, Pittsburgh, PA., September 14, 1989.

3. In the aggregate, the rise in earnings has kept up with inflation, but the rise in earnings hasn't been evenly distributed throughout the work force. It's gone to those at the top, and the majority have suffered a significant drop in earnings and therefore—without two incomes—a drop in their standard of living. In both cases—those who would otherwise suffer a significant drop in standard of living and those who have become much more affluent—it is the children who suffer from an overdose of surrogate care or inadequate day care or latchkey neglect—by their parents' full-time career involvement (the former from the real need of both parents to work and employer insistence that it be full-time, the latter from the seductive power of the materially good life).

4. Charles N. Siegel, "The Brave New World of Child Care," *New Perspectives Quarterly* (Winter 1990).

5. Joseph H. Pleck, *Working Wives/Working Husbands* (Beverly Hills, Calif.: Russell Sage Publications, 1985).

6. Cathy Trost, "Men, Too, Wrestle with Career-Family Stress," *The Wall Street Journal* (November 1, 1988).

7. Arlie Hochschield with Anne Maching, *The Second Shift*, op. cit.

INDEX